BABOK Revision Guide for
CBAP / CCBA

By Amit Lingarchani / Abhishek Srivastava

Second Edition: 2020 ISBN **9798-6648-706-64**, www.techcanvass.com

TECHCANVASS

Table of Contents

TECHCANVASS

TECHCANVASS

TECHCANVASS

From the Authors

It is our pleasure to present the second edition of this book. The first edition was released couple of years back. Since then we wanted to add several things to enable revision of BABOK more meaningful and quicker. So, here we are.

Our objective to write this book was to create a concise revision guide for Business Analysis Body of Knowledge (BABOK) guide v3.0. BABOK is a big book with around five hundred pages and revising BABOK can be cumbersome.

So, how does it help you in revising? One of the proven revision approaches is to create notes. We conceptualized this revision guide as notes. So, the first edition was written as notes based on BABOK. It simply summarized BABOK v3 and was much smaller than BABOK. However, we wanted to make it more meaningful for all the readers. So, we have now added *concept notes*, *mock questions*, *crosswords*, and *matchmaking*.

Most importantly, we have added *case studies* in this book, which are real-life case studies. Each case study explains the scenario and provides examples of the application of concepts. Each case study also has questions for you to practice.

We have also added examples at the end of Techniques chapter. The examples are added to help you see the real-life usage of the technique. It is added for *selected techniques*.

The guide is meant for professionals who are planning to undertake CCBA and CBAP certification examination. This revision guide covers these BABOK chapters - key concepts, all the six Knowledge Areas, Perspectives, and all the 50 Techniques.

For the best results, this revision guide must be picked up after you have gone through the BABOK guide *once*. You will find all the key aspects of BABOK in this guide. This means that you do not need to pick up BABOK again.

Cheers and all the best for your exam!

Abhishek Srivastava

Amit Lingarchani

Business Analysis Key Concepts

This chapter lays down the foundation for the business analysis body of knowledge guide by explaining and discussing the fundamental concepts used throughout the book. The chapter covers the core concept model and explains key terms used throughout the book.

Business Analysis Core concepts model (BACCM)

Business Analysis Core Concepts Model (BACCM) is the core framework integral to BABOK Guide v3. Core concepts are fundamental to the practice of business analysis as defined in BABOK guide. IIBA BABOK v3 is the new version of BABOK guide for the latest version of business analyst certifications. In this article, I am going to discuss the basics of business analysis core concepts model (BACCM).

None of the core concepts holds good in isolation. Each core concept is defined by the other five core concepts and cannot be fully understood until all the concepts are understood. None of the core concepts is more important than the other.

BUSINESS ANALYSIS CORE CONCEPT MODEL (BACCM)

CONTEXT
The environment where the change is taking place

NEED
A problem or opportunity that needs to be addressed.

VALUE
The tangible or intangible worth of the solution to a stakeholder.

CHANGE
It is a result of the actions taken to address the need.

STAKEHOLDER
Individuals or Group associated with the need, change or solution.

SOLUTION
A way of satisfying the needs in a given context

TECHCANVASS

Let us understand the concepts with examples.

Need

Need is defined by BABOK as:

A problem, opportunity, or constraint with potential value to a stakeholder (s)

A need can be thought of as the reason which starts a project. The need arises from the current state of the organization.

Example

An organization is receiving a lot of complaints from customers about the after-sales support provided. So, the organization needs to address the problem.

An organization is selling subscription software, where people subscribe to the software and pay monthly. In recent times, the drop out period and rates are very high. 60% of people stop paying after 1 month and 80% after 2 months. The organization needs to address the problem, and that's an example of a need.

What is not Need: Need is not a solution. Solutions are ways to address the need. So, in our first example, if we say that the company wants to automate its after-sales service process, it defines the solution and not the need.

Solution

The BABOK guide refers to this core concept as:

A specific way of satisfying one or more needs in a context.

Organizational needs can be satisfied or addressed through one or more than one solution. A solution to address the need can be specific to an organization as different organizations or situations may need different solutions.

Example

To address the need for resolving poor after-sales service, the organization may use a software application.

A need can be addressed in more than one way, which means that we can have more than one solution.

In our case, the organization can opt for a Software as a service (SaaS) CRM system, or a COTS (commercial off the shelf) CRM product or a completely custom-built software application.

So, how does a business analyst/organization decide which is the best solution? BA takes a decision based on multiple factors like cost, benefits, risks, etc.

Change

BABOK refers to this core concept as

The act of transformation in response to a need.

First, an organization recognizes the need. A need requires a solution. The organization chooses the solution, which is the best fit.

The organization implements the solution (internally or through a vendor). During the implementation of the solution, changes take place within the organization. The change includes team changes, process changes, and more.

Example

In our example, the support team, at the least, needs to learn how to use the new software? Are they ready? If not, they need to be skilled appropriately.

Stakeholder

A group or individual with a relationship to the change (or for whom the change is relevant), the need, or the solution

- A group or an individual who has an impact on the change initiative or can influence the outcome of this initiative.
- Stakeholders can be internal or external
- Business Analysts perform stakeholder analysis to identify the stakeholders for the project (change)

Example

Considering the loan processing system for the car agency, who are the stakeholders? For whom is this solution relevant or who are going to influence the change/project? Some stakeholders are:

- The Sales manager or front office staff dealing with customer
- The load approving officer
- Director of Car agency (as sponsor or sign off authority)

Value

The worth, importance, or the usefulness of something to a stakeholder within a context

- A value is the reason, why an Enterprise invests in a solution as an exercise to address the need.
- An enterprise can target tangible or intangible value.
- Increasing the revenue by 10% every year is an example of tangible value
- Improving the customer experience (by enhancing the user interface) is an example of intangible value

Example

The value for the stakeholders is the ability to close the sale deal faster & having a happier customer.

Context

The circumstances that influence is influenced by and provide an understanding of the change.

- A context defines everything that is relevant to a change, but not the change itself.
- A context includes enterprise background, demographics, culture, products, projects, etc.

Context and change initiative together present a unique situation to a business analyst.

Example

The loan processing system will be different if the car agency is not a single location agency but having a presence in multiple cities. The situation, in this case, demands an internet-enabled solution. It also demands approval and reporting facilities based on locations. That's the impact of a context in a solution.

Key Terms

Business Analysis

The BABOK® Guide describes and defines business analysis as the practice of enabling change in an enterprise by defining the needs and recommending solutions that deliver value to stakeholders.

This definition uses the six core concepts, as discussed in the previous section.

Business Analysis practice is clearly about enabling an organization to achieve its goals. The practice includes tasks like need identification to solution implementation and evaluation. BABOK describes the activities in the form of knowledge areas. There are six knowledge areas.

Business Analysis Information

The use of the term 'Business Analysis Information' is new to BABOK Version 3. In the previous versions, IIBA used 'Requirements' to represent the output produced by Business Analysts. However, this term was too restrictive.

A Business Analyst produces many work products during a project or career. Business Analysis information is a more apt word to indicate any outputs produced as a result of the business analysis work.

The Business Analysis information can be any of the following:

- Requirements
- Elicitation results
- Designs
- Solution Options
- Solution scope
- Change Strategy
- Business Case

Requirements and Design

It is important to understand the meaning of these two terms in the BABOK context.

A requirement is a usable representation of a need.

A design is a usable representation of a solution.

Design is used in a different context in this guide. In software parlance, design is referred to as the solution design representing technical design like table structures, code components, library design, interface design, etc.

Example of a requirement

The Sales head needs to view trends in sales for the last six months and performance in each sector.

Example of design

Creating a screen prototype to show the design of the above report/dashboard.

Enterprise and Organization

A differentiation has been made in the guide between an Enterprise and an organization.

An enterprise is a system of one or more organizations and the solutions they use to pursue a shared set of common goals.

An autonomous group of people under the management of a single individual or board, that works towards common goals and objectives.

As per the BABOK guide, an organization refers to a company that is created to run on a continuous basis.

An enterprise is a more heterogeneous grouping of organizations, legal entities, government bodies, etc. A change may span an enterprise going beyond just an organization. But an enterprise is a temporary phenomenon considered for the purpose of a change initiative, once the change is completed, it's disbanded.

Example

In India, Goods and Services Tax has been implemented by replacing the old multi-tax system. This change is not just for the tax body of the government but for all the partners as well as taxpayers. The government is not only upgrading the software, they have also launched massive training and awareness campaigns. This change spans an enterprise comprising of:

- *Tax bodies of government*
- *Partners*
- *Taxpayers*

Risk: Risk is a possibility of occurrence of an event, which is likely to have an impact on the change, solution, or the enterprise. Managing risks involves identification, assessment, prioritization or ranking by business analysts and the stakeholders.

Requirements Classification Schema

BABOK guide has the following classification of requirements:

Business Requirements

The requirements stating the primary reason (s) for change. This can include – Statements describing the goal, objectives and expected outcomes.

Example

We would like to automate our account opening process to eliminate duplicate data entries and reduce the time frame to open the account from 3 days to a single day.

This is an example of a business requirement for a bank. It is a high level yet objective statement of purpose.

Stakeholder Requirements

Stakeholders requirements are specific needs of stakeholders. They must be addressed by the solution to achieve business requirements.

Essentially BABOK establishes that stakeholders collectively and exhaustively represent the business requirements.

Example

Continuing the account opening system, a stakeholder may ask for a specific function as that concerns him/her. For example, we must ask for the account holder's spouse details as the stakeholder is part of the customer relationship team. Knowing more about the customer will help in making the communications more personalized.

Solution Requirements

It describes the capabilities and qualities of a solution that meets the stakeholder requirements. It is supposed to be detailed and carry information that will help the technology team in implementing it.

Solution requirements are of two types:

Functional Requirements: describe the capabilities that a solution must have in terms of the behaviour and information. In other words, this represents the way a user is going to interact with the system or view the information.

Example

The account holder's demographic data capturing is a feature that represents a functional requirement.

Non-Functional Requirements: Does not describe the behaviour of the system but concerns the conditions under which the system is expected to work effectively.

Example

Considering the banking environment, the account opening system should be a secured site.

Transition Requirements: Are temporary requirements, which arise because of the change becoming implemented. Once completed, they are not needed and are expired. All other types of requirements are managed throughout the change/project.

Example

In the account opening system, data for the existing account holders need to be captured into the new system. This is called data migration and is an example of transition requirements. Once the migration is finished, it is no longer needed.

Mock Questions

Q1. Ron is conducting requirements elicitation and has been talking to various stakeholders. During the discussions, many factors come up, which need further validation to be TRUE. How should Ron document these?

A. These should still be documented as needs

B. These should be documented as requirements

C. These should be documented as assumptions

D. These should not be documented till validated

Q2. BA Ajay is gathering the requirements and he wanted to explain the core concepts to the stakeholders so that they can discuss and refer to the requirements using common terms. Which of the following sets do not represent some of the core concepts as per BABOK?

A. Change, Need, solution and Value

B. Need, solution, stakeholder, and Context

C. Solution, stakeholder, architecture, and Change

D. Value, change, need and solution

Q3. A Business Analyst is studying the core concept model of business analysis so as to gain insight into his business analysis work. Which of the following is not TRUE about the core concepts model?

A. It helps in evaluating the relationships of key concepts in business analysis

B. It helps in communication about business analysis with a common terminology

C. It guides in setting the performance criteria for evaluating the business analysis work

D. It helps to perform better business analysis by holistically evaluating the relationships among these six concepts

Q4. A business analyst Alex is working on a mobile app. He arranges a session with all relevant stakeholders to gather the requirements. He also invites the implementation consultant, who was part of the previous project. Why does Alex involve him?

A. It helps in managing the day to day issues of the organization

B. It helps in providing various source data and documents related to the project

C. It helps in providing the knowledge regarding the implementation of one or more solution components

D. It helps in verifying the quality of the implemented solution with respect to the business need

Q5. Ronnie is a business analyst. He is eliciting, identifying, and managing the business analysis information for a project. Which of the following statement is NOT true for business analysis information?

A. Business analysis information can be used as an input to or output of business analysis work

B. It refers to the broad and diverse sets of information that business analysts analyze, transform, and report

C. Business analysis information is nothing but the requirements

D. Requirements, designs, solution scope, and change strategy are the examples of business analysis information

Q6. Identify which one of the following is a functional requirement?

A. All the screens must not take more than 2 seconds to load

B. The system should allow the users to login into the system using retina scan

C. The system should be able to support 1,00,000 concurrent users

D. The software should work on all the browsers including Android and iOS based mobile browsers

Q7. Daily stand-up meeting is a regular activity in an Agile project. What is the purpose of conducting the daily stand-up meeting?

A. To focus the team on getting issues solved

B. To discuss and share information one-to-one

C. To bring out issues that may be causing problems

D. To enable delivery management to allocate the work

Q8. During a requirement gathering meeting, a stakeholder told the business analyst, the application must be able to run on Windows, iOS and Android operating systems for all the versions released after 2018. Which of the following is true about this requirement?

A. This is a functional requirement

B. This is a non-functional requirement

C. This is not a requirement for a system

D. This is a constraint for the system

Q9. Customer relationship management software is being developed for an organization. This software will be used by Sales, Marketing, Customer services, and call centre employees. Who is the end-user in this case?

A) Sales Manager

B) Customer Service Executive

C) Finance Head

A. All three

B. Only B

C. B and C

D. A and B

ANSWERS

Q1. Answer C: As these are important factors, they should be documented as assumptions, till validated. Assumptions provide important context to the requirements and the proposed system and thus till the time, these are proved to be wrong, these will be treated as assumptions.
This question is based on the concept of assumptions as defined in the Glossary section of BABOK. So, the correct answer is option c.

Q2. Answer C: The six core concepts are - Change, Need, Solution, Stakeholder, Value, and Context. Now, options a, b, and d consist of a group of core concepts as per the BABOK whereas option C does not. So, the correct answer is option c. (Refer 2.1 of BABOK)

Q3. Answer C: Correct. The core concept model does not define any performance criteria. (Refer 2.1 of BABOK)

Q4. Answer C: Implementation SMEs help in providing the knowhow for the project implementation in the current context, as he/she is fully aware of the challenges and thus helps in gaining specialized knowledge regarding the implementation of one or more solution components. So, in this case, the correct answer is option c. (Refer 2.4.5 of BABOK)

Q5. Answer C: Choice c. Correct. Business analysis information is not just requirements, but any outputs produced during the business analysis activities. So, Business analysis information is more than just the requirements. Thus, in this case, the correct answer is option c. (Refer 2.2 of BABOK)

Q6. Answer B: Option B is correct because this requirement contains both the functional as well as a non-functional requirement. Retina scanning will separate hardware to work (Non-functional) but the interface needs to be developed in the software to use the result to allow login into the system (Functional Requirement).

Option A is a performance requirement, option C is a scalability requirement whereas option D is a compatibility requirement and is typically a non-functional requirement. (Refer to section 2.3)

Q7. Answer C: It is done to bring out issues that may be preventing the team working and needs attention. It is a general Scrum ceremony question and does not need direct BABOK reference.

Q8. Answer B: This requirement is a portability requirement and is categorized as a non-functional requirement. Non-functional requirements describe the conditions or qualities that a solution must have as mentioned in this case. So, option b is the correct answer. (Section 2.3 BABOK)

Q9. Answer D: Sales Manager and Customer service executives are going to use the software directly. The Finance department head will not interact with this software directly and hence is not an end-user. (Section 2.4.4)

Business Analysis Planning and Monitoring

This knowledge area describes the activities associated with planning the business analysis activities as well as measuring and finding ways to improve the performance of business analysis activities.

Deals with the definition and planning of the BA approach, governance, and monitoring

Describes how to improve business analysis performance

Produces outputs that are guidelines for other tasks

Key Concepts

Let us understand a few concepts related to this knowledge area. The image below shows four terms with the explanation and example.

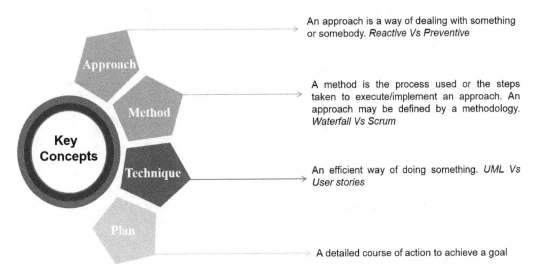

An approach is a way of dealing with something or somebody. *Reactive Vs Preventive*

A method is the process used or the steps taken to execute/implement an approach. An approach may be defined by a methodology. *Waterfall Vs Scrum*

An efficient way of doing something. *UML Vs User stories*

A detailed course of action to achieve a goal

Fig 3.1 Business Analysis planning and monitoring key concept

Business Analysis Planning and Monitoring Tasks

Business Analysis planning and monitoring knowledge area as five tasks as mentioned below:

01 **Plan business analysis approach**

02 **Plan Stakeholder engagement**

03 **Plan Business analysis governance**

04 **Plan Business Analysis Information Management**

05 **Identify Business Analysis Performance Improvements**

Task 1: Plan Business Analysis Approach

This task describes the following:

- Method or process to conduct the business analysis activities
- The schedule of activities
- What will be the output of the business analysis activities?

Purpose	Define an appropriate method to conduct business analysis activities
Description	➢ Business analysis approaches describe an **overall method** that will be followed --When **performing business analysis work** on a given initiative --How and when **tasks** will be performed **--Deliverables** that will be produced ➢ Business analysts may also identify an initial set of **techniques** to use. ➢ Business analysis approach may be defined by a **methodology** or by **organizational standards** that could be formalized into a repeatable business analysis process that can be leveraged for each effort. ➢ Business analysis approach should highlight --Align to overall goals of the change, --Coordinate the business analysis tasks with the **activities** and **deliverables** of the overall change, --Include tasks to manage any **risks** that could reflect the quality of the business analysis deliverables, --Leverage upon **approaches** and select **techniques** and **tools** that have historically worked well
Inputs	➢ **Needs** – Business analysis approach is shaped by the problem or opportunity faced by the organization.
Elements	➢ **Planning Approach** – Planning is an essential task to ensure value is delivered to an enterprise. It happens more than once on a given initiative as the plans are updated to address **changing business conditions.** **Predictive Approach** – Focus on minimizing upfront uncertainty and ensuring that the solution is defined before implementation begins to maximize control

and minimize risk. Best applied for the projects where requirements can effectively be defined ahead of implementation, the risk of incorrect implementation is unacceptably high, or when engaging stakeholders presents significant challenges. Very good approach for **traditional waterfall** methodology.

Adaptive Approach – Focus on rapid delivery of business value in short iterations in return for acceptance of a higher degree of uncertainty regarding the overall delivery of the solution. It is best applied when taking an exploratory approach to find the best solution or for incremental improvement of an existing solution. Very good approach for **agile** methodology.

- ➤ **Formality and Level of Detail of Business Analysis deliverables** – Business analysts need to consider the level of formality that is appropriate for the approach

  Predictive approach – Calls for a significant amount of formality and details.
  - o Information is captured at various levels of details using standard templates such as **Business Requirement Document (BRDs) and Functional Requirement Document (FRDs).**
  - o Activities required to complete deliverables are identified first and then divided into tasks.
  - o Tasks are performed in specific phases.

  Adaptive approach –
  - o Favours defining requirements and designs through **team interaction.**
  - o **Focuses on rapid feedback** from the stakeholders to use in the subsequent iterations
  - o Activities are divided into iterations.
  - o Tasks are performed iteratively.
  - o Formal documentation is often created after the implementation

  Some considerations that may affect the approach include:
  - o Very complex and risky changes
  - o The organization operates in heavily regulated industries
  - o Contracts or agreements necessitate formality
  - o Stakeholders are geographically distributed
  - o Resources are outsourced
  - o Staff turnover is high and / or team members may be inexperienced
  - o Requirements must be formally signed off
  - o Business analysis information must be maintained long term or handed over for use on future initiatives

- ➤ **Business Analysis Activities** – Incorporating business analysis activities within the business analysis approach includes:
  - o Identifying **activities** required to complete each deliverable and then breaking them into tasks
  - o Dividing the **work** into **iterations,** deliverables for each iteration and tasks and activities.

- ➤ **Timing of Business Analysis Work** – Planning includes determining whether the business analysis tasks will be performed primarily in specific phases or iteratively. Timing of business analysis activities can also be affected by:
  - o Availability of the resources
  - o Priority / urgency of the initiative

	o Other concurrent initiative
	o Constraints such as contract terms or regulatory deadlines
	➢ **Complexity and Risk** – Complexity, size of change and overall risk of the effort is to be considered while determining business analysis approach.
	    o Factors affecting **complexity** are – size of the change, number of business areas or systems affected, geographic and cultural considerations, technological complexities, and any other risks
	    o Factors impacting **risk** level are –
	        ▪ Experience level of business analyst,
	        ▪ Extent of domain knowledge held by the business analyst,
	        ▪ Level of experience stakeholders have in communicating their needs,
	        ▪ Stakeholder attitude about the change,
	        ▪ Amount of time allocated by a stakeholder to activities and any pre-selected framework, tool or technique,
	        ▪ Cultural norms of organization.
	    o Complexity and risk can be **better** handled in adaptive approach as compared to predictive approach.
	➢ **Acceptance** – Business analysis approach is reviewed and agreed upon by key stakeholders. Business analysis process must be tailored to a structure where key stakeholders ensure that all business analysis activities are identified, a realistic view of estimates is created, and proposed roles/responsibilities are correct. Stakeholders also play a vital role in **reviewing** and **accepting** changes to the approach.

Guidelines & Tools	➢ Business Analysis Performance Assessment – Provides results of previous assessments that should be reviewed and incorporated ➢ Business Policies – Define the limits within which decisions must be made. ➢ Expert Judgement – Expertise may be provided from a wide range of sources including stakeholders on the initiative, organizational centres of excellence, consultants, associations or industry groups and prior experiences of business analysts and other stakeholders. ➢ Methodologies and Framework – Methods, techniques, procedures, working concepts and rules shape up the approach ➢ Stakeholder Engagement Approach – Understanding stakeholders concerns and interest may influence decisions within the business analysis approach
Techniques	➢ **Brainstorming** – Identify possible business analysis activities, techniques, risks and other relevant items to build approach ➢ **Business Cases** – Used to understand time-sensitivity of the problem or opportunity or to find out uncertainty around elements of possible need or solution ➢ **Document Analysis** – Review existing organizational assets that might assist in planning the approach ➢ **Estimation** – Determine the time component to perform business analysis activities ➢ **Financial Analysis** – Used to assess how different approaches affect the value delivered ➢ **Functional Decomposition** – Used to break down complex business analysis processes into more feasible components ➢ **Interviews** – Used to help build the plan with an individual ➢ **Item Tracking** – Used to track any issues raised during planning activities with stakeholders

	➢ **Lessons Learned** – Used to identify an enterprise's previous experience with planning business analysis approach ➢ **Process Modelling** – Used to define and document the business analysis approach ➢ **Reviews** – Used to validate the selected approach with stakeholders ➢ **Risk Analysis and Management** – Used to assess risks in order to select proper business analysis approach ➢ **Scope Modelling** – Used to determine boundaries of solution as an input to planning and to estimating ➢ **Survey or Questionnaire** – Used to identify possible business analysis activities, techniques, risks, and other relevant items to build the approach ➢ **Workshops** – Used to help build the plan in a team structure
Stakeholders	➢ Domain Subject Matter Expert – Can be a source of risk if Domain SME is not available but required. ➢ Project Manager – Determines that the approach is **realistic** for the overall schedule and timelines. ➢ Regulator – May provide the approval for business analysis approach or tailoring it. ➢ Sponsor – Provides **needs** and **objectives** for the approach and makes sure that organizational objectives are followed.

Output	➢ **Business Analysis Approach** – Identifies the approach and activities that will be performed including
	    o Who will perform the activities?
	    o Timing and sequencing of the work
	    o Deliverables that will be produced
	    o Business analysis techniques that may be utilized

Task 2: Plan Stakeholder Engagement

This task describes the following:

- Approach for having an effective collaboration with the stakeholders to achieve the business objectives
- How to conduct stakeholder analysis
- Develop a stakeholder collaboration/management plan

Imp: It is not a one-time activity, but rather an ongoing activity as the project goes on.

Purpose	Plan an approach for establishing and maintaining effective working relationships with the stakeholders.
Description	➢ Planning stakeholder engagement involves conducting a thorough **stakeholder analysis** to identify all the involved stakeholders which help to plan for stakeholder risks. ➢ As number of stakeholders increases, the degree of complexity also increases. Why? Because, number of communication channels increases.
Inputs	➢ **Needs** – Understanding the business need helps in the identification of stakeholders.

	➢ **Business Analysis Approach** – Incorporating the overall business analysis approach into stakeholder analysis, collaboration and communication approaches are required to ensure consistency throughout the project.
Elements	➢ **Perform Stakeholder Analysis** – Stakeholder analysis involves **identifying the stakeholders** who will be directly or indirectly impacted by the change. It is NOT a one-time activity.

➢ **Perform Stakeholder Analysis** – Stakeholder analysis involves **identifying the stakeholders** who will be directly or indirectly impacted by the change. It is NOT a one-time activity.

- Not identifying stakeholders leads to missing critical needs or delayed discovery of requirements. This may cause **cost overrun** and **decreased stakeholder satisfaction**.
- Initial sources for identifying stakeholders:
  - Organizational chart
  - Any regulatory or governing bodies
  - shareholders,
  - Customers and suppliers
- **Roles** – This is identified by the business analysts to understand where and how the stakeholders will contribute to the initiative. For e.g. business owners and product owners.
- **Attitudes** – Stakeholders with positive attitudes may be strong champions and great contributors. Business analyst analyse stakeholder's attitudes about:
  - Business goals, objectives of the initiative and any proposed solutions
  - Business analysis in general
  - Level of interest in change
  - The sponsor, team members and other stakeholders as well as
  - Collaboration and a team-based approach
- **Decision Making Authority** – Identify the authority level a stakeholder possesses over business analysis activities, deliverables and changes to business analysis work.
- **Level of Power or Influence** – Understanding the influence and attitude each stakeholder may have can help develop strategies for obtaining **buy-in** and **collaboration**.

➢ **Define Stakeholder Collaboration** – Collaboration can be a **spontaneous event,** but most of the time, it is **considered** and **planned**, with specific activities and outcomes determined ahead of time in the form of **stakeholder collaboration plan**. The objective is to select the approaches that work best to **meet the needs of each stakeholder group** and ensure their **interest and involvement is maintained**. Some considerations while planning collaboration include:

- Timing and frequency of collaboration
- Location
- Available tools such as wikis
- Delivery method such as in-person or virtual
- Preferences of the stakeholders

➢ **Stakeholder Communication Needs** – Documented in the form of stakeholder communication plan. Evaluation of communication needs by business analyst includes:
- **What** needs to be communicated
- What is the appropriate **delivery method** (written or verbal)?

	• Who the appropriate **audience** is? • **When** communication should occur • **Frequency** of communication • **Geographic location** of stakeholders who will receive communications • **Level of detail** appropriate for the communication and stakeholder and • **Level of formality** of communications
Guidelines & Tools	➢ Business Analysis Performance Assessment – Provides results of previous assessments that should be reviewed and incorporated ➢ Change Strategy – Helps in the assessment of stakeholder impact and development of more effective stakeholder engagement strategies. ➢ Current State Description – Provides the context in which the work needs to be completed.
Techniques	➢ **Brainstorming** – Used to identify the stakeholder list and their roles and responsibilities ➢ **Business Rules Analysis** – Used to identify stakeholders who were the **source** of business rules ➢ **Document Analysis** – Used to review existing organizational assets for effective stakeholder engagement ➢ **Interviews** – Interact with specific stakeholders to gain more information or knowledge ➢ **Lessons Learned** – Used to identify an enterprise's previous successes and challenges while planning stakeholder engagement ➢ **Mind Mapping** – Identify potential stakeholders and help understand relationships between them ➢ **Organizational Modelling** – Used to determine if the organizational units or people listed have any unique needs and interests that should be considered. ➢ **Process Modelling** – Used to categorize stakeholders by the systems that support their business processes ➢ **Risk Analysis and Management** – Used to identify the risks to the initiative resulting from stakeholder attitudes. ➢ **Scope Modelling** – Used to develop scope models to show stakeholders that fall outside the scope of solution, but still interact with it. ➢ **Stakeholders List, Map or Personas** – Used to depict the relationship of stakeholders to the solution and to one another ➢ **Survey or Questionnaire** – Used to identify shared characteristics of the stakeholder group. ➢ **Workshops** - Used to interact with groups of stakeholders to gain more information
Stakeholders	➢ Customers – source of **external** stakeholders ➢ Domain Subject Matter Expert ➢ End User – source of **internal** stakeholders ➢ Project Manager ➢ Regulator – may require certain stakeholders to participate ➢ Sponsor - may request to involve specific stakeholders ➢ Supplier – source of **external** stakeholders.
Output	➢ **Stakeholder Engagement Approach** – Contains a list of stakeholders, their characteristics that were analysed and a listing of roles and responsibilities for the change.

Task 3: Plan Business Analysis Governance

Governance process defines how decisions and approvals take place in a change initiative.

This task describes the following:

- How a change request will be initiated and communicated (Responsible person and the process)
- How the change will be analyzed and impact analysis will be conducted (Impact Analysis)
- Who will approve the changes?
- The process of recording the changes (Change request logs for example)

A representative change control process could be as shown below:

Change Control Process

Process for requesting change
Applicability (Applies to all changes?)
Define the steps of initiating change.

Elements of change request
Cost & time estimates, Benefits, Risks,
Priority, Course of action

Prioritization of change
How the prioritization will happen

Documenting the change
Configuration Management and
traceability standards determine that

Communicating the Changes
Communication to stakeholders

Impact Analysis
Who is responsible for impact analysis

Authorization of change
Who can authorize

Purpose	Define how decisions are made about requirements and designs, including reviews, change control, approvals, and prioritization.

Description	➢ Business analysts ensure that a **governance process** is in place that identifies decision makers, process information and give a view on approach for approvals and prioritization decisions.
	➢ Business analysts identify following things when planning the governance approach:
	    ○ **How** business analysis work will be approached and prioritized
	    ○ **What** the process for proposing a change to business analysis information is
	    ○ **Who** has the **authority** and responsibility to **propose** changes and who should be **involved** in the change discussions?
	    ○ Who has the responsibility for **analysing** change requests?
	    ○ Who has the authority to **approve** changes?
	    ○ How changes will be **documented** and **communicated**

Inputs	➢ **Business Analysis Approach** – Incorporating overall business analysis approach into governance approach is required to ensure consistency ➢ **Stakeholder Engagement Approach** – Identifying stakeholder and understanding their communication and collaboration needs is useful to determine their participation in governance approach

Elements	

	➤ **Decision Making** – The decision-making process defines what happens when teams cannot reach consensus by identifying escalation paths and key stakeholders holding final decision-making authority. A stakeholder may serve in various roles in decision making process such as a **participant** in decision making discussions or **subject matter expert** lending experience and knowledge or a **reviewer** of information or an **approver** of decisions. The reviewer of information and/or approver of decisions might be different in predictive approach (e.g. Waterfall SDLC) as compared to adaptive approach (e.g. only one entity - Product owner in Agile methodology)
	
	➤ **Change Control Process** – When a business analyst develops a change control process, they:
	    ○ Determine the **process** for requesting changes – defining change control process to handle changes
	    ○ Determine the **elements** of change request
	        ▪ Cost and time estimates
	        ▪ Benefits
	        ▪ Risks
	        ▪ Priority
	        ▪ Course of action
	    ○ Determine how changes will be **prioritized** – priority is based on competing interests within initiative
	    ○ Determine how changes will be **documented** – configuration management and traceability standards
	    ○ Determine how changes will be **communicated** – communication plan for communicating changes
	    ○ Determine who will perform the **impact analysis** – identifying responsible parties to conduct analysis
	    ○ Determine who will **authorize** changes – include a designation of approvers with authority level
	
	➤ **Plan Prioritization Approach** – Timelines, expected value, dependencies, resource constraints, adopted methodologies and other factors influence prioritization. Following factors are considered in the prioritization process:
	    ○ **Formality** and **rigour** of the prioritization process
	    ○ **Participants** who will be involved in prioritization
	    ○ **Process** for deciding how prioritization will occur including which techniques will be used
	    ○ **Criteria** to be used for prioritization
	
	➤ **Plan for Approvals** – An approval formalizes the agreement between all stakeholders that the **content** and **presentation** of the requirements and designs are **accurate, adequate** and contain **sufficient detail** to allow for continued progress to be made.
	    ○ **Timing** and **frequency** of approvals are dependent on the size and complexity of the change and associated risks of foregoing or delaying approval.
	    ○ Business analyst must determine the **type** of requirements and design to be approved, **timing** for the approvals, **process** to be followed to gain approval and **who** will approve the requirements and designs.
	    ○ Business analysts consider the **organizational culture** and **type of information** is approved. New systems or processes in highly regulated industries will require **frequent** and **rigorous** review and **approval** of very detailed specifications. This is conducted by a

	change control board in traditional methodology whereas it is performed by product owner in agile. ○ **Schedule of events** for approvals and their **tracking mechanism** is included in planning for approvals. ○ **Stakeholder availability, attitude and willingness to engage** determine the efficiency of approval process.
Guidelines & Tools	➢ Business Analysis Performance Assessment – Provides results of previous assessments that should be reviewed and incorporated ➢ Business Policies – Define the limits within which decisions must be made. ➢ Current State Description – Provides the context within which the work needs to be completed which can help drive how to make better decisions ➢ Legal /Regulatory Information – Describes legislative rules or regulations that must be followed to develop a framework for sound decision making
Techniques	➢ **Brainstorming** – Used to generate an initial list of potential stakeholders' names who may need to be approvers in a defined governance process ➢ **Document Analysis** – Evaluate existing governance processes or templates ➢ **Interviews** – Used to identify possible decision making, change control, approval or prioritization approaches and participants with an individual or group ➢ **Item Tracking** – Used to track any issues that arise when planning a governance approach ➢ **Lessons Learned** – Used to find if past initiatives have identified valuable experiences with governance that can be leveraged on current or future initiatives ➢ **Organizational Modelling** – Used to understand roles /responsibilities within the organization in an effort to define a governance approach ➢ **Process Modelling** – Used to document the process or method for governing business analysis ➢ **Reviews** – Used to review the proposed governance plan with key stakeholders ➢ **Survey or Questionnaire** – Used to identify possible decision making, change control, approval or prioritization approaches ➢ **Workshops** - Used to identify possible decision making, change control, approval or prioritization approaches
Stakeholders	➢ Domain Subject Matter Expert – May be a possible **source** of a requested change or may be identified as needing to be involved in changing decisions ➢ Project Manager ➢ Regulator – May **impose** rules or regulations that need to be considered in determining the business analysis governance plan and can be a possible source of a requested change ➢ Sponsor – **Participates** in change discussions and **approves** proposed changes.
Output	➢ **Governance Approach** – Identifies the stakeholders who will have the responsibility and authority to make decisions, setting priorities and approving changes to business analysis information. It also lays down the process to manage requirements and design changes across the initiative.

Task 4: Plan Business Analysis Information Management

This task deals with the management (storage and access) of business analysis information. Business analysis information includes elicitation results, requirements, designs, solution options, solution scope, and change strategy.

Business analysis information

Comprises of all the information captured by a business analyst during elicitation, modelling, compilation and in any of the business analysis activities. Examples include functioning prototypes, Requirements specifications document, User stories, use cases, etc.

Planning of business analysis information includes detailing and formality of the information, the access to information, requirement architecture, identifying re-usability across the enterprise.

Purpose	Develop an approach for how business analysis information will be stored and accessed.

Description	➢ Business analysis information is comprised of formal requirement documents, user stories, and functioning prototypes, solution designs as well as solution options.
	 ➢ Information management helps ensure that business analysis information is organized in a **functional and useful manner, is easily accessible to appropriate personnel and is stored for the necessary length of time**.
	 ➢ Information management entails identifying:
	     o How information should be **organized**
	     o The **level of detail** at which information should be captured
	     o Any **relationships** between the information
	     o How information may be **used across multiple initiatives**
	     o How information should be **accessed and stored**
	     o **Characteristics** of the information that must be maintained

Inputs	➢ **Business Analysis Approach** – Incorporating overall business analysis approach into governance approach is required to ensure consistency ➢ **Stakeholder Engagement Approach** – Identifying stakeholder and understanding their communication and collaboration needs is useful to determine their participation in governance approach ➢ **Governance Approach** – Defines how changes are managed to requirements and designs, how decisions and approvals for business analysis deliverables will be made and how priorities will be set

Elements	➢ **Organization of Business Analysis Information** – Business analysis information must be organized in a manner that allows for **efficient access and use**, must be structured to be easily **located**, must not **conflict** with other information and must not be **duplicated**.
	 ➢ **Level of Abstraction** – Level of abstraction describes the breadth and depth of the information being provided. The **Needs of stakeholders, complexity of what is being explained and the importance of the change** are considered in determining the level of the detail provided to each stakeholder.
	 ➢ **Plan Traceability Approach** – Traceability approach is based on:
	     o The **complexity of the domain**
	     o The **number of views of requirements** that will be produced

- o Any requirement related **risks, organizational standards, applicable regulatory requirements**
- o An understanding of the **costs** and **benefits** involved with tracing

➢ **Plan for Requirements Reuse** – Business analyst identifies how best to **structure, store and access** requirements so they are usable and accessible for the future. Requirements must be clearly **named, defined and stored in a repository** that is available to other business analysts. Requirements that are potential candidates for long term use are of following types:

- o Regulatory requirements
- o Contractual obligations
- o Quality standards
- o Service level agreements
- o Business rules
- o Business processes
- o Requirements describing products the enterprise produces

➢ **Storage and Access** – Storage decisions depend on many factors such as **who** must access the information, **how often** they need to access it, and what **conditions** must be present for access.

- o **Organizational standards** and **tool availability** will also influence the storage and access decisions.
- o Tools may shape the selection of business analysis **techniques, notations** to be used and the **way that information is organized**.
- o The repository must be able to indicate the **status** of any stored information and **allow for modification** of that information over time.

➢ **Requirements Attributes** – Requirements attributes provide **information** about requirements, and aid in the **ongoing management** of the requirements throughout the change. Better trade-offs between requirements and identification of stakeholders affected by potential changes can be achieved via requirements attributes. Commonly used requirements attributes include:

- o **Absolute Reference** – Provides a unique identifier
- o **Author** – Name of the person to be consulted in case of ambiguous or unclear requirements found later
- o **Complexity** – Indicates how difficult the requirement will be to implement
- o **Ownership** – Individual or group that needs the requirement
- o **Priority** – Relative importance of requirements. Refers to the relative value of a requirement or sequence of implementation
- o **Risks** – Identifies uncertain events impacting requirements
- o **Source** – Identifies the origin of requirements
- o **Stability** – Indicates the maturity of requirements
- o **Status** – Indicates the state of requirement
- o **Urgency** – Indicates how soon the requirement is needed

Guidelines & Tools	➢ Business Analysis Performance Assessment – Provides results of previous assessments that should be reviewed and incorporated ➢ Business Policies – Define the limits within which decisions must be made. ➢ Information Management Tools – This refers to the tool that is used to store, retrieve and share business analysis information. Examples – simple whiteboard, complex global wiki, requirements management tool ➢ Legal/Regulatory Information – Legislative rules or regulations to be followed for managing business analysis information.

Techniques	<ul><li>**Brainstorming** – Used to help stakeholders uncover their business analysis information management needs</li><li>**Interviews** – Used to help specific stakeholders uncover their business analysis information management needs</li><li>**Item Tracking** – Used to track issues with current information management processes</li><li>**Lessons Learned** – Used to create a source of information for analyzing approaches for efficiently managing business analysis information</li><li>**Mind Mapping** – Used to identify and categorize the kinds of information that need to be managed</li><li>**Process Modelling** – Used to document process or method for managing business analysis information</li><li>**Survey or Questionnaire** – Used to ask stakeholders to provide input into defining business analysis information management</li><li>**Workshops** – Used to uncover business analysis information management needs in a group setting</li></ul>
Stakeholders	<ul><li>Domain Subject Matter Expert</li><li>Regulator – Defines rules and processes related to information management</li><li>Sponsor – Reviews, comments and approves business analysis information</li></ul>
Output	<ul><li>**Information Management Approach** – Includes the defined approach for how business analysis information will be stored, accessed and utilized during the change and after the change is complete.</li></ul>

Task 5: Identify Business Analysis Performance Improvements

This is an iterative task and happens throughout the software development lifecycle. Business analysis activities and processes are evaluated to identify improvement areas and incorporate them.

Organizational metrics can be used for measuring the performance of the business analysis activities.

Examples of metrics for measuring Business Analysis performance:

 Review Efficiency Index
How efficient was the review during requirements phase? Based on number of defects detected during post-coding phase, with origin of defect as "Requirements phase"

 Missing Requirements
Number of requirements added or modified after the baseline approval

 Stakeholder satisfaction Index
An interview/survey based metric, where a set of calibrated yet not-leading questions targeted to understand the satisfaction levels

 Schedule variance
The delay in completing the business analysis activities vs the planned schedule.

Purpose	Assess business analysis work and to plan to improve processes when required.
Description	<ul><li>Performance analysis is an ongoing task throughout an initiative. The improvements identified as part of this process will become guidelines for future task execution. To monitor and improve performance, it is necessary to<ul><li>**Establish** the performance measures</li><li>**Conduct** the performance analysis</li></ul></li></ul>

	o **Report** on the results of the analysis o **Identify** any necessary preventive and corrective actions
Inputs	➢ **Business Analysis Approach** – Identifies business analysis deliverables that will be produced, activities that need to be performed (including who and when) and techniques that will be used ➢ **Performances Objectives (external)** – Describes the desired performance outcomes that an enterprise is hoping to achieve

Elements	➢ **Performance Analysis** – Reports on business analysis performance can be **informal** and **verbal**, or they may include **formal** documentation and are **designed** and **tailored** to meet the needs of the various types of reviewers.
	➢ **Assessment Measures** – Business analysts may leverage measures if they are existing or may also elicit from stakeholders.
	  o Performance measures may be based on
	    ▪ **Deliverables due dates** as specified in the business analysis plan
	    ▪ **Metrics** such as frequency of changes to work products, number of review cycles required, task efficiency or
	    ▪ **Qualitative feedback** from stakeholders and peers regarding the business analyst's deliverables
	  o Measures may be both **qualitative** and **quantitative**
	  o **Qualitative** measures are **subjective** and can be heavily influenced by the **stakeholder's attitudes, perceptions, and other subjective criteria**.
	  o Some possible measures are:
	    ▪ Accuracy and Completeness
	    ▪ Knowledge
	    ▪ Effectiveness
	    ▪ Organizational Support
	    ▪ Significance
	    ▪ Strategic
	    ▪ Timeliness
	➢ **Analyze Results** – The analysis may be performed on the **business analysis process, resources involved and deliverables**. Certain bodies like line managers, Centre of Excellence may provide assessments and come up with those who have the authority to set the targets for measuring performance.
	➢ **Recommend Actions for Improvement** – Business Analyst engages appropriate stakeholders to identify the actions. These actions are likely to result in changes to the business analysis approach, repeatable processes, and tools. Actions could be as follows:
	  o **Preventive** – reduces the probability of an event with a negative impact
	  o **Corrective** – establish ways to reduce the negative impact of an event
	  o **Hybrid** – Combination of preventive and Corrective

Guidelines & Tools	➢ Organizational Performance Standards – Include performance metrics or expectations for business analysis work mandated by the organization.
Techniques	➢ **Brainstorming** – Used to generate ideas for improvement opportunities ➢ **Interviews** – Used to gather assessments of business analysis performance ➢ **Item Tracking** – Used to track issues occurring during the performance of business analysis

	➢ **Lessons Learned** – Used to identify recommended changes to organizational process assets that can be incorporated into current and future work ➢ **Metrics and Key Performance Indicators (KPIs)** – Identify metrics appropriate for assessing business analysis performance and how they may be tracked ➢ **Observation** – Used to witness business analysis performance ➢ **Process Analysis** – Used to analyse existing business analysis processes and identify opportunities for improvement ➢ **Process Modelling** – Used to define business analysis processes and understand how to improve those processes. ➢ **Reviews** – Used to identify changes to business analysis processes and deliverables that can be incorporated into future work ➢ **Risk Analysis and Management** – Used to identify and manage potential conditions and events that may impact business analysis performance ➢ **Root Cause Analysis** – Used to help identify the underlying cause of failures or difficulties in accomplishing business analysis work ➢ **Survey or Questionnaire** – Used to gather feedback from stakeholders about their satisfaction with business analysis activities and deliverables ➢ **Workshops** – Used to gather assessments of business analysis performance and generate ideas for improvement opportunities
Stakeholders	➢ Domain Subject Matter Expert ➢ Project Manager ➢ Sponsor – May require **reports** on business analysis performance to address the problems identified.

Output	➢ **Business Analysis Performance Assessment** – Includes a
	   ○ Comparison of planned versus actual performance
	   ○ Identifying the root cause of **variances** from the expected performance
	   ○ Proposed approaches to address issues
	   ○ Other findings to help understand the performance of business analysis performance

Glossary

- **Predictive** – Predictive refers to an approach that we can predict and act accordingly. This is mostly applied for traditional / Waterfall SDLC where there is a linear and structured plan to produce a decided outcome within a decided timeframe. As part of this approach, time and scope component remains static and pre-decided.
- **Adaptive** – Adaptive refers to an approach where the project keeps on evolving and changing conditions are encountered as part of the process. This is mostly applied for Agile SDLC where there is an unstructured plan and undetermined timelines to allow ultimate flexibility in directing the course of project. Time and scope component remain flexible and can be customized based on the need.
- **Governance** – It is an act of governing and monitoring by creating policies, rules as well as regulations and properly managing them.
- **Current State** – This is "as-is" state on which analysis is conducted and may need a change from a business perspective
- **Future State** – This is a "to-be" state in which business foresees itself in the upcoming future. This is the state which is an outcome of carrying out business analysis activities.
- **Agile** – A methodology that is characterized by division of work into short phases and frequently delivers the work in the form of short iterations.
- **Scrum** – Iterative and incremental agile development framework for managing product development.
- **Product Backlog** – A list of ideas from stakeholders, business sponsors and owners as part of agile methodology towards an initiative.
- **Backlog Refinement Sessions** – A session in which agile team discusses product backlog with the product owner and try to refine it to make it suitable for commencing work on the same.
- **Sprint Planning** – A scrum ceremony where team discusses and plans the work for the short iteration (so called sprint).
- **Stakeholder** - A group or person who has interests that may be affected by an initiative or influence over it
- **Stakeholder List** - An exhaustive list of stakeholders appropriately categorized and structured.
- **Stakeholder matrix -** Maps the level of stakeholder influence against the level of stakeholder interest
- **Requirements attributes -** Provide information about the requirements e.g. Author, Owner, Complexity, Priority, Absolute reference, status, etc.
- **Risk** - Risk refers to future uncertainty about deviation from the expected outcome. The impact could be positive or negative
- **Tailoring** - Tailoring means taking a deviation (change) from the standardized process or documentation. Tailoring a process means asking for a change in the process for a customer.
- **Approach** - It refers to a way of completing a task or achieving a goal.
- **Deliverable -** Any unique and verifiable work product/ service that a party has agreed to deliver

Case Study

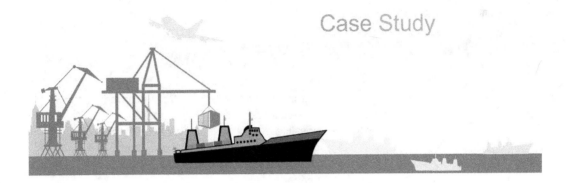

An e-commerce company, ComTel Inc, has hired an IT company to develop a customer tracking application to manage visitors who abandon the purchase cycle mid-way. The project management team wanted to monitor the performance of the project and key professionals including the business analyst.

The team decided to measure the following metrics:

Performance Measures	Expected value	Measurement Formula
Customer Acquisition success rate (CASR)	>=77%	Number of visitors completing purchases --- Number of visitors at Payments page
Number of defects	3 / Person Month	Total number of defects --- (Project months spent till then)
Schedule variance	<= 3%	(Actual end date – actual start date) * 100 --- (Scheduled end date – Scheduled start date)

Table 1: Performance Measures

The data was collected by the project tracking application and review was conducted every month. The analysis of data for December suggested that there are slippages. So, the Business analyst deliberated with the team to decide the approach to address the issues. The team decided to take a hybrid approach. The table below shows the correction and preventive actions as well as the data.

Activities	Expected value	Actual Value	Correction action	Preventive action
Number of defects	3 / Person Month	4 / Person month (Iteration 1completion)	Get the defects fixed	Conduct regular reviews to prevent defects
Schedule variance	<= 3%	5% (Iteration 1completion)	Communicate to the stakeholders for a possible overall project delay Evaluate for compensating as the variance is low	Weekly (or reduce the frequency of measurement) work activity tracking

Table 2: The Action plan

Case Study Questions

Q1. ComTel Inc team has identified the performance measures to assess the performance of the team and the project. Which of the following accurately measures the knowledge of the Business analysts in the team?

A. Customer Acquisition Success Rate (CASR)
B. Number of defects
C. Schedule variance
D. None of these

Q2. Schedule variance is one of the defined performance measures. The variance is measured against the planned schedule. What is the source of this planned schedule?

A. The planned schedule is provided by the Sponsor
B. The planned schedule is provided by the Project Manager
C. The planned schedule is the outcome of the business analysis planning
D. The planned schedule is based on the delivery schedule in the business case

Q3. Table 2 shows the proposed approaches to address the variances. The Business analyst is asked to record these. Where will the Business Analyst record these?

A. Business Analysis plan
B. Business Analysis Governance Plan
C. Information Management Approach
D. Business Analysis Performance Assessment

Case Study Answers

Q1 - Answer: None of the metrics defined in the section is specific to the performance of Business analysts. Defect Metrics concerns all the defects and not only business analysis defects. If the question would have mentioned the measurement after the requirements phase, this could have been the correct answer. But the question does not state that.

Schedule variance is also not specific to business analysis work and question does not mention when was it measured?

Customer Acquisition success rate (CASR) is a strategic goal and is not the right answer.

So, the correct answer is D. Section 3.5.4.2 of BABOK.

Q2 - Answer: The schedule is created by the Business analyst as the BA determines when the business analysis tasks need to be performed. As per section 3.5.4.4 of BABOK.

However, it must be pointed out that in most of the cases, the Project Manager prepares the project plan with inputs from Business Analysts.

Q3 - Answer: The root causes of variances from the expected performance and proposed approaches to address issues are included in the Business Analysis Performance Assessment. Section 3.5.8 of BABOK.

Exercises and Drills

Question 1: Match the following.

1. Project Complexity	A. Scheduling of tasks
2. Communication with stakeholders	B. Uniqueness of requirements, number of stakeholders, amount of risk etc.
3. Timing of Business Analysis work	C. Number of stakeholders
4. Work packages	D. Decomposition of tasks
5. Work breakdown structure (WBS)	E. Helps a BA to manage activities
6. Activity list	F. Interface between units

Question 2: Match the following.

1. Stakeholder analysis	A. Maps and shows the stakeholder's involvement with the proposed solution
2. Stakeholder matrix	B. Involves identifying stakeholders and their characteristics
3. Onion diagrams	C. Maps the level of stakeholder influence against the level of impact on stakeholders
4. RACI matrix	D. Shows the roles and responsibilities of a stakeholder in an initiative

Question 3: Match the following.

1. Change Request attributes	A. Timelines, expected value, dependencies, resource constraints, adopted methodologies
2. Business Analysis governance includes	B. Requirements and designs, reviews, change control, approvals, and prioritization
3. Factors influencing requirements and design prioritization are	C. Cost estimates, time estimates, benefits, risks, priority, course of action
4. Purpose of Plan business analysis governance is to define how decisions are made about	D. Decision making, Change control process, Plan prioritization approach, and Plan for approvals

Question 4: Solve this crossword puzzle.

Down

1. The value added by a change, a synonym (8)
3. Level of importance of change relative to the other factors (8)
5. A way of completing a task or achieving a goal (8)
6. A way of dealing with something (8)

Across

2. _____ Analysis of change requests (5)
4. Not a detailed format though it still represents what the customer wants (5)

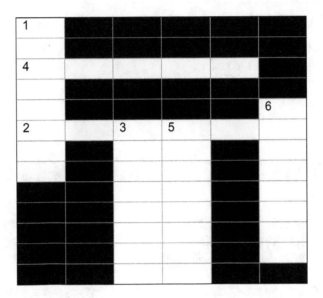

Question 5: Complete the crossword puzzle.

Across	Down
1. Deliverables are broken down into activities and each activity is broken into _____ (5).	2. An Approach that focuses on rapid delivery of business value in short iterations (8)
	4. The effect of uncertainty on the value of a change, a solution, or the enterprise (5)
	An influencing factor that cannot be changed, and that places a limit or restriction on a possible solution (11)
3. A planning Approach that calls for formal documentation and representations (10)	
5. The process of changing the organizational template or process to suit a project (9)	

ANSWERS:

Answer 1: 1 – B, 2 – C, 3 – A, 4 – F (Section 10.32.3.3), 5 – D, 6 – E

Answer 2: 1 – B, 2 – C, 3 – A, 4 – D

Answer 3: 1 –C, 2 – D, 3 – A, 4 – B

Answer 4:

1 B					
E					
4 N	E	E	D	S	
E					
F					6 S
2 I	M	3 P	5 A	C	T
T		R	P		R
S		I	P		A
		O	R		T
		R	O		E
		I	A		G
		R	C		Y
		T	H		
		Y			

Answer 5:

					4 R					
	3 P	R	E	D	I	6 C	T	I	V	E
1 T	2 A	S	K	S	S	O				
	D				K	N				
	A				S	S				
	P					T				
	5	A	I	L	O	R	I	N	G	
	T					A				
	I					I				
	V					N				
	E					T				
						S				

Mock Questions

Q1. A business analyst planned to upgrade an existing software system in the company. During the implementation phase, there was a technical challenge faced by the IT team, but the team was not clear on whom to go for resolving this impasse. What was not defined by the team in this case?

A. Stakeholder Engagement Approach
B. Business Analysis Governance plan
C. Requirements Architecture
D. Requirements Prioritization Approach

Q2. A junior BA is planning how to store the information, its complexity, details, and relationship amongst the information. Which of the following tasks act as an input for the ongoing work the BA is performing?

A. Define future state
B. Governance Approach
C. Specify and Modelling requirements
D. Assess solution limitations

Q3. Project Manager Ben asked the BA of the project to make a duplicate database to serve as a staging database and to allow system testing. He also asked the BA to keep the duplicate database in sync with the original one at all times. What kind of action is taken by Ben?

A. Corrective
B. Preventive
C. Improvement
D. Hybrid

Q4. Tanya Garg is preparing the business analysis approach. She is also considering the factors that can influence this approach as well as the decisions taken based on this approach. According to her list, which of the following factors does not affect the business analysis approach at all?

A. Business policies
B. Expert judgement
C. Business analysis performance assessment
D. Legal/ regulatory requirements

Q5. Akash is the business analyst of a project and is identifying the stakeholders. He is considering various factors to identify the stakeholders relevant to the project. Which of the following is NOT a factor in identifying the stakeholders?

A. Role in the organization
B. Recommendation from Sponsor
C. Role in the business processes
D. Availability of the stakeholder

Q6. As complexity and risk increase or decrease, the nature and scope of business analysis work can be altered and reflected in the business analysis approach. What is the impact on the BA approach, when the number of stakeholders increases?

A. No direct impact
B. Requirement of additional steps to manage BA work
C. Not enough information available to answer this question
D. Increase in the number of meetings with stakeholders

Q7. Rahim Bhimani is working on the business analysis approach for a retail banking project. It's a new age bank and the solution is also going to include some latest digital payments facility. He is not sure about the planning approach. Which all factors do he need to consider for this?

A) Level of uncertainty
B) Organization QMS (Quality Management System)
C) Historical references/Lessons learned.

A. A and B only

B. A Only

C. B and C

D. All the three

Q8. A sponsor is invited to participate in the meeting which is organized by a business analyst to plan and finalize the change control and approval process. What is the purpose of inviting a sponsor for this meeting?

A. The sponsor can provide needs and objectives for the approach and ensures that organizational policies are followed
B. The sponsor may require reports on business analysis performance to address problems as they are identified
C. The sponsor can impose his/her own requirements for how business analysis information should be managed
D. The sponsor will be responsible to review and approve the business case, solution or product scope, and all requirements and designs

Q9. A business analyst is planning to decide the approach for taking approvals from the stakeholders. The BA has to decide on the timing and frequency. Which of the factors should the BA consider deciding upon the timing and frequency of approvals?

A. Size and complexity of the change and associated risk of delaying the approval
B. Size and complexity of the change and availability of the stakeholder
C. Size and complexity of the change and role of the stakeholder in the organization
D. Associated risk of delaying the approval and availability of the stakeholder

Q10. Which type of stakeholder we need to keep satisfied throughout the project?

A. High influence and High impact
B. High influence and Low impact
C. Low influence and High impact
D. Low influence and Low impact

ANSWERS

Q1. Answer B: Choice A - Plan stakeholder engagement focuses on establishing and maintaining working relationships with stakeholders.
Choice B is correct (Section 3.3.4 BABOK): Governance plan defines how decisions are made about requirements, approvals, prioritization, etc, which was not defined in this case.

Choice C: This task ensures stakeholders have a shared understanding of business analysis information. Choice D: This deals with the prioritization of requirements and not the escalation path.

Q2. Answer B: The business analyst is involved in the plan business analysis information management activities where Governance Approach is an input for Plan business analysis information management task. (Section 3.4.4.1 primarily of BABOK and other elements of this task).

Choice a: Define future state is not an input for Plan business analysis information management.
Choice c: Specify and Modelling Requirements is not an input for Plan business analysis information management.
Choice d: Assess Solution limitations is not an input for Plan business analysis information management.
Thus, the correct answer is option b.

Q3. Answer B: choice B: This is a preventive action as it is reducing the probability of a negative impact. In this case, the Project Manager wants to avoid production issues. By creating the staging database, the testing team conducts the testing on an environment which is close to the actual production machine.

BABOK describes preventive action as one of the recommended actions to solve a problem. (Section 3.5.4.4)
Choice A: This is not a corrective action as no negative event has yet taken place.
Choice C: This is not a recommended action.
Also, Choice D is not correct as it includes corrective action also. Thus, option b is the correct answer.

Q4. Answer D: Choice a: Incorrect. Business policies do have an impact on the business analysis approach (Section 3.1.5 of BABOK)

Choice b: Incorrect. Expert judgement affects the business analysis approach.
Choice c: Incorrect. Performance assessment of business analysis affects the approach.
Choice d: Correct. Legal or regulatory requirements do not affect the business analysis approach. Thus, option d is the right answer.

Q5. Answer D: Stakeholders are selected based on their role in the organizational hierarchy as well as their role in the business processes. The Sponsor can also recommend the stakeholders. But availability is not a factor for identifying a stakeholder. It is considered while planning their engagement. (Section 3.2.4.1- 3rd Paragraph)

Q6. Answer B: (Refer 3.1.4.5 BABOK - Section complexity and risk) - An increase in the number of stakeholders may have additional steps for approval, reviews, and even elicitation meetings. Option D covers just one impact and is not the best answer but option b correctly defines the correct answer. So, option b is the correct answer.

Q7. Answer D: All the three options are correct as the level of uncertainty relating to requirements or any other inputs need to be considered. Organizational standards (present in QMS) is also used to determine the BA approach whereas experiences from the previous project are also valuable in determining the approach. Thus, correct answer is option d. (Refer section 3.1.4 BABOK)

Q8. Answer C: (Section 3.3.4 Elements of governance approach) - Option C: It describes the role of a sponsor in the task which includes defining change control and approval processes and this was the question whereas Change control and approval processes are the elements of business analysis governance process. So, it is the correct answer.

Option A describes the role of a sponsor in planning the Business Analysis Approach (A different task). So, it is incorrect.

Option B describes the role of a sponsor in Identifying Business Analysis Performance Improvements. So, it is incorrect.

Option D describes the role of a sponsor in Approving Requirements in the knowledge area - requirements life cycle management knowledge area. So, it is incorrect.

Q9. Answer A: Size and complexity of the change and associated risk of delaying the approval are two factors that should be considered in deciding the timing and frequency of the approvals. Thus, the correct answer is option a. (Section 3.3.4.4 of BABOK)

The role and availability are also considered but will not be the deciding factor. The last option is also incorrect as it has one correct and one incorrect answer.

Q10. Answer B: The figure shows that the strategy to handle high influence and low impact stakeholders is to keep them satisfied. As they are the key players in the change effort and have a high influence on the project, they can affect the project adversely if not kept satisfied. Thus, the correct answer is option b. (Refer to Fig 10.43.1 of BABOK)

Elicitation and Collaboration

The Elicitation and Collaboration knowledge area describes the tasks that business analysts perform to obtain and gather information from stakeholders and to confirm the results.

Elicitation is the **drawing forth** or **receiving** of the information from stakeholders or other sources which might involve interacting with stakeholders directly, performing research activities, conducting experiments, or using existing information to discover requirements and design information.

Collaboration is the act of two or more people working together towards a **common goal**. Elicitation and collaboration work are never a phase rather it is an ongoing activity if business analysis work is occurring.

Set of tasks used to gather information from Stakeholders for the change initiative

It's not a phase rather an ongoing activity of collecting and confirming information

It also describes the communication and collaboration with the stakeholders during and after the business analysis info is assembled

Elicitation activities can be **planned**, **unplanned** or **both**. Information derived from unplanned activity may require deeper exploration through a planned activity.

The usage and application of each of the core concepts within the context of Elicitation and Collaboration is as follows:

- **Change** – Use a variety of elicitation techniques to fully identify the characteristics of the change including concerns that stakeholders have about the change.
- **Need** – Elicit, confirm, and communicate needs and supporting business analysis information.
- **Solution** – Elicit, confirm, and communicate necessary or desired characteristics of proposed solutions.
- **Stakeholder** – Manage the collaboration with the stakeholders who participate in the business analysis work.
- **Value** – Collaborate with stakeholders to assess the relative value of the information provided through elicitation and apply a variety of techniques to confirm and communicate that value.
- **Context** – Apply a variety of elicitation techniques to identify the information about the context that may affect the change.

Elicitation and Collaboration Tasks

01 **Prepare for Elicitation**

02 **Conduct Elicitation**

03 **Confirm Elicitation Results**

04 **Communicate Business Analysis Information**

05 **Manage Stakeholder Collaboration**

Task 1: Prepare for Elicitation

Purpose	To understand the scope of the elicitation activity, select appropriate techniques and plan for appropriate supporting materials and resources.
Description	➤ The preparation for elicitation is done by defining the **desired outcomes** of the activity, considering the **stakeholders** involved and the **goals** of the initiative. This includes deciding on: 　○ **Work products** that will be produced using results, 　○ **Techniques** that are best suited to product results, 　○ Establishing the elicitation **logistics**, 　○ Identifying any supporting **materials** needed, 　○ Understanding circumstances to foster **collaboration** during an elicitation activity
Inputs	➤ **Needs** – Provides guidance for preparation in terms of scope and purpose of elicitation activities. ➤ **Stakeholder Engagement Approach** – Understanding stakeholder's communication and collaboration needs to help plan and prepare for elicitation events.
Elements	➤ **Understand the Scope of Elicitation** – Business analysts consider business domain, overall corporate culture, stakeholder and their locations, expected outputs the elicitation activities will feed, skills of the business analysis practitioner, strategy, solution approach, scope of the future solution and possible sources of the business analysis information to determine the type of the business analysis information and techniques that may be used. 　○ Understanding the scope of elicitation activity helps to keep the activity within intended **scope** and to recognize if **people** and **material** are available as well as when the activity is **complete**. ➤ **Select Elicitation Techniques** – Choosing the right techniques and ensuring each technique is performed correctly is extremely important for the success of elicitation activity. **Table 2.1 describes the factors for selecting elicitation techniques** ➤ **Set Up Logistics** – Logistics are planned prior to an elicitation activity. This includes identifying activity goals, participants and their roles, scheduled resources, locations, communication channels, techniques, languages used

	by stakeholders and may sometimes involve creating an agenda if other stakeholders are involved.
	➤ **Secure Supporting Material** – Business analysts identify **sources** of information which include people, systems, historical data, materials and **documents** such as existing system documents, relevant business rules, regulations, contracts as well as **supporting materials** in form of outputs of analysis work to conduct the elicitation activity.

	➤ **Prepare Stakeholders** – Business analysts may need to explain a particular elicitation technique to stakeholders who are not involved in this activity if they feel that it is not aligned to their individual objectives or are not able to understand process or are confused about it. There is a need to have **buy-in** from all stakeholders in order to conduct elicitation. In order to avoid issues,
	
	    ○ Business analysts may ask stakeholders to **review** required supporting material upfront so that elicitation activity can be conducted effectively.
	    ○ An **agenda** may be published in advance so that stakeholders come prepared for the activity
	    ○ In case of elicitation that is conducted via research or exploration, a business analyst is a solo participant for it.

Guidelines & Tools	➤ Business Analysis Approach – Sets the general strategy to be used to guide the business analysis work which involves methodology, types of stakeholders and their involvement, the timing of work and expected format as well as the level of detail of results. ➤ Business Objectives – Describe the desired direction needed to achieve the future state. ➤ Existing Business Analysis Information – Helps in preparing for elicitation by providing a better understanding of goals ➤ Potential Value – Describes the value to be realized by implementing the proposed future state.
Techniques	➤ **Brainstorming** – Used to collaboratively identify and reach consensus about sources that need to be consulted and techniques that might be most effective. ➤ **Data Mining** – Used to identify information or patterns which require further investigation. ➤ **Document Analysis** – Used to identify and assess candidate sources of supporting materials. ➤ **Estimation** – Used to estimate the time and effort required for elicitation and associated cost. ➤ **Interviews** – Used to identify concerns about the planned elicitation and can be used to seek authority to proceed. ➤ **Mind Mapping** – Used to collaboratively identify and reach consensus about sources that need to be consulted and techniques that might be most effective. ➤ **Risk Analysis and Management** – Used to identify, assess and manage conditions that could disrupt the elicitation or affect the quality and validity of elicitation results. ➤ **Stakeholder List, Map or Personas** – Used to determine who should be consulted while preparing for elicitation and who should participate in the event.
Stakeholders	➤ Domain Subject Matter Expert ➤ Project Manager

	➤ Sponsor – Has the **authority** to approve or deny a planned elicitation event and to authorize and require the **participation** of certain stakeholders.
Output	➤ **Elicitation Activity Plan** – Used for each elicitation activity to include logistics, scope, selected techniques, and supporting materials.

Factors considered for Selecting Elicitation techniques

Parameters	Meaning	Selection
Cost and Time constraints	How rigid is the schedule and budget for the change initiative?	Budget constraints leads to more efficient techniques like Workshops, Questionnaires
Stakeholders Diversity	Heterogeneous, Homogeneous, Mixed	
Stakeholders Locations	Single location, Multi-locational	Multi-locational stakeholders make it difficult to involve them physically. Surveys or Questionnaires or any group meeting techniques help
Project Complexity	Technical complexity, Functional complexity, Stakeholders/Management complexity	
Project Domain	Is the change initiative - replacing the existing processes or is new?	
Domain Knowledge	Does the change initiative require an understanding of the domain or it's a generic domain and does not require additional effort?	Observation, Prototyping, use case scenarios and even interviews help in understanding domain well
Project Criticality	Any special requirement like 24x7 availability or redundancy or security etc.	
Chosen Perspectives	What is the perspective? – Agile, BPM, Business architecture etc	Personas, Story boarding etc

Task 2: Conduct Elicitation

Purpose	To draw out, explore and identify information relevant to the change.

Description	➢ Stakeholders may collaborate in elicitation by participating and interacting as part of an activity or by researching, studying and providing feedback on documents, models, and interfaces.
	➢ There are 3 common types of elicitation:
	   o **Collaborative** – Direct interaction with stakeholders and relies on their experiences, expertise, and judgement.
	   o **Research** – Involves systematically discovering and studying information from materials or sources that are not directly known by stakeholders involved in the change.
	   o **Experiments** – Involves identifying information that via controlled test such as observational studies, proofs of concept and prototypes.

Inputs	➢ **Elicitation Activity Plan** – Includes the planned elicitation activities and techniques, activity logistics, scope and available sources for background information.

Elements	➢ **Guide Elicitation Activity** – The format of business analysis information defined in planning helps ensure that the elicitation activities are producing intended information at the desired level of detail.
	   o In order to help guide and facilitate towards the expected outcomes, business analysts consider:
	     ▪ Elicitation activity goals and agenda,
	     ▪ Scope of the change
	     ▪ The forms of output generated,
	     ▪ Other representations that activity results will support,
	     ▪ Integration of output into what is already known,
	     ▪ Source provider of information, consumer of information and the process by which that information will be used.
	➢ **Capture Elicitation Outcomes** – On the basis of the scope, elicitation is conducted iteratively and in multiple parallel or in sequence sessions. Capturing the elicitation outcomes helps to ensure that the information produced during elicitation is recorded for later reference and use. These outcomes are documented in requirements management tools. By using a tool, we can make sure that requirements will be available for future use too.

Guidelines & Tools	➢ Business Analysis Approach – Influences how each elicitation activity is performed, as it identifies the types of outputs that will be needed based on the approach. ➢ Existing Business Analysis Information – May guide the questions posed during elicitation and the approach to draw out information from various stakeholders. ➢ Stakeholder Engagement Approach – Provides collaboration and communication approaches that might be effective during elicitation. ➢ Supporting Materials – Includes any materials to prepare for elicitation as well as any information, tools or equipment to be used during elicitation.
Techniques	➢ **Benchmarking and Market Analysis** – Used as a source of business analysis information by comparing it with some external baseline such as a standard created by an industry association. Market analysis is used to determine what customers want and what competitors provide. ➢ **Brainstorming** – Used to generate, organize and prioritize a number of ideas from a group of stakeholders in a short period.

	➢ **Business Rules Analysis** – Used to identify the rules that govern decisions in an organization.
	➢ **Collaborative Games** – Used to develop a better understanding of a problem or to stimulate creative solutions.
	➢ **Concept Modelling** – Used to identify key terms and ideas of importance and define relationships between them.
	➢ **Data Mining** – Used to identify relevant information and patterns.
	➢ **Data Modelling** – Used to understand entity relationships during elicitation.
	➢ **Document Analysis** – Used to review existing systems, policies and standards.
	➢ **Focus Groups** – Used to identify and understand ideas and attitudes from a group.
	➢ **Interface Analysis** – Used to understand the interaction between two entities such as two systems, people or roles.
	➢ **Interviews** – Used to ask questions to uncover needs, identify problems or discover opportunities.
	➢ **Mind Mapping** – Used to generate, organize and prioritize many ideas in a short time.
	➢ **Observation** – Used to gain insight into how the work is currently done.
	➢ **Process Analysis** – Used to understand current processes and to identify opportunities for improvement in those processes.
	➢ **Process Modelling** – Used to elicit processes with stakeholders during elicitation activities.
	➢ **Prototyping** – Used to elicit and validate stakeholder's needs through an iterative process that creates a requirements model.
	➢ **Survey or Questionnaire** – Used to elicit business analysis information from a group of people in a structured way and in a short period of time.
	➢ **Workshops** – Used to elicit business analysis information from a group of people in a collaborative, facilitated way.
Stakeholders	➢ Customer – Will **provide** valuable business analysis information during elicitation.
	➢ Domain Subject Matter Expert
	➢ End User
	➢ Implementation Subject Matter Expert
	➢ Sponsor – Authorizes and ensures that the stakeholders necessary to participate in elicitation are involved.
	➢ Any stakeholders
Output	➢ **Elicitation Results (unconfirmed)** – Captured information in a format that is specific to the elicitation activity.

Task 3: Confirm Elicitation Results

Purpose	To check the information gathered during an elicitation session for accuracy and consistency with any other information.
Description	➢ Elicited information is **compared** against their **source** and other **elicitation results** and **confirmed** to identify any **problems** and **resolve** them before resources are committed to use the information. Committing resources to business analysis activities based on unconfirmed elicitation results may mean that stakeholder expectations are not met. ➢ Confirming the elicitation results is a much **less rigorous** and formal review than it occurs during analysis.
Inputs	➢ **Elicitation Results (unconfirmed)** – Capture information in a format specific to the elicitation activity.

Elements	➢ **Compare Elicitation Results Against Source Information** – Follow up meetings can be arranged by the business analysts to correct and verify elicitation results. On the other hand, it can be done independently too by stakeholders.
	➢ **Compare Elicitation Results Against Other Elicitation Results** – Results collected through multiple elicitation activities are compared to find out if the information gathered is consistent and accurately represented. Variations in results are identified and resolved in collaboration with stakeholders.
	    o In some cases, historical data is also compared to confirm recently collected elicitation results.
	    o Inconsistencies are uncovered when business specifications and models are created which can be removed by improving collaboration with stakeholders.

Guidelines & Tools	➢ Elicitation Activity Plan – Used to guide which alternative sources and which elicitation results are to be compared. ➢ Existing Business Analysis Information – Can be used to confirm the results and draw out more detailed information.
Techniques	➢ **Document Analysis** – Used to confirm elicitation results against existing documents. ➢ **Interviews** – Used to confirm the business analysis information that is collected is correct. ➢ **Reviews** – Informal or formal reviews to confirm on the set of elicitation results. ➢ **Workshops** – Used to conduct reviews of the drafted elicitation results using any level of formality.
Stakeholders	➢ Domain Subject Matter Expert ➢ Any Stakeholder
Output	➢ **Elicitation Results (confirmed)** – Integrated output that the business analyst and other stakeholders agree correctly reflects captured information and confirms it is relevant and useful as an input to further work.

Task 4: Communicate Business Analysis Information

Purpose	To ensure that the stakeholders have a shared understanding of business analysis information.
Description	➢ Appropriate information must be communicated to stakeholders at the right **time** and in **formats** that meet their needs. ➢ Consideration is given to expressing the information in **language, tone, and style** that is appropriate to the **audience**. ➢ Communication of information is usually **bi-directional** and **iterative**. It involves determining recipients, explaining the content, providing the right context and expecting an outcome out of it. ➢ Business analysts act on any **discrepancies** that are identified and work on resolving them. This could also be due to the method of delivering the information as stakeholders may not be able to understand it.
Inputs	➢ **Business Analysis Information** – Any kind of information at any level of detail that is used as an input or output of business analysis work. This is the best input when the need is to be communicated as information to stakeholders. ➢ **Stakeholder Engagement Approach** – Describes stakeholder groups, roles, and general needs regarding communication of business analysis information.

Elements	➢ **Determine Objectives and Format of Communication** – The primary goal of developing a package is to **convey** information **clearly** and in a **usable** format for continuing change activities.
	   o Business analysis information packages may be prepared for several reasons such as below:
	      ▪ Communication of requirements and designs to stakeholders,
	      ▪ Early assessment of quality and planning,
	      ▪ Evaluation of possible alternatives,
	      ▪ Formal reviews and approvals,
	      ▪ Inputs to solution design,
	      ▪ conformance to contractual or regulatory obligations and
	      ▪ Maintenance for reuse.
	   o The package must-have a combination of material that can convey a cohesive and effective message as a whole. Such packages can be stored in different online or offline repositories including documents and tools.
	   o Possible form of packages includes:
	      ▪ **Formal Documentation** – Usually based on the template used by the organization to provide a stable, easy to use, long term record of information.
	      ▪ **Informal Documentation** – Documented as part of the change process, but not as part of a formal organizational process.
	      ▪ **Presentations** – A high level overview to show understanding of goals of a change, functions of a solution or supported information for decision making purpose.
	➢ **Communicate Business Analysis Package** – The purpose of communicating the business analysis package is to provide an **appropriate level of detail about the change** so they can understand the information it contains. Stakeholders are given the opportunity to review the package,

	comment as well as raise any concerns they may have. Communication can be done via the following ways: ○ **Group Collaboration** – Communicate the package to a group of stakeholders at the same time. This allows immediate discussion about information and issues. ○ **Individual Collaboration** – Used to communicate the package to a single stakeholder at a time. Very beneficial when an individual understanding is required. ○ **Email or other non-verbal methods** – Best when to communicate highly matured and self-explanatory information to support it.
Guidelines & Tools	➢ Business Analysis Approach – Describes how various information will be disseminated. Includes level of details, formality, communication frequency and its impact on geographically distributed stakeholders. ➢ Information Management Approach – Helps determine how the information will be packaged and communicated to stakeholders.
Techniques	➢ **Interviews** – Used to individually communicate information to stakeholders. ➢ **Reviews** – Used to provide stakeholders with an opportunity to express feedback, request changes, agree or provide approvals. Reviews can be used during **group** or **individual** collaboration. ➢ **Workshops** – Best fit for group collaboration and provides stakeholders with an opportunity to express feedback and to understand adjustments, responses, actions, gaining consensus and providing approvals.
Stakeholders	➢ End User ➢ Customer ➢ Domain Subject Matter Expert ➢ Implementation Subject Matter Expert ➢ Tester ➢ Any stakeholder
Output	➢ **Business Analysis Information (communicated)** – It is considered as communicated when the target audience reaches a state of understanding of its content and implications.

Task 5: Manage Stakeholder Collaboration

Purpose	To encourage stakeholders to work towards a common goal.
Description	<ul><li>Managing stakeholder collaboration is an **ongoing** activity.</li><li>New stakeholders can be identified at **any point** during an initiative. As new stakeholders are identified, their role, influence, and relationship to the initiative are analyzed. Each stakeholder's role, responsibility, influence, attitude, and authority may change over time.</li><li>Business analysts manage stakeholder collaboration to **capitalize** on positive reactions and **mitigate** or avoid negative reactions. Stakeholder's attitude needs to be monitored and assessed to determine if it is affecting their participation in business analysis activities. Outcomes of poor relationships with stakeholders could be as follows:<ul><li>Failure to provide quality information,</li><li>Strong negative reactions to setbacks and obstacles,</li><li>Resistance to change,</li><li>Lack of support and participation in business analysis work and ignorance of business analysis information.</li></ul></li><li>A strong, positive, and trust-based relationships need to be managed with stakeholders who:<ul><li>Provides service to business analyst</li><li>Depends on the services provided by business analyst</li><li>Participate in the execution of business analysis tasks.</li></ul></li></ul>
Inputs	<ul><li>**Stakeholder Engagement Approach** – Describes the type of expected engagement with stakeholders and how they might need to be managed.</li><li>**Business Analysis Performance Assessment** – Provides key information about the effectiveness of business analysis tasks being executed, including those focused on stakeholder engagement.</li></ul>
Elements	<ul><li>**Gain Agreement on Commitments** – Stakeholders may be participating in activities that involve investing time and commitments from resources. This needs to be identified and agreed upon as early as possible.<ul><li>Explicit understanding of expectations and desired outcomes of the commitment needs to be communicated formally or informally. In case of issues with the terms and conditions of the commitments, effective **negotiation, communication, and conflict-resolution skills** need to be used.</li></ul></li><li>**Monitor Stakeholder Engagement** – Business analysts continually monitor the participation and performance of stakeholders as well as risks.<ul><li>Continuous monitoring of participation and performance ensures that:<ul><li>Right subject matter experts are participating effectively,</li><li>Stakeholder attitudes and interest are improving,</li><li>Elicitation results are confirmed within time,</li><li>Agreements and commitments are maintained</li></ul></li><li>Following types of risks are monitored:<ul><li>Stakeholders being diverted to other work,</li><li>Elicitation activities not providing quality of information required,</li><li>Delayed approvals</li></ul></li></ul></li><li>**Collaboration** – Stakeholders are more supportive of change if business analysts collaborate with them to allow the flow of information, ideas, and innovations. Collaboration involves regular and frequent communication in</li></ul>

	the form of free flow of information around obstacles and to promote a shared effort to resolve problems and achieve desired outcomes.	
Guidelines & Tools	➤ Business Analysis Approach – Describes the nature and level of collaboration required from each stakeholder group. ➤ Business Objectives – Describe the desired direction needed to achieve the future state. ➤ Future State Description – Defines the future state and expected value it delivers while keeping the focus on common goals. ➤ Recommended Actions – Communicating what should be done to improve the value of the solution can help to galvanize support and focus on common goal. ➤ Risk Analysis Results – Stakeholder related risks will need to be addressed to ensure stakeholder collaboration activities are successful.	
Techniques	➤ **Collaborative Games** – Used to stimulate teamwork and collaboration by immersing participants in a safe and fun situation to explore and share the knowledge. ➤ **Lessons Learned** – Used to understand stakeholder's satisfaction or dissatisfaction and offer them an opportunity to help improve working relationships. ➤ **Risk Analysis and Management** – Used to identify and manage risks. ➤ **Stakeholder List, Map, or Personas** – Used to determine who is available to participate in business analysis work and who needs to be consulted about different kinds of business analysis information.	
Stakeholders	➤ All Stakeholders	
Output	➤ **Stakeholder Engagement** – Willingness of stakeholders to engage in business analysis activities and interact with the business analyst when necessary.	

Glossary

- **Requirements Management Tools** – Tools provide a continuous process of managing requirements and managing them throughout the lifecycle of those requirements. A couple of examples of such tools are IBM Rational Rose, IRIS Business Architect, and Enterprise Architect.
- **Focus group:** It is used to identify and understand ideas from a group
- **Elicitation:** Is to draw forth or bring out something for further analysis and understanding. Requirement elicitation refers to a set of activities to extract business needs from the stakeholders
- **Scope:** Defines the extent of responsibility for a team, but it does not refer to the requirements or functionality scope. Scope of work in the software world refers to the activities needed to be completed for a software project (or change).
- **Value:** The benefit resulting from a change. The benefit could be monetary or non-monetary
- **Sponsor:** A stakeholder who is responsible for initiating the effort to define a business need and develop a solution that meets that need. They authorize the work to be performed and control the budget and scope for the initiative.
- **RACI Matrix:** Responsible, Accountable, Consulted, and Informed matrix (RACI matrix): A tool used to identify the responsibilities of roles or team members and other stakeholders
- **Proof of concept (POC):** A proof of concept is a controlled test conducted to check the viability of a concept or to identify information. It's a type of experiments.
- **Business analysis information package:** The primary goal of developing a package is to convey information clearly and in a usable format for continuing change activities.
- **Informal documentation:** It may include text, diagrams, or matrices that are used during a change but are not part of a formal organizational process.
- **Formal documentation:** It may include text, diagrams, or matrices that are used during a change based on an organizational template

Case Study

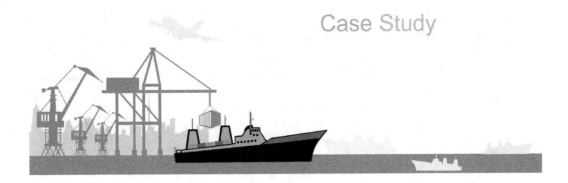

Trac LLC is an automobile spare parts manufacturing plant. They supply spare parts to the car manufacturing companies. The company wants to implement SAP (Top ERP product) for managing its production as well as inventory.

It has hired AG software Inc to implement the modules. AG Software has given a timeline of 10 months and has submitted the implementation plan.

Robert Weiss is the Business Analyst of the project. Robert is creating the stakeholder communication and management plan.

Robert studied the organizational chart and talked to the General manager and came up with the first list of the stakeholders.

Stakeholder Name	Designation	Contact Email Id	Contact Number
Mr. George Smith	General Manager	George.smith@trac-s.com	+1 234-546-710
Mr. Rakesh Garg	Chief Financial Officer (CFO)	Rakesh.garg@trac-s.com	+1 234-546-720
Ms. Silvia Paris	Purchase Manager	Silvia.paris@trac-s.com	+1 234-546-723
Mr. Wills Miles	Warehouse Manager	Walls.miles@trac-s.com	+1 234-546-745

Table 1: Stakeholder List

The AG software team, led by Robert, went to the Trac headquarters for requirements elicitation. Robert had further discussions and came up with the following stakeholder communication and management plan.

Stakeholder Name	Impact (Low, Medium, High)	Influence (Low, Medium, High)	What is important to the stakeholder?	How could the stakeholder contribute to the project?	How could the stakeholder block the project?	Strategy for engaging the stakeholder
Mr. George Smith	High	High	Maintaining the production as scheduled as well as managing inventory	He is the decision maker and approver	Stops or delays sign offs	Keeping him informed through a call on a weekly basis. He wants to be on top of things.
Mr. Rakesh Garg	Low	High	No project cost overruns	Not significantly but providing cost control	By not releasing payments	Keeping him informed by milestone completion progress
Ms. Silvia Paris	Low	High	Getting raw materials for not allowing any impact on production schedule	Proving requirements related to her department	Not approving the delivered modules, if not found appropriate	Sending her weekly status report

Table 2: Stakeholder Management Plan

This stakeholder communication and management plan is maintained throughout the project and collaboration with the stakeholders is managed.

Case Study Questions

Q1. Robert Weiss has prepared the stakeholders list as shown in Table 1. What would be the sources of identifying the stakeholders for Robert?

1. Meeting with Sponsor
2. Organizational Chart
3. Business processes

Choose the correct answer

A. All three
B. 1 and 2
C. 1 and 3
D. 2 and 3

Q2. Mr. Rakesh Garg is a stakeholder with high influence but low impact. The last column in Table 2 describes the collaboration strategy for Rakesh Garg. Is this strategy correct?

A. No, since Mr. Rakesh is influential, he needs to be involved in all the requirements meeting also
B. No, since Mr. Rakesh is influential, he needs to be informed of his needs being met regularly
C. Yes, by keeping him informed of milestone completion his needs are satisfied
D. Yes, by keeping him informed of milestone completion he will feel satisfied

Q3. A Subject matter expert (SME) with extensive knowledge of the ERP product is also hired as a consultant to guide Robert. Where will you place the SME in the Influence and impact matrix?

A. High Influence and Low impact

   B. High Influence and High impact

   C. Low Influence and Low impact

   D. Low Influence and High impact

Q4. Rachel is also a Business Analyst and she advised Robert to create a RACI matrix instead of a Stakeholder management plan as in Table 2. Is she right?

   A. Yes, RACI matrix is a more powerful stakeholder analysis approach

   B. Yes, RACI matrix provides more accurate information about the stakeholders

   C. No, RACI matrix does not capture the responsibilities of Stakeholders

   D. No, RACI matrix does not provide enough details to strategize about collaboration

Case Study Answers

Answer – Q1. The case study clearly mentions that Robert prepared the Stakeholder list (as in Table 1) using inputs from the Sponsor and the Organizational chart. So, the correct answer is B.

Answer – Q2. Refer to Section 10.43.3.2: Stakeholder Matrix. These stakeholders have needs that must be met and they should be satisfied with the progress. Informing them about only the milestone is not enough. They should be kept informed and engaged regularly. So, the Correct answer is B.

Answer - Q3. Correct answer is A. A Subject Matter Expert is hired as a specialist and is going to have a significant level of authority within the domain of change (ERP implementation). This indicates a high influence. However, the Subject matter expert is a consultant and is likely to work on multiple projects. This means that there will be a low impact on the SME. So, the correct answer is A. Section 10.43.2.

Answer – Q4. RACI matrix only captures the responsibilities of stakeholders as Responsible, Accountable, Consulted, and Informed. This information is not sufficient to plan for effective collaboration with the Stakeholders. Correct answer is D. Section 10.43.3.3, BABOK.

Exercises and Drills

Question 1: Match the following Descriptions of elicitation techniques with the techniques.

Involves groups of people giving multiple inputs, and the solution direction unclear	A. Prototyping
Taking an independent view on the processes when stakeholders not able to provide required inputs	B. Brainstorming
Stakeholders lack the clarity on processes and its details	C. Job Shadowing
Involves groups of people giving varied inputs, but the direction is clear	D. Surveys
Involves large number of stakeholders and is used to quickly cover all of them	E. Focus Groups

Question 2: Match the following tasks with their respective descriptions.

1. Process Models	A. Type of business analysis information package
2. Email	B. Business Analysis Information package
3. Screen prototypes	C. Common communication platform
4. Communicate business analysis information	D. Monitoring stakeholder collaboration
5. Domain SME availability	E. Provides stakeholders with the information they need; at the time they need it

Question 3: Match the elements on the left with their usage.

1. Existing Business Analysis Information	A. Guides the preparation for elicitation
2. Business Analysis approach	B. To identify Stakeholder related risks
3. Risk Analysis results	C. Aids in the preparation of elicitation
4. Risk Analysis and Management	D. To manage conditions or situations that could disrupt the elicitation process.

Question 4: Complete the crossword puzzle.

Across	Down
2. A focused event with a group of stakeholders (8)	1. Composed of pre-qualified individuals whose purpose is to discuss on a topic under the guidance of a trained facilitator (10) 4.Used to elicit and validate stakeholders' needs through an iterative process that creates a model of requirements or designs (11)
3. Used to elicit BA information from many people in a relatively short period of time (6)	

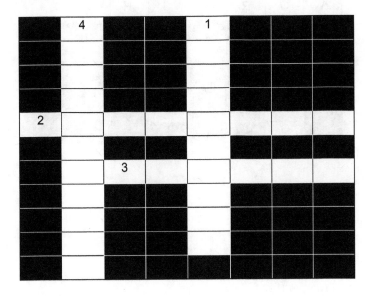

TECHCANVASS

ANSWERS:

Answer 1: 1 – B, 2 – C, 3 – A, 4 – E, 5 – D

Answer 2: 1 – B, 2 – C, 3 – A, 4 –E, 5 – D

Answer 3: 1 – C (BABOK Section 4.1.5), 2 – A (BABOK Section 4.1.5), 3 – B (Section 4.5.5), 4 – D (Section 4.1.6. BABOK)

Answer 4:

	4 P			1 F			
	R			O			
	O			C			
	T			U			
2W	O	R	K	S	H	O	P
	T			G			
	Y	3S	U	R	V	E	Y
	P			O			
	I			U			
	N			P			
	G						

TECHCANVASS

Mock Questions

Q1. In her project, a BA is facing challenges because of a poor relationship with stakeholders. What can be the possible effect on her business analysis work?

A) Strong negative reactions to small issues
B) Failure to provide quality information
C) Resistance to change
D) Incomplete research of business analysis information

      A. A and B

      B. B and D

      C. C and D

      D. A and D

Q2. Max Connors is a business analyst for an ongoing project. He prepares a package of documents to be shared with the stakeholders including text and matrices. He looked at the quality management system repository to search for an appropriate template but could not find it. What should he do?

      A. He can present the details in a format of his own

      B. He needs to ask the QA team to come up with a template, else he can't present it

      C. He will inform the stakeholders about the delay, till he gets a template

      D. None of these

Q3. A business analyst prepared a set of questions to understand the business processes. The BA sent questions to the stakeholders. The stakeholders sent the answers. However, the BA found the answers to be too short and didn't help in understanding the processes at all. Did the BA make some mistake in framing the questions?

      A. Yes, he included open ended questions mostly

      B. Yes, he used close ended questions mostly

      C. No, the BA didn't make any mistakes

      D. Yes, the BA lacked the domain knowledge

Q4. A business analyst is conducting elicitation for an e-commerce website for PLUS size garments. The proposed application will need to be integrated into ANSIN bank's payment gateway. BA talks to ANSIN bank to know more about the payment gateway and how it can be integrated. What is the BA doing?

      A. Interface Analysis

      B. Concept Modelling

      C. Proof of Concept

      D. Requirements Elicitation

Q5. Satish Garg is the BA for an Enterprise Application Integration (EAI) project for a bank. This involves many stakeholders. Even though he has conducted several meetings, he can sense that some of the stakeholders don't look happy. What can Satish do to understand the dissatisfaction and improve the working relationships with them?

      A. Conducting collaborative Games

      B. One on one meetings & interviews

C. Arranging a lesson learned session with them

D. Meeting the Sponsor to seek inputs

Q6. A business analyst is preparing the stakeholders for conducting elicitation. What can be done by the BA to make the process efficient and easier?

1) Educate them on the elicitation technique being used

2) Provide them an agenda

3) Ask them to review materials relating to the system

4) Ask them to conduct research on the topic and best practices. Choose the right option.

    A. Options 1 and 2

    B. All options are correct

    C. Options 1 and 3

    D. Options 1, 2 and 3

Q7. A business analyst is preparing for elicitation to be conducted for a project. He needs to study more and conduct research to understand industry practices. Whom would he consult for the materials, he can use for research and study?

    A. Implementation subject matter expert

    B. Sponsor

    C. Project Manager

    D. Domain subject matter expert

Q8. During the requirements elicitation phase, the stakeholders provided details of the existing system (which is going to be replaced). How will the business analyst use this information?

    A. By conducting document analysis to understand more about existing systems

    B. By using it as a reference document in the SRS document

    C. By keeping it but not doing anything with it as it is for the system, which is going to be replaced

    D. By defining the change strategy

Q9. A project team is preparing the business analysis approach and plan. One of the key elements of this is to choose the right elicitation technique(s). How is the elicitation technique decided?

    A. By the Project Manager using organizational project database

    B. By the Business Analyst using organizational project database and past experience

    C. By the Project Manager and business analyst using their experience and historical data

    D. By collaborating with appropriate stakeholders

Q10. Multiple techniques are used during an elicitation activity. Choosing the right techniques and ensuring each technique is performed correctly, is extremely important for the success of the elicitation activity. Which of the following factors are important for making the right selection?

A) Business Domain of the proposed project

B) Techniques used in a similar type of projects in the past

C) Scope of future solution

Choose the correct option which identifies the factors.

    A. A and B
    B. B and C
    C. A and C
    D. All the three

ANSWERS

Q1. Answer A: Choice A: Options a and b are the correct answer. Let us consider the wrong options first. Point C is incorrect as resistance to change does not depend on the relationships with stakeholders (it is a human characteristic). Point D is also incorrect as research of information does not involve stakeholders. (Section 4.2.2)

Now, regarding the points A and B. Poor relationships create strong reactions to small issues, because of a lack of trust and respect. Stakeholders may not provide all the information because of poor relationships.

Q2. Answer A: (Section 4.4.4.1) The business analyst can also use an informal format. So, in this case, he can create a format of his own and present the information to the stakeholders. As long as the format suits the expectations of the stakeholders, it is acceptable. This is called informal documentation. Thus, option a is the right answer.

Q3. Answer B: The question does provide a hint about the questions being close-ended - the BA found the answers to be too short. Close ended questions result in short answers (e.g. Yes/No) and don't provide process details. Hence option B is correct and option A is incorrect.

Option D is not correct because a BA with a lack of domain knowledge is likely to create wrong questions but not necessarily close-ended questions. (Refer to section 10.25.3.3, BABOK) Option C is incorrect as BA did make a mistake by asking close ended questions mostly.

Q4. Answer A: Interface Analysis is used to understand the interaction, and characteristics of that interaction between two entities, such as two systems, two organizations, or two people or roles. (Section 4.2.6, BABOK)

Q5. Answer C: It is used to understand stakeholders' satisfaction or dissatisfaction and to offer them an opportunity to help improve the working relationships. These techniques can also be beneficial at the close of any milestone within the effort meaning you can apply it after an interaction and phase also. (Section 4.5.6 and 10.27 - Lessons Learned)

Q6. Answer D: Eliciting through research or exploration may be a solo activity for the business analyst and does not require preparing the stakeholders. (Section 4.2.2)

Section 4.1.4.5 of BABOK describes what should be done to prepare the stakeholders. So, 1,2 and 3 are correct and 4 is not correct.

Q7. Answer D: Domain subject matter expert provides supporting materials as well as guidance about which other sources of business analysis information to consult. It may also help to arrange research, experiments, and facilitated elicitation. (Section 4.1.7, BABOK)

Q8. Answer A: Document analysis is a process that is used to understand the processes of existing systems, business procedures and policies, standards and regulations, and also to understand the issues, which can be improved in the new system. Thus, option A is the right answer.

(Section 4.2.6, BABOK) Option C is an obvious wrong answer. Option B is also not wrong but not the best use of existing system details. Option D is wrong because change strategy can't be defined without studying the future state.

Q9. Answer D: Mind mapping and brainstorming are used to collaborate and discuss the selection of elicitation techniques. That means it is decided by collaborating with stakeholders.

Option C is a close choice but generally more stakeholders will be involved as the selection of elicitation techniques depends on multiple factors. This will be requiring the presence of other stakeholders also. Hence D is the best choice. (Section 4.1.6 BABOK)

Q10. Answer D: All the factors are necessary. (Refer to the 4.1.4.1 and 4.1.4.2 sections) Section 4.1.4.1 lists down business domain and scope of the future solution as two of the factors which are considered for selecting business analysis techniques. Option B is taken from section 4.1.4.2. It mentions that to select an elicitation technique, Business analyst considers techniques commonly used in similar initiatives and that makes option B also correct. Thus, d is the correct option.

Requirements Life Cycle Management

Requirements Life Cycle Management knowledge area describes the tasks that business analysts perform to **manage** and **maintain** requirements and design information from inception to retirement.

The purpose of requirements life cycle management is to maintain traceability between business, stakeholder and solution requirements and designs and solution implements them. It also involves control of the requirements and its implementation in the actual solution.

Requirements life cycle **begins** with a representation of business need as a requirement, **continues** through the development of a solution and ends when a solution and requirements that represent it are **retired**.

Activities associated with the complete life cycle of requirements, from inception to	RLCM begins with the representation of a business need as a requirement.

RLCM continues through the development of a solution & ends when a solution & the requirement that represent it, are retired.

The usage and application of each of the core concepts within the context of Requirements Life Cycle Management is as follows:

- **Change** – Manage how proposed changes to requirements and designs are evaluated during an initiative
- **Need** – Trace, prioritize and maintain requirements to ensure that the need is met
- **Solution** – Trace requirements and designs to the solution components to ensure that the solution satisfies the need
- **Stakeholder** – Work closely with key stakeholders to maintain understanding, agreement, and approval of requirements and designs
- **Value** – Maintain requirements for reuse in future
- **Context** – Analyse the context to support tracing and prioritization activities

Requirements Life Cycle Management Tasks

01 **Trace Requirements**

02 **Maintain Requirements**

03 **Prioritize Requirements**

04 **Assess Requirements Change**

05 **Approve Requirements**

Task 1: Trace Requirements

Purpose	Requirements and designs at different levels are aligned to one another and to manage the effects of change to one level on related requirements.
Description	➢ Requirements traceability identifies and documents the lineage of each requirement, including its **backward** traceability, its **forward** traceability, and its **relationship** to other requirements. ➢ **Traceability** is used to help ensure that the solution confirms to requirements and to assist in **scope, change, risk, time, cost, communication management**, to detect any **missing functionality** and to identify if the implemented functionality is **not supported** by any requirement. In addition, it also supports both **requirements allocation** and **release planning** by providing a direct line of sight from the requirement to expressed need.
Inputs	➢ **Requirements** – May be traced to other requirements, solution components, visuals, business rules, and other work products ➢ **Designs** – May be traced to other requirements, solution components, and other work products

Elements	➢ **Level of Formality** – Value delivered by tracing requirements, nature and use of traceability relationships created help to decide the formality level. When the requirements and related relationships grow, an effort to trace them also increases significantly.
	➢ **Relationships** – Several types of relationships that business analyst considers when defining traceability approach:
	   ○ **Derive** – Used when a requirement is derived from another requirement. For e.g., a solution requirement derived from a business or a stakeholder requirement
	   ○ **Depends** – Used when one requirement is dependent on another. Types of dependency relationships include:
	      ▪ **Necessity** – When it makes **sense** to implement a requirement if a related requirement is also implemented
	      ▪ **Effort** – When a requirement is **easier** to implement if a related requirement is also implemented
	   ○ **Satisfy** – Relationship between an implementation element and the requirements it is satisfying

	o **Validate** – Relationship between a requirement and another element to identify whether a solution fulfils the requirement. ➤ **Traceability Repository** – It is recommended to use **Requirements management tools** to reap benefits when we are tracing a large number of requirements as compared to manual approaches. Some examples of requirements management tools are IBM Rational Rose, JIRA, Rally, etc.
Guidelines & Tools	➤ Domain Knowledge – Knowledge and expertise in the business domain needed to support traceability ➤ Information Management Approach – Provides decisions form planning activities ➤ Legal / Regulatory Information – Describes legislative rules or regulations that must be followed ➤ Requirements Management Tools/Repository – Used to store and manage business analysis information
Techniques	➤ **Business Rules Analysis** – Used to trace business rules to requirements ➤ **Functional Decomposition** – Used to break down solution scope into smaller components for allocation ➤ **Process Modelling** – Used to visually show future state process and tracing requirements to the same ➤ **Scope Modelling** – Used to visually depict scope to the area of scope the requirement supports
Stakeholders	➤ Customers ➤ Domain Subject Matter Expert ➤ End User ➤ Implementation Subject Matter Expert ➤ Operational Support ➤ Project Manager ➤ Sponsor – Required to **approve** the various relationships ➤ Suppliers ➤ Tester – Need to understand **how** and **where** requirements are implemented when creating test plans and test cases
Output	➤ **Requirements (Traced)** – Have clearly defined relationships to other requirements, solution components, or releases, phases or iterations within a solution scope ➤ **Designs (Traced)** - Have clearly defined relationships to other requirements, solution components, or releases, phases or iterations within a solution scope

Task 2: Maintain Requirements

Purpose	Retain requirement accuracy and consistency throughout and beyond the change during entire requirements lifecycle to support its reuse in other solutions

Description	➤ To maximize the benefits of maintaining and reusing requirements, the requirements should be:
	   o Consistently represented
	   o Reviewed and approved for maintenance using a standardized process that defines proper access rights and ensures quality
	   o Easily accessible and understandable

Inputs	➤ **Requirements** – Includes goals, objectives, business, stakeholder, solution and transition requirements that need to be maintained throughout the lifecycle ➤ **Designs** – Maintained throughout the lifecycle as needed

Elements	➤ **Maintain Requirements** – After an approved change, requirements are kept **correct** and **current** for future initiatives. This is achieved via requirements management tools.
	   o Requirements need to be clearly **named**, **labelled**, **defined** and easily accessible to stakeholders.
	   o Relationships among requirements, sets of requirements and associated business analysis information are maintained to ensure the **context** and **original intent** of requirement are preserved.
	   o Repositories with accepted **taxonomies** assist in establishing and maintaining links between maintained requirements and facilitate requirements and design traceability.
	➤ **Maintain Attributes** – Attributes such as requirement's **source**, **priority** and **complexity** aid in managing each requirement throughout the lifecycle.
	➤ **Reusing Requirements** – Requirements for future initiatives need to be named, labelled, defined and stored in a manner easily accessible to stakeholders. Requirements at a higher level of abstraction may be written with limited reference to specific solutions whereas those represented in a **general manner** tend to be more reusable. Requirements that are intended for **reuse** reflect the **current state** of the organization. Requirements can be reused:
	   o Within the current initiative
	   o Within similar initiatives
	   o Within similar departments
	   o Throughout the entire organization

Guidelines & Tools	➤ Information Management Approach – Indicates how requirements will be managed for reuse
Techniques	➤ **Business Rules Analysis** – Used to identify business rules that may be similar across the enterprise to facilitate reuse ➤ **Data Flow Diagrams** – Used to identify information flow ➤ **Data Modelling** – Used to identify data structure that may be similar across the enterprise to facilitate reuse ➤ **Document Analysis** – Used to analyze existing documentation for reusing requirements ➤ **Functional Decomposition** – Identify requirements associated with components and available for reuse ➤ **Process Modelling** – Identify requirements associated with processes that are available for reuse

	➢ **Use Cases and Scenarios** – Used to identify a solution component that may be utilized by more than one solution ➢ **User Stories** – Identify requirements associated with the story that may be available for reuse
Stakeholders	➢ Domain Subject Matter Expert ➢ Implementation Subject Matter Expert – Utilize maintained requirements when **developing regression tests** and **conducting impact analysis** for an enhancement ➢ Operational Support ➢ Regulator ➢ Tester
Output	➢ **Requirements (maintained)** – Defined once and available for long team usage as **organizational process assets** to be used in future initiatives. **A requirement that was not approved or implemented may be maintained for possible future initiative.** ➢ **Designs (maintained)** – Maybe reusable once defined.

Task 3: Prioritize Requirements

Purpose	Rank Requirements in the order of relative importance.
Description	➤ Prioritization is the act of **ranking** requirements to determine their relative importance to stakeholders. ➤ Priority can refer to the **relative value** of a requirement, or to the **sequence** in which it will be implemented. ➤ It is an **ongoing** process with priorities changing as context changes ➤ **Interdependencies** between requirements are identified and used as the basis for prioritization. ➤ It is a critical exercise that seeks to ensure the maximum **value** is achieved.
Inputs	➤ **Requirements** – Any requirements in the form of text, matrices or diagrams that are ready to prioritize. ➤ **Designs** – Any design in a form that is ready to prioritize.

Elements	➤ **Basis for Prioritization** – Typical factors that influence prioritization include:
	   ○ **Benefit** – Advantage accrued to stakeholders as a result of requirement implementation as measured against the goals and objectives for the change. **Conflict resolution and negotiation** may be employed to come to a consensus on overall benefit.
	   ○ **Penalty** – Consequences that result from not implementing a given requirement. It may also refer to the **negative consequence** of not implementing a requirement that improves customer experience.
	   ○ **Cost** – Effort and resources needed to implement the requirement.
	   ○ **Risk** – Uncertainty about requirement not been met at all or requirement not delivering potential value. A proof of concept in the form of **prototype** or **spike** is created to gain confidence in high-risk options.
	   ○ **Dependencies** – Relationships between the requirements where one requirement cannot be fulfilled unless the other requirement is fulfilled.
	   ○ **Time Sensitivity** – A date after which implementation of specific requirement loses value.
	   ○ **Stability** – Likelihood that the requirement will change due to need to do further analysis or because stakeholders have not reached a consensus about it
	   ○ **Regulatory or Policy Compliance** – Requirements to meet regulatory or policy demands which may take precedence over stakeholder interests.
	➤ **Challenges of Prioritization** – **Relative value** is assessed as part of prioritization. There are chances that stakeholders might prioritize all requirements as high or may indicate a priority to influence the result according to their desired outcome.
	➤ **Continual Prioritization** – Priorities may shift as **context** evolves and as more **information** becomes available. Initially, prioritization is done at a higher level of abstraction and once requirements are further refined, it is done at a more granular level.

Guidelines & Tools	➤ Business Constraints – Obligations or business policies that may define priorities ➤ Change Strategy – Provides information on costs, timelines and value realization which are used to determine the priority of requirements

	➢ Domain Knowledge – Understanding of business domain to support prioritization ➢ Governance Approach – Outlines the approach for prioritizing requirements ➢ Requirements Architecture – Understand the relationships with work products and other requirements ➢ Requirements Management Tools/Repository ➢ Solution Scope
Techniques	➢ **Backlog Management** – Compare requirements within backlog to be prioritized ➢ **Business Case** – Assess requirements against identified business goals and objectives ➢ **Decision Analysis** – Identify high value requirements ➢ **Estimation** – Produce estimates which can be base for prioritization ➢ **Financial Analysis** – Assess the financial value of the requirements set and how the timing of delivery will affect that value. ➢ **Interviews** – Gain an understanding of a small group of stakeholders that can provide a base for prioritization ➢ **Item Tracking** – Track issues raised by stakeholders ➢ **Prioritization** – Facilitate the process of prioritization. ➢ **Risk Analysis and Management** – Understand the risks for the basis of prioritization ➢ **Workshops** – Gain an understanding of stakeholder's basis of prioritization
Stakeholders	➢ Customer ➢ End User – Verifies that prioritized requirements will deliver **value** from a customer ➢ Implementation Subject Matter Expert ➢ Project Manager ➢ Regulator ➢ Sponsor
Output	➢ **Requirements (prioritized)** – Ranked requirements available for additional work by making sure that requirements with the **topmost value** are addressed first. ➢ **Designs (prioritized)** – Ranked designs available for additional work.

Task 4: Assess Requirements Changes

Purpose	To evaluate the implications of proposed changes to requirements and designs.

Description	➤ This task is performed as new **needs** or possible **solutions** are identified.
	➤ Assessment is needed to determine whether a proposed change will increase the **business value of the solution** and the necessary **action** that needs to be taken for applying the same.
	➤ It is utmost necessity to **trace** back a proposed change to a need to understand the background. When assessing changes, the proposed change is considered if it:
	   o Aligns with overall strategy
	   o Affects value delivered to business or stakeholder group
	   o Impacts the time or resources required to deliver value
	   o Alters any risks, opportunities or constraints associated with overall initiative

Inputs	➤ **Proposed Change** – Can be identified at any time and impact any aspect of business analysis work or deliverables completed to date. ➤ **Requirements** – Identify the impact of proposed change ➤ **Designs** – Assessed to identify the impact of a proposed modification.

Elements	➤ **Assessment Formality** – Formality of assessment process will be determined based on the information available, importance of the change and the governance process.
	   o **Predictive Approach** – It requires a **formal** assessment of proposed changes. There is a high chance of **rework** of already completed work due to the impact of change as it is following a step by step approach in the waterfall cycle.
	   o **Adaptive Approach** – It requires **less formality** in the assessment of proposed changes. Iterative and incremental implementation techniques (**agile frameworks**) helps to minimize the impact of changes and in turn, may reduce the need for formal impact assessment.
	➤ **Impact Analysis** – This is conducted to **assess** and **evaluate** the effect of a change for which traceability is considered as a useful tool. Impact of the proposed change must be assessed by considering:
	   o **Benefit** – Benefit that will be gained by accepting a change
	   o **Cost** – Total cost to make the changes
	   o **Impact** – Customer or business processes that are affected by the change
	   o **Schedule** – Impact to existing delivery commitments
	   o **Urgency** – Level of importance of the change
	➤ **Impact Resolution** – All impacts and resolutions resulting from the change are to be documented and communicated to all stakeholders.

Guidelines & Tools	➤ Change Strategy – Describes the purpose and direction of changes as well as identify critical components for change. ➤ Domain Knowledge – Knowledge of the business domain needed to assess proposed requirements changes. ➤ Governance Approach – Provides guidance regarding the change control and decision-making processes ➤ Legal / Regulatory Information – Describes legislative rules or regulations that must be followed.

	➢ Requirements Architecture – Examine and analyze requirement relationships to determine which requirement will be impacted by requested requirement change. ➢ Solution Scope – Considered to fully understand the impact of the proposed change.
Techniques	➢ **Business Cases** – Required for justification of proposed change ➢ **Business Rules Analysis** – Used to assess changes to business policies and develop revised guidance. ➢ **Decision Analysis** – Help to facilitate the change management process ➢ **Document Analysis** – Analyze any existing documents that facilitate understanding of the impact of change ➢ **Estimation** – Determine the size of the change ➢ **Financial Analysis** – Financial impact of a proposed change ➢ **Interface Analysis** – Identify interfaces that can be affected by a change ➢ **Interviews** – Used to gain an understanding of the impact on the organization and its assets ➢ **Item Tracking** – Used to track any issues or conflicts discovered during impact analysis ➢ **Risk Analysis and Management** – Determine the level of risk associated with the change ➢ **Workshops** – Understand the impact of change in a group setting
Stakeholders	➢ Customer – Provides **feedback** on the impact of the change will have on value. ➢ Domain Subject Matter Expert ➢ End User ➢ Operational Support ➢ Project Manager ➢ Regulator ➢ Sponsor ➢ Tester
Output	➢ **Requirements Change Assessment** – Recommendation to **approve**, **modify** or **deny** a proposed change to requirements. ➢ **Designs Change Assessment** – Recommendation to approve, modify or deny a proposed change to one or more design components.

Task 5: Approve Requirements

Purpose	Obtain agreement on and approval of requirements and designs to proceed on business analysis work and/or solution construction.
Description	➢ Clear **communication** of requirements, designs and other business analysis information to key stakeholders is responsible for **approving** that information ➢ Business Analysts work with key stakeholders to gain consensus on new and changed requirements, communicate the outcome of discussion and track as well as manage the approval. ➢ Predictive approach performs approvals at the **end of a phase** or during planned control meetings. ➢ Adaptive approach typically approve requirement when the solution matching those requirements is ready to be taken into the construction phase.
Inputs	➢ **Requirements (verified)** – A set of requirements that have been matching sufficient quality to be used for further work ➢ **Designs** – A set of designs that are ready to be used for further specification and development.

Elements	➢ **Understand Stakeholder Roles** – Business analysts are responsible for obtaining stakeholder approvals and must be able to identify the parties holding **decision-making** responsibility versus those having **authority for sign-off** across the initiative. An example of the same in the agile world is product owner versus external stakeholders.
	➢ **Conflict and Issue Management** – Stakeholder groups have varying point of view and conflicting priorities. A conflict may arise among stakeholders due to varying interpretations of requirements.
	    o Conflict resolution and issue management may occur **quite often** while aiming to secure sign off.
	➢ **Gain Consensus** – Business analysts are responsible for ensuring that stakeholders with approval authority **understand** and **accept** requirements.
	➢ **Track and Communicate Approval** – Requirements maintenance and tracking tool is used to record approval decisions and to keep accurate records of current approval status. Audit history of changes to requirements refers to the following:
	    o What was changed
	    o Who made the changes?
	    o The reason for change
	    o When was the change made

Guidelines & Tools	➢ Change Strategy – Provides information in managing stakeholder consensus regarding stakeholder needs. ➢ Governance Approach – Identify the stakeholders who have authority and responsibility to approve business analysis information ➢ Legal / Regulatory Information – Legislative rules to be followed. ➢ Requirement Management Tools/ Repository – Tool to record requirements approvals ➢ Solution Scope – Must be considered while approving requirements.
Techniques	➢ **Acceptance and Evaluation Criteria** – Used to define approval criteria ➢ **Decision Analysis** – Used to resolve issues and gain agreement ➢ **Item Tracking** – Used to track issues identified during the agreement process ➢ **Reviews** - Used to evaluate requirements

	➢ **Workshops** – Used to facilitate obtaining approvals
Stakeholders	➢ Customer – May play an active role in **reviewing** and **approving** requirements to ensure needs are met ➢ Domain Subject Matter Expert ➢ End User – People who **use** the solution ➢ Operational Support ➢ Project Manager ➢ Regulator ➢ Sponsor ➢ Tester
Output	➢ **Requirements (approved)** – Requirements that are agreed to by stakeholders and are ready for use. ➢ **Designs (approved)** – Agreed by stakeholders and ready for use.

Glossary

- **Traceability** – Traceability provides the ability to track the relationships between sets of requirements and designs. It helps to support change control by ensuring the source of requirement that can be identified and those potentially affected by a change are known.
- **Forward Traceability** – This refers to tracing requirements and designs to the solution that will implement them.
- **Backward Traceability** – This refers to tracing requirements and designs back to stakeholder needs and related goals and objectives for verification purposes.
- **Change Control Board (CCB):** A group of stakeholders who discuss and make decisions regarding the treatment of change requests/ changing requirements.
- **Requirements Traceability Matrix (RTM):** A matrix used to trace requirements relationships. It is a grid that links requirements from their origin to the deliverables that satisfy them.
- **MoSCoW Analysis:** Must have, should have, could have, won't have categorization of requirements based on priority.
- **Impact analysis:** Performed to assess/ evaluate the effect of a change.
- **Acceptance and evaluation criteria:** These are important techniques which are used to define the requirements approval criteria.

Case Study

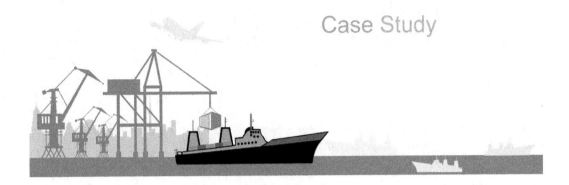

Case Study

Antik private Ltd is launching an e-commerce website and its team is developing the software. Rahul is the Business Analyst of the project. The team has already released the first version of the software.

New modules will be added to the software, so Rahul has decided to maintain the requirements using a Requirement traceability matrix (RTM). The RTM also maintains the relationships amongst the requirements. Below is a snapshot of the RTM for the project.

S. No	Business Requirements	Functional Requirements	Software Component	Test Suite/Cases	Relationship
	A	B	C	D	
1.1	Only registered users could use the premium facility of the website	User registration		Test case Number 10.1, 10.2, 10.3, 10.4	1.2 (Necessity/Depends)
1.2		Menu (with premium feature options) enabling based on user category	Code page 1.2		
1.3.1	Complete details of user actions on the page as well as purchase history – for a period, weekly and monthly	Create sketches of all the reports			

1.3.2	Each report in 1.3.1 must-have sorting and filtering options	Create a re-usable table with sorting and filtering feature			

Table 1: Requirements Traceability Matrix

Case Study Questions

Q1. Rahul wanted to make sure that his traceability approach is in line with the defined project approach. Which of the following documents he should refer to?

A. Business Analysis Approach
B. Governance approach
C. Information Management Approach
D. Stakeholder Engagement Approach

Q2. Functional requirements and business requirements are related to each other. Which type of relationship these two have?

A. Derive
B. Satisfy
C. Parent-Child
D. Necessity

Q3. Table 1 shows not only the requirements but also the software component details of the developed solution. Which of the following correctly represents the relationship between business requirements and the software components?

A. Derive
B. Satisfy
C. Validate
D. Necessity

Case Study Answers

Answer – Q1. The traceability approach is an element of the information management approach as described in section 3.4.4.3 BABOK. So, the correct answer is C.

Answer – Q2. Functional requirements are derived from business requirements (Column A and B) and so the correct answer is A. Section 3.4.4.2 BABOK.

Answer – Q3. Software elements/components satisfy the functional/business requirements (Columns B and C). So, the correct answer is B. Section 3.4.4.2 BABOK.

Exercises and Drills

Question 1: Identify the correct relationship of terms mentioned in the first column and choose the relationship type from the second column.

1. Test cases – Functional Requirements	A. Attribute
2. Functional Requirements – Business Requirements	B. None
3. User Registration Screen – Functional Requirements	C. Validate
4. Functional Requirements – Non-Functional Requirements	D. Satisfy
5. Functional Requirement – Date of completion	E. Derive

Question 2: Match the following relationships with their description.

Relationship	Description
1. Satisfy	A. Relationship between a requirement and a test case
2. Necessity	B. A requirement that is easy to implement only if another requirement is implemented
3. Validate	C. A requirement derived from another requirement which is usually on a different level of abstraction
4. Derive	D. Relationship between an implementation element and the requirement it is satisfying
5. Effort	E. A requirement that only makes sense to implement if another related requirement is also implemented
6. Subset	F. A requirement is decomposed from another requirement

Question 3: Match the description with the correct choices in the right column.

1. Used to store and manage business analysis information.	A. Information Management Approach
2. How requirements will be managed for reuse	B. Requirements Traceability Matrix
3. How to prioritize requirements	C. Requirements Management Tools
4. Impacted requirements by a requested change	D. Solution Scope
5. Must be considered when approving requirements	E. Governance Approach

Question 4: Complete the below crossword.

Across

2. The process of analyzing and maintaining the relationships between requirements, designs, solution components, and other work products (7)
3. Name the relationships between requirements, when a requirement is easier to implement if a related requirement is also implemented.

Down

1. A point-in-time view of requirements that have been reviewed and agreed upon to serve as a basis of further development (8)
4. A place where things are stored and can be found

TECHCANVASS

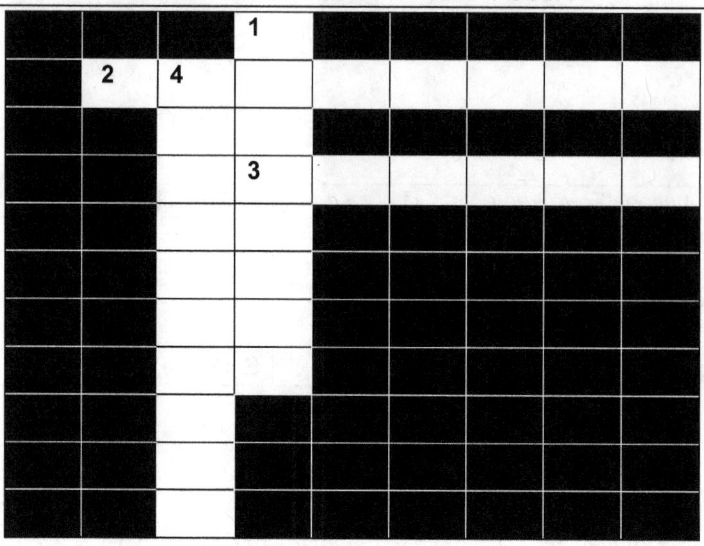
1
2
4
3

ANSWERS:

Answer 1: 1 – C, 2 – E, 3 – D , 4 – B, 5 – A

Answer 2: 1 - D, 2 – E, 3 - A, 4 - C, 5 – B, 6 – F

Answer 3: 1-C (Section 5.1.5 BABOK), 2-A (Section 5.2.5 BABOK) , 3-E (Section 5.3.5 BABOK), 4-B, 5-D (Section 5.5.5 BABOK)

Answer 4:

			1B					
	2T	4R	A	C	I	N	G	
		E	S					
		P	3E	F	F	O	R	T
		O	L					
		S	I					
		I	N					
		T	E					
		O						
		R						
		Y						

Mock Questions

Q1. Password rotation policy enforced by IAM in the CloudHop enterprise was linked to the Login Policy. Which of the below relationships best associate these two policies?
A. Depends
B. Necessity
C. Effort
D. Satisfy

Q2. Requirement R-51, which involved the development of Customer Feedback form was deprioritized and parked for the next release. This resulted in negative consequences because the partner organization discontinued the contract. Which of the below was considered/not considered during the Prioritization exercise?

A. Risk
B. Dependencies
C. Penalty
D. Time Sensitivity

Q3. The merger of Zion Gmb with Helsinki based Suess Int has led to a massive restructuring program which integrates the ERP systems of both the enterprises. This has put ambiguity in most of the rollouts planned for the first quarter. The change control board has lowered the Priority of most of the requirements in the pipeline. What has impacted this decision?

A. Risk
B. Dependency
C. Time Sensitivity
D. Stability

Q4. What is a value chain, which is at the top of the hierarchy in the process traceability chart as shown in the diagram?

A. A value chain is the overall outcome of the proposed business processes
B. A value chain is an abstract concept and is used to refer to the business strategy of the firm, resulting in the proposed system
C. A set of activities of a firm to deliver a valuable product or service
D. The grouping of all outputs resulting from a traced business process

Q5. Ron Powell is facing an obstacle in a project. There is a serious conflict amongst the stakeholders regarding the prioritization of requirements. Stakeholders are not ready to budge from their positions. But it's not possible to proceed further without prioritizing the requirements. He is considering the following techniques:

A) Budgeting and Time-boxing
B) Grouping
C) Negotiation
Choose the option, which can be used by Ron in this scenario.

A. All the three are valid options
B. A and B
C. A and C
D. B and C

Q6. Sally Sams is working on a project. She is conducting the impact analysis for the proposed changes. Which of the following she may need to contact for inputs?

A) End Users
B) Domain SME
C) Operational Support
D) Implementation SME

A. A, B and C
B. A, C and D
C. B, C and D
D. All the four

Q7. The basis on which requirements are prioritized is agreed upon by relevant stakeholders as defined in the Business Analysis Planning and Monitoring knowledge area. Typical factors that influence prioritization excludes:

A. Stakeholders need for specific functionality, quality, or business objectives
B. The requirements related to policy implementations
C. The uncertainty about requirements not achieving the desired value
D. The requirements related to the external interfaces

Q8. In a retail banking system, the software team is developing a virtual keyboard so that people can safeguard their passwords from phishing. It is one of the key security requirements for this software. What kind of relationship exists between the feature and the way it is being implemented?

A. Satisfy
B. Necessity
C. Effort
D. Validate

Q9. Which are the top challenges in prioritization of requirements? Select the best option from the given ones below:

A) Stakeholder's conflicting Requirements
B) Cost
C) Risk
D) Domain
E) Technology

A. 1, 2 and 4
B. 1, 2 and 3
C. 1 & 2
D. All of these

Q10. A business analyst has created a document that describes the requirements, its details, and the relationships amongst these. Which of the following is being referred to here?

A. Design document
B. System requirements specifications (SRS) document
C. Requirements Architecture
D. Requirements traceability Matrix

Answers:

Q1. Answer B: Password rotation policy will only exist if the login policy will exist. Password policy does not have any significance without the login policy. For example, 15 days password expiry policy can only be used if somebody tries to log in, 15 days after a password change.

Thus, the correct answer is option b. (For justification Refer to Section 5.1.4 of BABOK.)

Q2. Answer C: The penalty or negative consequences of not implementing a particular functionality. In this case, the partner organization cancelled the contract as the terms were not adhered to and so penalty is the correct answer, which is option C. (Justification Refer to section 5.3.4.1.)

Q3. Answer D: Stability or rather lack of stability (because of the merger) is generally associated with frequent changes or uncertainty as far as requirements are concerned. So, the change board has lowered the priority so that teams can wait to let the requirements stabilize. (For Justification Refer Chapter 5.3.4.1 - Stability of BABOK)

Q4. Answer C: Value chain is not output. Instead, it is a set of activities that produces an output, which is higher in value as compared to input costs. Thus, option c is the correct answer. (Fig 5.1.1: BABOK)

Q5. Answer C: Conflict amongst the stakeholders is one of the challenges of prioritization. In this case, Ron can use the budgeting to help the stakeholders understand the organizational constraint and enable them to reconsider their position for re-prioritization. Ron can also use negotiations to convince the stakeholders so that a prioritized list can be prepared. Thus, option c is the correct answer. (Section 5.3.4.2 and 10.33.3 of BABOK)

Q6. Answer A: End users are needed to use a solution and tell about the impact of change on their activities. Operational Support provides input on supporting the operation of the solution. Domain SME can provide inputs on how the change impacts the solution. However, the implementation SME is not listed as a stakeholder and does not provide any inputs for the impact analysis. Thus, the correct answer is option A. (Refer to section 5.4.7)

Q7. Answer D: First three options are - Benefit, Regulatory or Policy Compliance and risks. These are three valid factors for prioritizing the requirements.

Option D is never a basis for prioritization unless an interface is required. The question does not provide any details whether there is any requirement for an interface. So, option D is not valid and hence is the correct answer. (Section 5.3.4.1)

Q8. Answer A: Satisfy relationship refers to the relationship between an implementation element and the requirements. In this case, use of virtual keyword is an implementation example while preventing phishing of passwords is an example of a requirement. Thus, the correct answer is option a. (Section 5.1.4.2 of BABOK)

Q9. Answer B: It's challenging to make a decision about priority because of conflicting priorities. This and other challenges in the prioritization of requirements are listed in section 5.3.4.2 in BABOK. The domain is not on the list because it does not have any impact on priority. So, point 4 is not valid.

Technology has an obvious impact in a few cases and is an easy decision. If a project feature has a technology dependency, then that technical piece is given the same priority as the feature. There is no challenge in deciding. So, point 5 is not valid as it's not a challenge. This means 1,2, and 3 are valid, and so option B is correct.

Q10. Answer D: As per section 5.1.2 of BABOK. Requirements traceability identifies and documents the lineage of each requirement, including its backward traceability, its forward traceability, and its relationship to other requirements. Requirements traceability Matrix is used to capture these details. SRS captures details of all the requirements, but its purpose is very different. so, option B is incorrect.

Design document in fact is made to capture the design details. So, option A is also incorrect. Requirements Architecture is a close option. However, architecture does not contain the requirements attributes as mentioned in the question. So, option C is also incorrect.

Strategy Analysis

Strategy Analysis knowledge area describes the business analysis work that is required to be carried out to identify a **business need**, enable the enterprise to address that need and align the resulting strategy for the change.

Describes business analysis work performed to collaborate with stakeholders to identify a need of strategic or tactical importance	Describes how to enable enterprises to address that need & align the resulting strategy for the change with higher & lower level strategies

Focuses on identifying the current state, the future state where the organizations want to reach and the gaps which **need** to be addressed

Strategic analysis focuses on defining the **future** and **transition** states needed to address the business need and the work required to achieve that state.

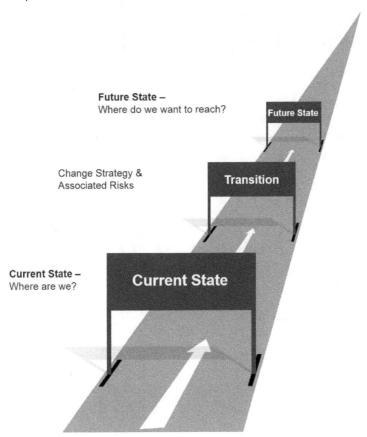

Future State –
Where do we want to reach?

Change Strategy &
Associated Risks

Current State –
Where are we?

Fig 6.1 Current State to Future State

Strategy analysis should be performed as a **business need is identified**. This allows stakeholders to make the determination of whether to address that need or not. Strategy analysis is an **ongoing** activity that assesses any changes in that need, in its context, or any new.

A strategy may be captured in a **strategic plan, product vision, business case, product roadmap** or other artefacts.

Usage and application of each of the core concepts within the context of Strategy Analysis is as follows:

- **Change** – Define the future state and develop a change strategy to achieve the future state.
- **Need** – Identify needs within the current state and prioritize needs to determine the desired future state.
- **Solution** – Define the scope of the solution as part of developing a change strategy.
- **Stakeholder** – Collaborate with stakeholders to understand the business need and to develop a change strategy and future state that will meet those needs.
- **Value** – Examine the potential value of the solution to see if a change can be justified.
- **Context** – Consider the context of the enterprise in developing a change strategy.

Strategy Analysis Tasks

01 **Analyze Current State**

02 **Define Future State**

03 **Assess Risks**

04 **Define Change Strategy**

Task 1: Analyse Current State

Purpose	To understand the reasons why an enterprise needs to change some aspects of how it operates and what would be directly or indirectly affected by the change.
Description	➢ The starting point for any change is an understanding of **why the change** is needed. Potential change is triggered by problems or opportunities that cannot be addressed without altering the current state. ➢ Change always occurs in the context of existing stakeholders, processes, technology and policies which constitute the current state of the enterprise. The **current state** is explored in just enough detail to validate the need for a change or change strategy. ➢ The scope of the current state describes the important existing characteristics of the environment. The current state of an enterprise is **rarely static** while a change is being developed and implemented.
Inputs	➢ **Elicitation Results** – Used to define and understand the current state ➢ **Needs** – The problem or opportunity faced by an enterprise or organization often launches business analysis work

Elements	➢ **Business Needs – Problems** or **opportunities** faced by enterprises leading to strategic outcomes are termed as business needs.
	   o A business need may be identified at many different levels of enterprise:
	      ▪ Achieving a strategic goal via a **top-down** approach. This includes starting from the goal definition and finding out the required steps to achieve it by drilling it down to smallest possible.
	      ▪ Problem with the current state of a process, function or system via a **bottom-up** approach
	      ▪ From **middle management** needing additional information to make sound decisions to meet business objectives
	      ▪ In the form of **external drivers** such as customer demands or business competition in the marketplace
	   o The definition of business needs is frequently the most **critical** step in any business analysis effort. A **solution** must satisfy the business needs to be considered successful.
	   o The approach to determine a business need includes identification of **alternative solutions**, identifying **stakeholders** for consultation and solution **approaches** that will be evaluated.
	   o Business needs are always expressed from the **perspective of the enterprise, not that of any stakeholder**. Business needs will drive overall analysis of the **current state**.
	   o Factors that business analyst may consider for the solution:
	      ▪ Adverse impacts the problem is causing within the organization
	      ▪ Expected benefits from any potential solution
	      ▪ How quickly the problem could potentially be resolved, or the opportunity could be taken
	      ▪ The underlying source of the problem
	➢ **Organizational Structure and Culture – Formal relationships** between people working in an enterprise is termed as organizational structure.
	   o Organizational culture is the **beliefs, values, and norms** shared by the members of the organization which drive the actions taken by the organization.

o Business analysts perform a cultural assessment to:
- Identify if the goals that need to be achieved need any cultural changes
- Identify if stakeholders understand the value delivered as well as rationale behind the current state
- Ascertain if current state needs any change or is it in a satisfactory state

➢ **Capabilities and Processes** – Activities performed by an enterprise are termed as capabilities and processes. It is due to these capabilities and processes, an enterprise can be a unique player in a particular area. They are measured by performance indicators that can be used to assess the benefits of the change. There are 2 views that an enterprise may apply:

o **Capability-Centric view** – This is applied when looking for innovative solutions that combine existing capabilities to produce a new outcome. It is very useful to identify the gaps while maintaining the functional hierarchy of the capabilities.

o **Process-Centric view** – This is applied when an enterprise is looking for ways to improve the performance of current activities. The processes are organized in such a way that the change, in fact, increases performance.

➢ **Technology and Infrastructure** – Information systems used by the enterprise support people in executing processes, making decisions, and in interactions with suppliers and customers. The infrastructure describes the enterprise's environment with respect to physical components and capabilities.

➢ **Policies** – Policies define the **scope of decision making** at different levels of an enterprise. They generally address routine operations rather than strategic change. The scope of solution space and any constraints on the type of action will be impacted by the identification of relevant policies.

➢ **Business Architecture** – It is very important to understand how the elements of current state fit together to support one another in order to recommend changes that will be effective. Existing business architecture is a combination of **business** and **stakeholder** needs.

➢ **Internal Assets** - Tangible or intangible resources used in a current state are identified as enterprise assets. For e.g. patents, reputation, brand names and financial resources

➢ **External Influencers** – Usually present constraints, dependencies or drivers on the current state. Sources include:
o Industry Structure
o Competitors
o Customers
o Suppliers
o Political and Regulatory Environment
o Technology
o Macroeconomic Factors

Guidelines & Tools	➢ Business Analysis Approach – Guides how the business analyst undertakes an analysis of current state
	➢ Enterprise Limitation – Used to understand the challenges that exist within the enterprise
	➢ Organizational Strategy – A set of goals and objectives that provide a vision of a future state

	➢ Solution Limitation – Understand the current state and challenges of existing solutions ➢ Solution Performance Goals – Measure the current performance of an enterprise or solution ➢ Solution Performance Measures – Describe the actual performance of existing solutions ➢ Stakeholder Analysis Results – Stakeholders contributing to an understanding and analysis of the current state.
Techniques	➢ **Benchmarking and Market Analysis** – Provides an understanding of where the opportunities for improvement are in the current state. Available frameworks to conduct this technique include 5 Force Analysis, PEST, STEEP, CATWOE ➢ **Business Capability Analysis** – Identifies gaps and prioritizes them in relation to value and risk ➢ **Business Model Canvas** – Provides an understanding of the value proposition that enterprise satisfies for its customers, critical factors in delivering that value and resulting cost and revenue streams. ➢ **Business Cases** – Capture information regarding business need and opportunity ➢ **Concept Modelling** – Capture key terms and concepts in the business domain and define the relationships between them ➢ **Data Mining** – Used to obtain information on the performance of an enterprise ➢ **Document Analysis** – Analyse any existing documentation about the current state ➢ **Financial Analysis** – Understand the profitability of the current state and financial capability to deliver change ➢ **Focus Groups** – Solicits feedback from customers or end users ➢ **Functional Decomposition** – Breaks down complex systems or relationships in the current state ➢ **Interviews** – Facilitate dialogue with stakeholders to understand the current state and any needs evolving from the same ➢ **Item Tracking** – Tracks and manages issues discovered about the current state ➢ **Lessons Learned** – Enables the assessment of failures and opportunities for improvement in past initiatives ➢ **Metrics and Key Performance Indicators** – Assesses performance of the current state of an enterprise ➢ **Mind Mapping** – Explore relevant aspects of current state and factors affecting the business need ➢ **Observation** – May provide insights into needs within the current state which may have been missed previously ➢ **Organizational Modelling** – Describes the roles, responsibilities and reporting structure existing in current state organization ➢ **Process Analysis** – Identify opportunities to improve current state ➢ **Process Modelling** – Describes how work occurs within the current solution ➢ **Risk Analysis and Management** – Identifies risks to current state ➢ **Root Cause Analysis** – Understanding of underlying causes of any problems in the current state to clarify a need ➢ **Scope Modelling** – Helps define the boundaries on current state description ➢ **Survey or Questionnaire** – Gain an understanding of the current state from a large, varied, or disparate group of stakeholders

	➢ **SWOT Analysis** – Evaluates the strengths, weaknesses, opportunities, and threats to the current state in an enterprise ➢ **Vendor Assessment** – Assessment of vendors on making sure that commitments are met or if any changes are needed ➢ **Workshops** – Engage stakeholders to collaboratively describe the current state and their needs
Stakeholders	➢ Customers – Makes **use** of existing solution and might have input about **issues** with a current solution ➢ Domain Subject Matter Expert ➢ End User – Directly **uses** a solution and might have input on **issues** with the current solution ➢ Implementation Subject Matter Expert ➢ Operational Support ➢ Regulator ➢ Sponsor ➢ Supplier ➢ Tester
Output	➢ **Current State Description** – The context of the enterprise's scope, capabilities, resources, performance, culture, dependencies, infrastructure ad relationships between these elements ➢ **Business Requirements** - The problem, opportunity or constraint is defined based on an understanding of the current state.

Task 2: Define Future State

Purpose	To determine the set of necessary conditions to meet a business need
Description	➤ Business analysts work to ensure that the **future state** of the enterprise is well defined, that it is achievable with the **resources** available and that key **stakeholders** have a shared consensus vision of the outcome. The future state will be defined at a level of detail that: 　○ Allows to identify and assess competing strategies to achieve that future state 　○ Provides a clear definition of the outcomes that will satisfy the business needs 　○ Detail the scope of the solution space 　○ Allows for value associated with the future state to be assessed and 　○ Enables a consensus to be achieved among key stakeholders ➤ The future state description can describe the **new, removed, and modified components** of an enterprise. It can include changes to the **boundaries** of the organization, or it can be simple changes to **existing** components of an organization. ➤ Changes may be needed to various components of enterprise such as business processes, functions, lines of business, organization structures, staff competencies, knowledge and skills, training, facilities, desktop tools, organization locations, data and information, application system and/or technology infrastructure. ➤ Describing the future state allows stakeholders to understand the **potential value** that can be realized from a solution which can be used as part of the decision-making process regarding the change strategy. ➤ For a **predictable** approach, where the outcome is predictable and where there are a large number of possible changes that can increase value, the purpose of future state analysis is to gather sufficient information to make the **best possible choices** amongst available options. This also requires conducting a **cost-benefit analysis** of the options. ➤ For **adaptive** approach, where it is difficult to predict the value realized by a change, the future state may be defined by the identification of appropriate **performance measures** and exploring multiple **options**.
Inputs	➤ **Business Requirements** – Problems, opportunities or constraints that the future state will address.
Elements	➤ **Business Goals and Objectives** – Business goals and objectives describe the ends that the organization is seeking to achieve. 　○ Goals and objectives can relate to changes that the organization wants to **accomplish** or current conditions that it wants to **maintain**. 　○ Goals are **longer term, ongoing and qualitative statements** of a state or condition that the organization is seeking to establish and maintain. Certain examples of business goals are: 　　▪ Create a new capability such as new product/service to gain a competitive advantage 　　▪ Improve revenue by increasing sales or reducing cost 　　▪ Increase customer satisfaction 　　▪ Increase employee satisfaction 　　▪ Comply with new regulations 　　▪ Improve safety 　　▪ Reduce time to deliver a product or service

TECHCANVASS

- As goals are analyzed, they are converted into more **descriptive, granular, specific objectives and linked to measures** that make it possible to assess if the objective can be achieved. A common test for assessing objectives is to ensure they are **SMART**:
  - **Specific** – describing something that has observable outcome
  - **Measurable** – Tracking and measuring the outcome
  - **Achievable** – Testing the feasibility of effort
  - **Relevant** – Aligning with enterprise's vision, mission, and goals
  - **Time-Bounded** – Define a timeframe that is consistent with the need
- **Example** – For an organization investing heavily in digital initiatives, the **goal** can be to "increase traffic on an online portal by enabling self-service" and **objective** can be to "increase traffic by 50% and reduce incident calls to call centre by 50% within 1 year".

➢ **Scope of Solution Space** – Decisions must be made about the range of solutions that will be considered to meet the business goals and objectives. The scope of the solution space defines which kinds of options will be considered when investigating possible solutions, including changes to **organizational structure or culture, capabilities, and processes, technology and infrastructure, policies, products or services** or even creating or changing **relationships** with organizations currently outside the scope of an enterprise.
  - In case of multiple future states meeting the business needs, goals and objectives, it is necessary to determine which ones to be considered and that consideration will be dependent on **overall objectives of the enterprise, qualitative and quantitative value of each option, the time needed to achieve** each future state and the opportunity cost to the enterprise.

➢ **Constraints** – Constraints describe aspects of the current state and planned future state that may not be **changed** by the solution or mandatory elements of the design. Constraints may reflect any of the following:
  - Budgetary restrictions,
  - Time restrictions
  - Technology & infrastructure
  - Policies
  - Limits on the number of resources available
  - Restrictions based on skills of team and stakeholders
  - A requirement that certain stakeholders may not be affected by the implementation of the solution
  - Compliance with regulations and
  - Any other restriction

➢ **Organizational Structure and Culture** –The formal and informal working relationships that exist within the enterprise may need to change to facilitate the desired future state. In addition, changes to reporting lines can encourage teams to work more closely together to achieve goals and objectives.

➢ **Capabilities and Processes** – New or changed capabilities and processes will be needed to **deliver** new products and services, to **comply** with new regulations or to **improve** the performance of the enterprise.

➤ **Technology & Infrastructure** – There could be technical constraints imposed on the design of solution on the basis of existing technology and infrastructure. **Technical constraints** may describe **restrictions** such as resource utilization, message size and timing, software size, maximum number of and size of files, records and data elements. It includes any **IT architecture standards** that must be followed.
  o A very good **example** of technical constraint could be "System should be able to show 50 transactions at a time". This describes the technical constraint on size of the file retrieved by the system from backend.

➤ **Policies** – **Policies** are a **common source of constraints** on a solution or on the solution space. Depending on approval levels, the approach used to obtain approval, necessary criteria used to receive funding, business policies may mandate what solutions will be implemented.

➤ **Business Architecture** – Elements of future state must effectively support one another, and all contribute to meeting the business goals and objectives.

➤ **Internal Assets** – When analysing resources, business analysts examine the resources needed to maintain the current state and implement the change strategy and determine what resources can be used as part of the desired future state.

➤ **Identify Assumptions** – Assumptions must be identified and clearly understood, so that appropriate decisions can be made if the assumption later proves invalid. These assumptions need to be tested as early as possible so that a decision can be taken to either redirect or terminate an initiative. **Example** – Test environment must be available at start of the project.

➤ **Potential Value** – Potential value must be evaluated to see if it is sufficient to justify a change. **The potential value of the future state is the net benefit of the solution after operating costs are accounted for.** It is possible that future states can show a decrease in value for certain stakeholders or at an enterprise level.
  o When determining the future state, business analysts consider varying potential value from:
    ▪ External opportunities revealed in assessing external influences
    ▪ Unknown strengths of new partners
    ▪ New technologies or knowledge
    ▪ Potential loss of a competitor in a market and
    ▪ Mandated adoption of a change component
  o Business case for the change should reflect the potential value in the form of costs and benefits in case of no change is made.
  o In most cases, future state will not address all of the **opportunities for improvement**. Those opportunities that are not addressed will be taken as **enhancements** in future analysis.
  o In addition, the analysis should consider the acceptable level of **investment** to reach the future state. It helps to guide the selection of possible strategies.

Guidelines & Tools	➤ Current State Description – Provides the context within which the work needs to be completed. It is often used as a **starting point** for future state.

	➤ Metrics and Key Performance Indicators (KPIs) – Key performance indicators and metrics will determine if the desired future start has been achieved ➤ Organizational Strategy – Describes the approach an organization will take to achieve the desired future state.
Techniques	➤ **Acceptance and Evaluation Criteria** – Used to identify what may make the future state acceptable or how options may be evaluated ➤ **Balanced Scorecard** – Used to set targets for measuring the future state ➤ **Benchmarking and Market Analysis** – Used to make decisions about future state business objectives ➤ **Brainstorming** – Used to collaboratively come up with ideas for the future state. ➤ **Business Capability Analysis** – Used to prioritize capability gaps in relation to value and risk ➤ **Business Cases** – Used to capture the desired outcomes of the change initiative ➤ **Business Model Canvas** – Used to plan strategy required to fulfil the value proposition to customers in the desired future state ➤ **Decision Analysis** – Used to compare different future state options and understand which one is the best ➤ **Decision Modelling** – Used to model complex decisions regarding future state options ➤ **Financial Analysis** – Used to estimate potential financial returns to be delivered by a proposed future state ➤ **Functional Decomposition** – Used to break down complex systems within the future state ➤ **Interviews** – Used to talk to stakeholders to understand the future state they want to achieve ➤ **Lessons Learned** – Used to determine which opportunities for improvement will be addressed and how the current state can be improved upon ➤ **Metrics and Keys Performance Indicators (KPIs)** – Used to determine when the organization has succeeded in achieving business objectives ➤ **Mind Mapping** – Used to develop ideas for the future state and understand relationships between them ➤ **Organizational Modelling** – Used to describe the roles, responsibilities, reporting structures that would exist within the future state organization ➤ **Process Modelling** – Used to describe how work would occur in the future state ➤ **Prototyping** – Used to describe how work would occur in the future state ➤ **Scope Modelling** – Used to define the boundaries of the enterprise in the future state ➤ **Survey or Questionnaire** – Used to understand stakeholder's desired future state they want to achieve including needs they want to address and desired business objectives they want to meet ➤ **SWOT Analysis** – Used to evaluate strengths, weaknesses, opportunities and threats that may be exploited or mitigated by future state ➤ **Vendor Assessment** – Used to assess potential value provided by vendor solution options ➤ **Workshops** – Used to work with stakeholders to collaboratively describe the future state
Stakeholders	➤ Customers

	➢ Domain Subject Matter Expert ➢ End User ➢ Implementation Subject Matter Expert ➢ Operational Support ➢ Project Manager ➢ Regulator ➢ Sponsor – **Authorizes** and ensures **funding** to support moving towards the future state. ➢ Supplier ➢ Tester
Output	➢ **Business Objectives** – Desired direction that the business wishes to pursue in order to achieve the future state. ➢ **Future State Description** – Future state description includes boundaries of the proposed, new, removed, and modified components of the enterprise and the potential value expected from future state. ➢ **Potential Value** – The value that may be realized by implementing the proposed future state.

Task 3: Assess Risks

Purpose	To understand the undesirable consequences of internal and external forces on the enterprise during a transition to or once in the future state. An understanding of the **potential impact** of those forces can be used to make a recommendation about a course of action.
Description	<ul><li>Assessing risks includes **analyzing** and **managing** them. Risks might be related to the current state, a desired future state, a change itself, a change strategy, or any tasks being performed by the enterprise.</li><li>The risks are analyzed for the possible **consequences** if the risk occurs, **impact** of those consequences, **likelihood** of the risk and **potential time frame** when the risk might occur.</li><li>A **risk assessment** can include choosing to accept a risk if either the effort required to modify the risk or the level of risk outweighs the probable loss.</li></ul>
Inputs	<ul><li>**Business Objectives** – Describing the desired direction needed to achieve the future state can be used to identify and discuss potential risks</li><li>**Elicitation Results (confirmed)** – Understanding of what the various stakeholders perceive as risks to the realization of a desired future state</li><li>**Influences** – Factors inside the enterprise and factors outside of the enterprise which will impact the realization of the desired future state</li><li>**Potential Value** – Describing the value to be realized by implementing the proposed future state provides a benchmark against which risks can be assessed.</li><li>**Requirements (prioritized)** – Depending on their priority, requirements will influence the risks to be defined and understood as part of solution realization.</li></ul>
Elements	<ul><li>**Unknowns** – When assessing a risk, there will be **uncertainty** in the likelihood of it occurring, and the **impact** if it does occur. Business analysts should be able to estimate the impact of unknown events if possible.<ul><li>The lessons learned from **past changes** and **expert judgement** from stakeholders assist in guiding the team in deciding the impact and likelihood of risks for the current change.</li></ul></li><li>**Constraints, Assumptions, and Dependencies** – If the constraint, assumption, and dependency is related to an aspect of the change, it can be restated as a **risk** by identifying the event or condition and related consequences.</li><li>**Negative Impact to Value** – Risks refer to uncertainties that may increase the chances of a negative impact of value. Business analysts clearly identify and express each risk and estimate its **likelihood** and **impact** to determine the level of risk. Overall risk level can be quantified in **financial terms, or in the amount of time, effort** or other measures.</li><li>**Risk Tolerance** – It is the measure that shows the willingness to accept the uncertainty against value delivered out of it. There are three broad ways of describing attitude towards risk:<ul><li>**Risk-aversion** – This refers to a state where risk is not acceptable. It includes avoiding the action that can cause risk or invest more to reduce the chance of risk.</li><li>**Neutrality** – Some levels of risk are acceptable, provided the course of action does not result in a loss even if the risks occur.</li><li>**Risk-seeking** – A state where risk is accepted against higher potential value.</li></ul></li></ul>

	➢ **Recommendation** – A change to the current state of enterprise or to the strategy is required to manage risk. The recommendation usually falls into one of the following categories:
	  ○ Pursue the benefits of the change **regardless** of risk,
	  ○ Pursue the benefits of a change while investing in **reducing risk**,
	  ○ Seek out ways to **increase** the benefits of a change to **outweigh** a risk,
	  ○ Identify ways to **manage** and **optimize** opportunities,
	  ○ Do not pursue the **benefits** of the change.

Guidelines & Tools	➢ Business Analysis Approach – Guides how the business analyst analyses risks. ➢ Business policies – Define the limits within which decisions must be made. ➢ Change Strategy – Provides the plan to transition from current state to the future state and achieve desired business outcomes. ➢ Current State Description – Provides the context within which the work needs to be completed. ➢ Future State Description – Determines risks associated with the future state ➢ Identified Risks – Can be used as a starting point for a more thorough risk assessment. ➢ Stakeholder Engagement Approach – Understanding stakeholders helps identify and assess the potential impact of internal and external forces.
Techniques	➢ **Brainstorming** – Used to collaboratively identify potential risks for assessment ➢ **Business Cases** – Used to capture risks associated with alternative change strategies. ➢ **Decision Analysis** – Used to assess problems. ➢ **Document Analysis** – Used to analyze existing documents for potential risks, constraints, assumptions, and dependencies ➢ **Financial Analysis** - Used to understand the potential effect of risks on the financial value of solution. ➢ **Interviews** – Used to understand what stakeholders might think be risks and related factors ➢ **Lessons Learned** – Used as a foundation of past issues that might be risks ➢ **Mind Mapping** – Used to identify and categorize potential risks and understand their relationships ➢ **Risk Analysis and Management** – Used to identify and manage risks ➢ **Root Cause Analysis** – Used to identify and address the underlying problem creating a risk ➢ **Survey or Questionnaire** – Used to understand what stakeholders might think be risks ➢ **Workshops** – Used to understand what stakeholders might think be risks
Stakeholders	➢ Domain Subject Matter Expert ➢ Implementation Subject Matter Expert ➢ Operational Support ➢ Project Manager ➢ Regulator ➢ Sponsor – Needs to understand risks as part of **authorizing** and **funding** change. ➢ Supplier ➢ Tester

Output	➢ **Risk Analysis Results** – An understanding of the risks associated with achieving future state and the mitigation strategies which will be used to prevent them, reduce the impact of risk or reduce the likelihood of the risk occurring.

Task 4: Define Change Strategy

Purpose	To develop and assess alternative approaches to the change and then select the recommended approach.

Description	➢ Developing a change strategy is simpler when the **current** state and the **future** state are already defined because they provide some context of the change.
	➢ The change strategy clearly describes the nature of the change in terms of:
	  o Context of the change
	  o Identified alternative change strategies
	  o Justification for why a change strategy is the best approach
	  o Investment and resources required to work toward the future state
	  o How the enterprise will realize value after the solution is delivered
	  o Key stakeholders in the change and
	  o Transition states along the way
	➢ The change strategy might be presented as part of a **business case, Statement of Work (SOW), an enterprise's strategic plan** or in other formats.
	➢ Various strategies are identified as part of defining change strategy and based on common decisions pertaining to a situation, a particular strategy is selected and applied. This should be providing information on which parts of the completed solution are going to provide value and needs a change.

Inputs	➢ **Current State Description** – Provides context about the current state and includes assessments of internal and external influences to the enterprise under consideration ➢ **Future State Description** – Provides context about the desired future state ➢ **Risk Analysis Results** – Describe identified risks and exposure of each risk ➢ **Stakeholder Engagement Approach** – Understanding stakeholder's communication and collaboration needs can help identify change related activities and should be included as part of the change strategy.

Elements	➢ **Solution Scope** – The solution is the **outcome** of a change that allows an enterprise to satisfy a need. Best solution approach is selected and justified as part of the analysis of multiple solution options.
	  o The solution scope defines the **boundaries** of the solution and enables stakeholders to understand which new capabilities the change will deliver as well as how it will enable future state's goals. It also defines 'out of scope' solution components.
	  o The solution scope might be described in different ways, including the use of capabilities, technology, business rules, business decisions, data, processes, resources, knowledge and skills, models and descriptions of markets, functions, locations, networks, organizational structures, workflows, events, sequence, motivations or business logic.
	➢ **Gap Analysis** – A gap analysis identifies the difference between **current** and **future** states using the same technique. The gaps will be **addressed** in transition and future states.

- o Gap analysis can help identify the gaps that prevent the enterprise from meeting **needs** and achieving **goals**. No change is required if no capability gaps are identified. In order to create the missing capabilities, a **change strategy** is needed.
- o The capabilities analyzed in a gap analysis can include processes, functions, lines of business, organizational structures, staff competencies, knowledge and skills, training, facilities, location, data, application systems, and technology infrastructure.

➢ **Enterprise Readiness Assessment** – The readiness assessment considers the enterprise's capacity to **make** the change, use and **sustain** the solution and **realize value** from the solution. The assessment also factors in:
- o Cultural readiness of the stakeholders
- o Operational readiness in making the change
- o Timeline from when the change is implemented to when value can be realized and
- o Resources available to support the change effort

➢ **Change Strategy** – A change strategy is a high-level plan of key **activities** and **events** that will be used to transform the enterprise from current state to future state in form of a sequence of projects or as improvement efforts.
- o Several options are explored and described in enough detail to determine **feasibility**. A preferred change strategy should be selected considering:
  - Organizational readiness to make the change
  - Major costs and investments needed
  - Timelines to make the change
  - Alignment to the business objectives
  - Timelines for value realization and
  - Opportunity costs of the change strategy
- o The **options** considered and rejected are an important component of the final strategy, providing stakeholders with an understanding of pros and cons of various approaches.
- o If the **investment** for making the change is unbearable then the enterprise may skip this opportunity and look to invest in something else.
- o The **potential value**, including the cost-benefit analysis, is the key component to making a business case for the change.

➢ **Transition States and Release Planning** – Future states will need to be achieved over time rather than through a single change in many cases, meaning that enterprises will have to operate in one or more transition states.
- o **Release planning** is concerned with determining which requirements to include in each release, phase or iteration of the change. **Business analysts** help **facilitate** release planning discussions to help stakeholders reach decisions.
- o **Factors** guiding these decisions are overall budget, deadlines or time constraints, resource constraints, training schedules and ability of the business to absorb the changes within a defined time frame by adhering to organizational constraints or policies.
- o **Timing** of the implementation is also decided in order to cause minimal disruption to business activities and to ensure that all parties understand the impact of an organization.

Guidelines & Tools	➢ Business Analysis Approach – Guides how the business analyst defines a change strategy ➢ Design Options – Describe the various ways to satisfy the business needs. ➢ Solution Recommendations – Identifying the possible solutions which can be pursued in order to achieve the future state
Techniques	➢ **Balanced Scorecard** – Used to define the metrics that will be used to evaluate change strategy ➢ **Benchmarking and Market Analysis** – Used to make decisions about which change strategy is appropriate ➢ **Brainstorming** – Used to collaboratively come up with ideas for change strategies ➢ **Business Capability Analysis** – Used to prioritize capability gaps in relation to value and risk ➢ **Business Cases** – Used to capture information about the recommended change strategy that were assessed, but not recommended ➢ **Business Model Canvas** – Used to define the changes needed to achieve potential value ➢ **Decision Analysis** – Used to compare different change strategies and choose an appropriate one ➢ **Estimation** – Used to determine timelines for activities within the change strategy ➢ **Financial Analysis** – Used to understand the potential value associated with change strategy and evaluate strategies against targets for return on investments. ➢ **Focus Groups** – Used to bring customers together to solicit their input on solution and change strategy ➢ **Functional Decomposition** – Used to break down components of the solution into parts ➢ **Interviews** – Used to talk to stakeholders to fully describe the solution scope and change scope and to understand their suggestions ➢ **Lessons Learned** – Used to understand what went wrong in past changes in order to improve change strategy ➢ **Mind Mapping** – Used to develop and explore ideas for change strategies ➢ **Organizational Modelling** – Used to describe organizational structure necessary for the change and is part of the solution ➢ **Process Modelling** – Used to describe how work would occur in the solution scope or during the change. ➢ **Scope Modelling** – Used to define boundaries on solution scope and change scope descriptions. ➢ **SWOT Analysis** – Used to make a decision about which change strategy is appropriate ➢ **Vendor Assessment** – Used to determine whether any vendors are part of change strategy for implementation ➢ **Workshops** – Used to work with stakeholders to collaboratively develop change strategies
Stakeholders	➢ Customer ➢ Domain Subject Matter Expert ➢ End User ➢ Implementation Subject Matter Expert ➢ Operational Support ➢ Project Manager ➢ Regulator

	➢ Sponsor – **Authorizes** and ensure **funding** for solution delivery and **champions** the change. ➢ Supplier ➢ Tester
Output	➢ **Change Strategy** – Approach that the organization will follow to guide change ➢ **Solution Scope** – Solution scope that will be achieved through execution of the change strategy

Glossary

- **Strategy** – A plan of action designed to achieve a long-term aim for an enterprise or for a function within an enterprise.
- **Tactics** - Concrete steps or initiatives to achieve smaller steps or goals, part of a long-term plan. Strategy is a long-term vision and tactics represent short term actions.
- **PEST** – PEST analysis refers to an approach to widely analyze the Political, Economic, and Socio-Cultural and Technological changes in your business environment. PEST analysis looks at high level factors that has the potential to influence a decision, market or any potential new business.
- **5 Forces Analysis** – The framework allows a business to identify and analyze the important forces that determine the profitability of an industry. Those 5 forces are – a) Competitive Rivalry, b) Threat of New Entrants, c) Threat of Substitutes, d) Bargaining Power of Buyers, e) Bargaining Power of Suppliers.
- **Business case** - It is a justification for investment. In other words, it is the evaluation of qualitative and quantifiable data to decide to move or not move forward with a particular solution to the proposed change. Comprises primarily of Cost, Benefit, Risk and Schedule aspects of the proposed change.
- **Assumptions** - Are factors that are believed to be true but have not been confirmed.
- **Constraints** - Are restrictions/ limitations on the delivery of the solution.
- **SWOT analysis** - Strengths, Weaknesses, Opportunities, and Threats Analysis is used to make decisions about which change strategy is appropriate.
- **Pilot testing** - It is a type of testing, which is conducted by a group of end users to ascertain the working of major functionality before it is deployed on the production machine. Please note that doing a pilot is not the same as pilot testing.
- **Beta release** - Beta releases are early versions of the next major release. They follow the alpha releases.
- **Capability** - Capability refers to the potential and competency of an organization. A business analyst may evaluate an organization using capability centric view during strategy analysis.

Case Study

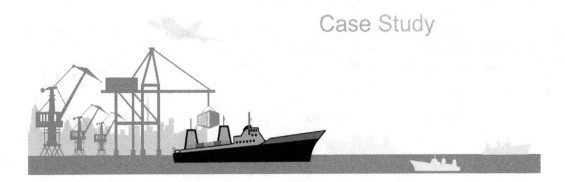

Cavalier group LLC is a medical equipment manufacturer. The company is seeing a surge in the market demand. The company board reviewed the analysis submitted by the Sales and marketing analysis team. The board observed that the marketing spend was increasing rapidly but not the Sales. The board passed a resolution to retain BACS Consulting to help them address the problem.

BACS Consulting sent a team led by Nikhil Jain, the lead business analyst. The team conducted the initial study to understand the current state of the organization.

Current State

Nikhil and his team found that the Cavalier group had automated most of its Sales, marketing, and the lead management systems, but these systems were developed over the last few years and these were working in Silos. The Sales and Marketing business heads did not have unified views to understand and to analyze the data.

Here is a summary of their current state findings:

- Multiple disparate systems for lead acquisition, lead assignment and management
- Marketing campaigns and lead management systems integration is patchy
- Customer database is managed using Excel
- The lead conversion data is not accurate
- The Sales and Marketing teams are not getting a complete picture of leads to the Sales cycle

Change Strategy

The BACS team conducted meetings with the Senior Management. Purpose of these meetings was to understand the constraints and to validate their findings. BACS team observed that the company had many field sales operatives. As they were considering using an ERP system to streamline the sales and marketing processes, it was important that the Cavalier's employees were motivated enough to use it.

The BACS team came up with the following change strategy:

- Implement Microsoft Dynamics 365 Sales, marketing, and customer service modules
- Develop a mobile app for the field sales team
- Create learning modules for the employees for using the system effectively

- Create performance measures to track the progress using the measures

Following key metrics were selected to measure and to track:

- Lead acquisition cost (This would help in knowing the effectiveness of campaigns and spend)
- Funnel Conversion rate (For sales funnel optimization)
- Customer Lifetime value (The ability to retain a customer and effectiveness of 3 functions)

Following diagram summarizes the complete strategy analysis exercise done by BACS consulting:

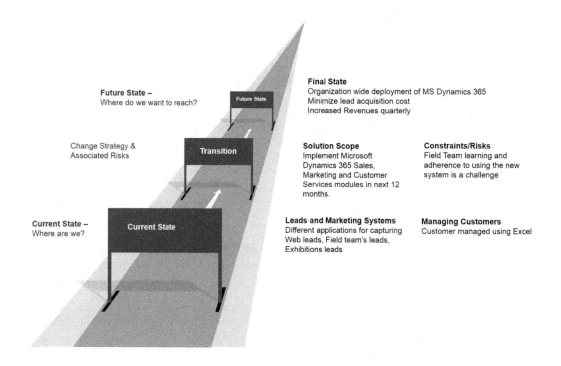

Fig 6.2: Transition Strategy

Case Study Questions

Q1. Nikhil and his team described the current strategies after having discussions with the senior management team. They came up with the findings as mentioned in the case. Which of the following they should also prepare while analyzing the current state?

A) Business Case
B) Business Requirements document
C) Business Analysis approach

Choose the right option from below:

A. Only 1
B. 1 and 2
C. 2 and 3
D. All three

Q2. BACS Consulting team was hired to help Cavalier group LLC address the problem they were facing. At which level this need was identified?

A. From the top-down
B. From the bottom-up
C. From middle management
D. From external drivers

Q3. BACS has identified that compliance with field agents may be a challenge. How will BACS determine that this challenge should be dealt with as a risk?

A. Based on the assessment of risk impact
B. Based on the likelihood and risk impact
C. Based on the reputation of the risk
D. None of these

Case Study Answers

Answer – Q1. Business requirements document is an output of the task – Analyze current state. Business case document can be initiated at this stage, but it can only be completed once the change strategy (solution options and risks) are also determined. So, the correct answer is A. (Section 6.1.8, BABOK)

Answer – Q2. Even though the board passed the resolution to hire BACS consulting, it was based on the findings of the marketing and sales analysis team. The board simply reviewed the need and passed a resolution to hire BACS. Typically, the analysis team will be middle management professionals as they consolidate the data from all the field or executive level staff. So, the correct answer is C. (Section 6.1.4.1, BABOK)

Answer – Q3. Analysis of risk can be based on likelihood and its impact. The analysis can also be based on factors like Reputation, Social responsibility, etc. Out of the four options, the best answer is to consider the impact and its likelihood. Both factors are important. So, the correct answer is B. (Section 10.38.3.2, BABOK)

Exercises and Drills

Question 1: Match the following tasks with their respective description.

1. Analyse current state	A. To determine the set of necessary conditions required to meet the business need
2. Define future state	B. To perform a gap analysis between the current and target state and then to select the best approach after having assessed various alternative approaches to the change
3. Assess risks	C. To understand the reason why a change is needed and what would be affected by the change
4. Define change strategy	D. To understand the uncertainties around the change and the consequences of such uncertainties
	E. To assess the impact of the change

Question 2: Match the following.

1. Business needs	A. Are the activities that an organization performs
2. Organizational structure	B. Suppliers, competitors, customers, technology, macroeconomic factors
3. External influencers	C. Are problems or opportunities or Compliance/ regulatory requirements
4. Organizational culture	D. Defines the formal relationships between people working in the organization
5. Capabilities and processes	E. Is the beliefs, values, norms shared by people working in an organization

Question 3: Match the following risk tolerance attitudes with their description.

1. Risk aversion	A. Indicates that some level of risk is acceptable, provided it does not result in a loss even if the risk occurs
2. Neutrality	B. Indicates low tolerance to risks i.e. there is willingness to accept uncertainty
3. Risk seeking	C. Indicates that tolerance to risk is high

Question 4: Match the column one descriptions with the right match in column two.

1. Challenges that exist within which may pose risk for the solution implementation	A. Organizational Strategy
2. Approach an enterprise or organization will take to achieve its desired future state	B. Enterprise Limitations
3. It guides how the business analyst analyses risks.	C. Design Options
4. It describe various ways to satisfy the business needs.	D. Business Analysis Approach

ANSWERS:

Answer 1: 1 – C, 2 – A, 3 – D, 4 –B

Answer 2: 1 – C, 2 – D, 3 – B, 4 – E, 5 – A

Answer 3: 1 – C, 2 – A, 3 – B

Answer 4: 1-B, 2-A, 3-D (Section 6.3.5 BABOK), 4-C (Section 6.4.5 BABOK)

Mock Questions

Q1. An Organization has developed a software product that will help users to order food online from certain Food chains. After launching this application, the market response is not that good as was expected during the inception of the project. In the next phase of the project, the Business Analyst looked at the business objectives and alignment of the software with it. The BA wants to make sure that the enhanced version will be able to deliver what is valuable for the customers. Which of the techniques needs to be used by the Business Analyst?

    A. Document Analysis
    B. Brainstorming
    C. Benchmarking and Market Analysis
    D. SWOT analysis

Q2. John is appointed as a Business analyst and he is creating the AS-IS model to understand the business processes. Next up, he plans to create a TO-BE model. Which of the following techniques will be used for TO-BE model?

    A. Process Modelling
    B. State Modelling
    C. Concept Modelling
    D. None of these

Q3. A Business Analyst, Robert, is evaluating a few solutions for an organization. The organization has provided timelines, budget, and data privacy expectations. His analysis suggests that one of the solutions is going to address the problem and will provide returns over a three-year period. However, the estimated cost is very high. What should the business analyst recommend?

    A. He should advise the customer to go ahead with the investment
    B. He should advise the customer to let it go as the cost is very high
    C. He should still prepare the business case and let the customer make the decision
    D. He should ask the customer to get a detailed financial analysis done

Q4. A business analyst has been assigned to a project that started recently. He started by studying the current state. Why does a BA need to study and analyze the current state for carrying out the change?
    A. Because it's a suggested step
    B. Because it helps in validating the need for a change
    C. Because without understanding the current state, it is difficult to understand the future state
    D. Current state provides information about the organization

Q5. A business analyst is developing a strategy for a new initiative for an Oil and Gas company. He has identified a couple of solutions and would like to validate his solution with an expert. Which of the following stakeholders would be helpful?
    A. Project Manager
    B. Business Analyst
    C. Subject Matter Expert
    D. Sponsors

Q6. Consider a scenario in which an organization is intending to get an Enterprise resource planning (ERP) solution. They have hired a business analyst to help them take the right decision. What should the business analyst do first?

    A. Determine the approach to implement the ERP solution
    B. Define the scope of the ERP solution
    C. Conduct the cost-benefit analysis for the ERP implementation

D. Define the business need that the ERP package is intended to address

Q7. Which of the following activities involves assessing and defining the business functions to be added/modified, capabilities to be built, need for systems, and tools?

    A. Scope modelling
    B. Impact Assessment for a change
    C. Functional decomposition
    D. Strategy analysis

Q8. A business analyst is planning and developing a strategy for a digital project. Looking at the organizational capabilities, she has concerns about the success of the project. What should she do?

    A. She should continue with the strategy planning and come out with the change strategy roadmap
    B. She should assess the risk and come out with a risk management plan
    C. She should assess the risk and come out with a risk management plan and should ensure regular review
    D. She should advise the organization to be risk-averse and start the initiative at an opportune time

Q9. A Business Analyst has been working in an Investment Bank. He got involved in a consulting program for Merger & Acquisition of a large Retail chain client. After the initial analysis, the Business Analyst has prepared a list of companies, which can be acquired by his company. During cost-benefit analysis, which category of cost is mostly under consideration in this analysis?

    A. Total Cost of Ownership
    B. Opportunity Cost
    C. Sunk Cost
    D. Operational Cost

Q10. A business analyst discovers that there is a low tolerance for risks in the organization. The BA reviews the Risk register to identify the high probability and high impact risks. What should Alex do with these risks?

    A. He should put in place the contingency plan
    B. He should put in place the mitigation plan
    C. Risks should only be dealt with when it realizes
    D. The project can be stalled till risks become low in probability

Answers

Q1. Answer C: (Section 6.2.6) Benchmarking and market analysis helps to study the competition and customer expectations. Since this technique enables us to take effective decisions regarding future business objectives so by using this technique, the enhanced version can be more effective. Thus, the correct answer is option c.

Q2. Answer A: Both AS-IS and TO-BE models are part of process modelling where the AS-IS model is used to define the current state of a process and the TO-BE model is used to define the potential future state as to provide what is desired to happen in the future state. So, the correct answer is process Modelling. (Section 10.35.2 - Last Paragraph)

Q3. Answer D: Solution option recommendation is an element of the change strategy. In this case, the returns are over a period of three years, it can't be compared with the cost (to assess cost-benefit). Even if the question states that the cost is very high, there are no numbers provided. So, the best strategy is to get a financial analysis done (an NPV analysis will provide the correct information) to understand cost-benefit before a recommendation can be made. Thus, option d is the correct answer. (Refer to 6.4.4.4 of BABOK)

Q4. Answer B: The starting point for any change is an understanding of why the change is needed. The current state is explored in just enough detail to validate the need for a change and/or the change strategy. Understanding the current state of the enterprise prior to the change is necessary to identify what needs to be changed to achieve a desired future state and how the effect of the change will be assessed. Thus, option b is the correct answer. (BABOK Section 6.1.2)

Q5. Answer C: While developing a change strategy for a project, several options are identified, explored, and described in enough detail to reach a consensus to help select the best feasible option. These options can also be identified through brainstorming or by consulting the subject matter experts (SMEs). Thus, the correct answer is option c. (BABOK Section 6.4.4.4 Second paragraph)

Q6. Answer D: This comes under the task Analyze Current State. The business analyst should get the clarity on business needs and objectives for the desire to implement the ERP solution. Any solution approach and subsequent business case must have clearly defined objectives. The strategy analysis knowledge area describes the transition strategy for an organization to go through a change initiative. Refer to Section 6.1.3, the input to start the activities (studying the current state) is needs. So, option D is correct.

Q7. Answer A: The scope modelling defines the limits or boundaries and places the respective elements inside or outside of it. The determination of the elements is done by assessing various factors which are listed as bullet points in section 10.41.3.2. Business functions to be added/modified, capabilities to be built, need for systems, and tools are included in this list and hence the answer A is correct. (Section 10.41.1 and 10.41.3.2)

Q8. Answer C: (The paragraph below Fig 6.0.1. As per BABOK) - When there is uncertainty regarding the outcome of a change initiative, the strategy may need to focus more on mitigating risk, testing assumptions, and changing course until a strategy that will succeed in reaching the business goals can be identified or until the initiative has ended. This means that creating a risk management plan and reviewing it for any changes is the correct strategy. hence option C is correct.

Q9. Answer B: Correct option B - In evaluating alternatives, a Business analyst considers opportunity cost. It provides if investing an option is beneficial. The opportunity cost of any design option is equal to the value of the best alternative not selected. (Section 6.4.4.4)

Q10. Answer B: When an organization has a low tolerance for risks, it is better to get mitigation strategies in place so that the risks impact, as well as probability, can be minimized or avoided whereas stalling projects do not make sense as it will be over-reaction and unwarranted. Thus, the correct answer is option b. (Refer 6.3.4.4 of BABOK)

Requirements Analysis and Design Definition

The Requirements Analysis and Design Definition knowledge area describes the tasks that business analysts perform to **structure** and **organize requirements** discovered during elicitation activities, **specify** and **model** requirements, **validate** and **verify** information, identify **solution options** that meet business needs, and estimate the **potential value** that could be realized for each solution option.

It covers the **incremental** and **iterative** activities ranging from the initial concept and exploration of the need through the transformation of those needs into a recommended solution.

Business analyst's role is instrumental in modelling needs, requirements, designs, and solutions as well as conducting thorough analysis and communicating them with other stakeholders. The form, level of detail, and what is being modelled are all dependent on the **context**, **audience,** and **purpose**.

Business analysts analyze the potential value of both requirements and designs. Solution options can be evaluated to recommend the best solution option that meets the need and brings the most value in collaboration with the **implementation subject matter expert**.

Usage and application of core concepts within the context of Requirements Analysis and Design Definition are as follows:

- **Change** – Transform elicitation results into requirements and design in order to define the change.
- **Need** – analyze the need to recommend a solution that meets the needs.
- **Solution** – Define solution options and recommend the one that is most likely to address the need and has most value.
- **Stakeholder** – Tailor the requirements and designs so that they are understandable and usable by each stakeholder group.
- **Value** – Analyze and quantify the potential value of the solution options.
- **Context** – Model and describe the context in formats that are understandable and usable by all stakeholders.

Key Concepts

Before we move forward, lets understand three key terms – Needs, Requirements and Design.

Terms	Description	Example
Needs	What does a business want? To address a problem, opportunity or issue or risk	A bank's retail lending division wants to use bank's customer to cross sell and upsell their products, so that they grow 10% every quarter
Requirements	A useful representation of needs. Detailing the needs by collaborating with the stakeholders	The system will identify the suitable customers based on average balance and net worth. The system will then send emails every 15 days to them using email templates.
Design	A useful representation of requirements from the solution perspective. Multiple design options are possible	Create an algorithm to identify the customers for sending marketing emails. The customer details will be displayed to the marketing manager in a UI for approval.

TECHCANVASS

		Create a CRON job to send emails to shortlisted customers. The CRON job will run every 1st and 15th of the month

Table 7.1: RADD Key Concepts

Requirements Analysis and Design Definition Tasks

01 Specify and Model Requirements

02 Verify Requirements

03 Validate Requirements

04 Define Requirements Architecture

05 Define Design Options

06 Analyze Potential Value and Recommend Solution

Task 1: Specify and Model Requirements

Purpose	To analyze, synthesize and refine elicitation results into requirements and designs.
Description	➢ This task describes the practices for **analyzing** elicitation results and **creating representations** of those results. ➢ The outputs are referred to as **requirements** when the focus of the specifying and modelling activity is on **understanding** the need and it is referred to as **designs** when the same activity is focused on **solution**. ➢ All business deliverables are referred to as requirements whereas the word 'design' is used specifically for technical designs. ➢ This task captures information about **attributes** or **metadata** about the requirements as well as the models used to represent the requirements.
Inputs	➢ **Elicitation Results (any state)** – Modelling can begin with any elicitation result and may lead to the need for more elicitation to clarify or expand upon requirements. **Elicitation and modelling may occur sequentially, iteratively, or concurrently**.

Elements	➢ **Model Requirements** – A model is a descriptive way to convey information to a specific audience to support analysis, communication, and understanding.
	    o Models may also be used to confirm knowledge, identify information gaps and identify duplicate information. One or more of the following modelling formats are chosen:
	        ▪ **Matrices** – A matrix is used in modelling a requirement or set of requirements that have a **complex but uniform structure** that can be broken down into elements that apply to every entry in the table. Matrices are used for prioritizing requirements and recording requirements attributes and metadata. Data dictionaries, requirements traceability or gap analysis are the areas where matrices are applied.
	        ▪ **Diagrams** – A diagram is a visual, often pictorial, representation of a requirement. It is used to depict **complexity** in a way that would be difficult to do with words. They can be used to define boundaries for business domains, to categorize and create hierarchies of items and to show components of objects such as data and their relationships.
	    o Model categories can include:
	        ▪ **People and Roles** – Represent **organizations, roles and their relationships** within an enterprise and to a solution. Techniques include Organizational Modelling, Roles and Permissions Matrix and Stakeholder List, Map or Personas
	        ▪ **Rationale** – Represent "**why**" of a change. Techniques include Decision Modelling, Scope Modelling, Business Model Canvas, Root Cause Analysis, and Business Rules Analysis.
	        ▪ **Activity Flow** – Represent a **sequence** of actions, events or a course that may be taken. Techniques include Process Modelling, Use Cases and Scenarios, and User Stories.
	        ▪ **Capability** – Focus on **features** or **functions** of an enterprise or a solution. Techniques include Business Capability Analysis, Functional Decomposition, and Prototyping.

- **Data and Information** – Represent the **characteristics** and the **exchange** the information within an enterprise or a solution. Techniques include Data Dictionary, Data Flow Diagrams, Data Modelling, Glossary, State Modelling, and Interface Analysis.
- ➤ **Analyze Requirements** – Analysis of requirements is dependent on the level of decomposition required, level of detail to be specified, knowledge of stakeholders, potential for misunderstanding and organizational standards. Information gathered is decomposed into components to further examine for:
  - o Anything that must change to meet the business needs
  - o Anything that should stay the same to meet the business need
  - o Missing components
  - o Unnecessary components,
  - o Any constraints or assumptions that impact the components
- ➤ **Represent Requirements and Attributes** – As part of specifying requirements, they can also be categorized according to the schema described in task Requirements Classification Schema. Categorizing requirements can help ensure the requirements are fully understood, a set of any type is complete, and that there is appropriate traceability between the types.
- ➤ **Implement Appropriate Levels of Abstraction** – The level of requirement varies based on the **type** of requirement and **audience** for the requirement. It is appropriate to produce different **viewpoints** of requirements to represent the same need for different stakeholders. Special care needs to be taken to maintain the **meaning** and **intent** of the requirements over all representations.

Guidelines & Tools	➤ Modelling Notations/Standards – Allow requirements and designs to be precisely specified as is appropriate for the audience and purpose of the models. ➤ Modelling Tools – Software products that facilitate drawing and storing matrices and diagrams to represent requirements. ➤ Requirements Architecture – Requirements and interrelationships can be used to ensure models are complete and consistent. ➤ Requirements Life Cycle Management Tools – Software products that facilitate recording, organizing, storing and sharing requirements and designs. ➤ Solution Scope – Boundaries of the solution provide boundaries for the requirements and design models.
Techniques	➤ **Acceptance and Evaluation Criteria** – Used to represent attributes of requirements. ➤ **Business Capability Analysis** – Represent the features and functions of an enterprise ➤ **Business Model Canvas** – Describe the rationale for requirements ➤ **Business Rules Analysis** – Analyze business rules so that they can be specified and modelled alongside requirements. ➤ **Concept Modelling** – Used to define terms and relationships relevant to change and enterprise ➤ **Data Dictionary** – Used to record details about the data involved in the change ➤ **Data Flow Diagrams** – Used to visualize data flow requirements ➤ **Data Modelling** – Used to model requirements to show how data will be used to meet stakeholder information needs

	➤ **Decision Modelling** – Used to represent the decisions in a model in order to show the elements of decision making required ➤ **Functional Decomposition** – Used to model requirements in order to identify constituent parts of an overall business function ➤ **Glossary** – Used to record the meaning of relevant business terms ➤ **Interface Analysis** – Used to model requirements in order to identify and validate inputs and outputs of the solution ➤ **Non-Functional Requirement Analysis** – Used to define and analyze the quality of service attributes ➤ **Organizational Modelling** – Used to allow business analysts to model the roles, responsibilities, and communications within an organization ➤ **Process Modelling** – Used to show the steps or activities that are performed in the organization ➤ **Prototyping** – Used to assist the stakeholders in visualizing the appearance and capabilities of a planned solution. ➤ **Roles and Permissions Matrix** – Used to specify and model requirements concerned with the separation of duties among users and external interfaces ➤ **Root Cause Analysis** – Used to model root cause of a problem ➤ **Scope Modelling** – Used to visually show a scope boundary ➤ **Sequence Diagrams** – Used to specify and model requirements to show how processes operate and interact with one another ➤ **Stakeholder List, Map or Personas** – Used to identify the stakeholders and their characteristics ➤ **State Modelling** – Used to specify the different state of a part of the solution throughout a life cycle in terms of events ➤ **Use Cases and Scenarios** – Used to model the desired behaviour of a solution by showing user interactions with the solution, to achieve a specific goal or accomplish a particular task. ➤ **User Stories** – Used to specify requirements as a brief statement about what people do or need to do when using a solution.
Stakeholders	➤ Any stakeholder – Business Analysts may choose to perform this task themselves and communicate the requirements to stakeholders for their review and approval.
Output	➤ **Requirements (specified and modelled)** – Any combination of requirements and designs in the form of text, matrices, and diagrams.

Task 2: Verify Requirements

Purpose	To ensure that requirements and design specifications and models meet quality standards and are usable for the purpose they serve.
Description	➢ Verifying requirements ensures that the requirements and designs have been **defined** correctly and constitutes a **check** that they are ready for validation, and provides the information needed for further work to be performed. ➢ A high-quality **specification** is a well written and easily understood by its intended **audience**. A high-quality **model** represents **reality**. ➢ The most important characteristic is **fitness for use** by the stakeholders who will use them for a particular purpose.
Inputs	➢ **Requirements (specified and modelled)** – Any requirement, design or set of those may be verified to ensure that text is well structured, and that matrices and modelling notation are used correctly.

Elements	➢ **Characteristics of Requirements and Designs Quality** – Acceptable quality requirements exhibit many of the following characteristics:
	   ○ **Atomic** – Self-contained and capable of being understood independently
	   ○ **Complete** – Enough to guide further work and at an appropriate level of detail for work to continue. The level of completeness required differs based on **perspective** or **methodology** and **point in the life cycle** where the requirement is being examined or represented.
	   ○ **Consistent** – Aligned with the identified needs of the stakeholders and not conflicting with other requirements.
	   ○ **Concise** – Contains no extraneous and unnecessary content.
	   ○ **Feasible** – Reasonable and possible within the agreed upon risk, schedule, budget or considered feasible enough to investigate further through prototypes.
	   ○ **Unambiguous** – Requirement must be clearly stated in such a way to make it clear whether a solution does or does not meet the associated need.
	   ○ **Testable** – Able to verify the requirement has been fulfilled.
	   ○ **Prioritized** – Ranked, grouped or negotiated in terms of importance and value against all other requirements
	   ○ **Understandable** – Represented using common terminology of the audience
	➢ **Verification Activities** – Verification activities are typically performed iteratively throughout the requirement analysis process. They include:
	   ○ Checking for **compliance** with organizational performance standards for business analysis, such as using right tools and methods,
	   ○ Checking for the **correct use** of modelling notations, templates or forms,
	   ○ Checking for **completeness** within each model,
	   ○ **comparing** each model against other relevant models, checking for elements that are mentioned in one model but are missing in other models, and **verifying** that the elements are referenced consistently,
	   ○ Ensuring the terminology used in expressing the requirement is **understandable** to stakeholders and consistent with the used of those terms within the organization and **adding examples** where appropriate for clarification.

	➢ **Checklists** – Checklists are used for **quality control** when **verifying** requirements and designs. o The purpose of a checklist is to **ensure** that items determined to be important are included in the final requirements deliverables, or that **steps** required for the verification process are followed.
Guidelines & Tools	➢ Requirements Life Cycle Management Tools – Some tools have the functionality to check for issues related to many of the characteristics such as atomic, unambiguous, and prioritized.
Techniques	➢ **Acceptance and Evaluation Criteria** – Used to ensure that requirements are stated clearly enough to devise a set of tests that can prove that the requirements have been met. ➢ **Item Tracking** – Used to ensure that any problems or issues identified during verification are managed and resolved. ➢ **Metrics and Key Performance Indicators (KPIs)** – Used to identify how to evaluate the quality of requirements. ➢ **Reviews** – Used to inspect requirements documentation to identify requirements that are not of acceptable quality.
Stakeholders	➢ All Stakeholders – Business analyst in conjunction with the domain and implementation subject matter experts, has the primary responsibility for determining that the task has been completed.
Output	➢ **Requirements (verified)** – Set of requirements or designs that are of sufficient quality to be used as a basis for further work.

Task 3: Validate Requirements

Purpose	To ensure all the requirements and designs align with the business requirements and support the delivery of needed value.
Description	➤ Requirements validation is an **ongoing** process to ensure that stakeholder, solution, and transition requirements align with the business requirements and that the designs satisfy the requirements. ➤ The overall **goal** of implementing the requirements is to **achieve** the stakeholder's desired future state. Conflicts in needs, differences in views amongst stakeholders can be identified when requirements are validated.
Inputs	➤ **Requirements (specified and modelled)** – Validation applies to **any type** of requirements and designs. Validation activities may begin **before** requirements are completely **verified** but **cannot be completed** before requirements are completely verified.
Elements	➤ **Identify Assumptions** – If an organization is launching an unprecedented product/service, it may be necessary to make assumptions about **customer or stakeholder response** as there are no previous similar experiences on which to rely. o Stakeholders may be expecting certain benefits from requirements implementation. Such assumptions need to be recorded and detailed down so that associated **risks** can be managed. ➤ **Define Measurable Evaluation Criteria** – Business Analysts define the **evaluation criteria** that will be used to evaluate how successful the change has been after the solution is implemented. **Baseline metrics** might be established based on the **current state**. Target metrics can be developed to reflect the achievement of the business objectives or some other measurement of success. ➤ **Evaluate Alignment with Solution Scope** – A requirement that does not deliver **benefit** to a stakeholder is a strong candidate for **elimination**. When requirements do not align, either the future state must be re-evaluated and the solution scope changed, or the requirement removed from the solution scope. Similarly, if a design cannot be validated to support a requirement, there might be a missing or misunderstood requirement, or the design must change.
Guidelines & Tools	➤ Business Objectives – Ensure the requirements deliver the desired business benefits. ➤ Future State Description – Helps to ensure the requirements that are part of the solution scope do help achieve the desired future state. ➤ Potential Value – Can be used as a benchmark against which the value delivered by requirements can be assessed. ➤ Solution scope – Ensures the requirements that provide benefits are within the scope of the desired solution.
Techniques	➤ **Acceptance and Evaluation Criteria** – Used to define the quality metrics that must be met to achieve acceptance by a stakeholder. ➤ **Document Analysis** – Used to identify previously documented business needs in order to validate requirements. ➤ **Financial Analysis** – Used to define the financial benefits associated with requirements. ➤ **Item Tracking** – Used to ensure that any problems or issues identified during validation are managed and resolved.

	➢ **Metrics and Key Performance Indicators (KPIs)** – Used to select appropriate performance measures for a solution, solution component or requirement ➢ **Reviews** – Used to confirm whether or not the stakeholder agrees that their needs are met. ➢ **Risk Analysis and Management** – Used to identify possible scenarios that would alter the benefit delivered by a requirement.
Stakeholders	➢ All Stakeholders – All project stakeholders are involved in this task. **Business analysts in conjunction with customers, end user, and sponsors** has the primary responsibility for determining whether or not requirements are validated.
Output	➢ **Requirements (validated)** – Validated requirements and designs are those that can be demonstrated to deliver benefit to stakeholders and align with the business goals and objectives of the change. If a requirement or design cannot be validated, then it either doesn't benefit an organization or doesn't fall within solution scope or both.

Task 4: Define Requirements Architecture

Purpose	To ensure that the requirements collectively support one another to fully achieve the objectives.

Description	➢ A requirements architecture fits the individual models and specifications together to ensure that all of the requirements form a **single whole** that supports the overall business objectives and produces a useful outcome.
	   o Requirements architecture is used to:
	      ▪ Understand which **models** are appropriate for the domain, solution scope, and audience,
	      ▪ Organize requirements into **structures** relevant to different stakeholders
	      ▪ Illustrate how requirements and models **interact** with and **related** to each other and show how parts fit together into a meaningful whole,
	      ▪ Ensure the requirements **work together** to achieve the overall objectives, and
	      ▪ Make **trade-off decisions** about requirements while considering the overall objectives.
	   o Requirements architecture is focused on showing how elements work in harmony to support business requirements and to align the viewpoint of different stakeholders.
	   o **Traceability** is used to represent and manage these relationships. It proves that every requirement links back to an objective and shows how an objective was met.

Inputs	➢ **Information Management Approach** – Defines how the business analysis information will be stored and accessed. ➢ **Requirements (any state)** – Every requirement should be stated once and only once and incorporated into requirements architecture so that the entire set may be evaluated for completeness. ➢ **Solution scope** – Must be considered to ensure the requirements architecture is aligned with solution boundaries.

Elements	➢ **Requirements Viewpoints and Views** – A viewpoint is a set of **conventions** that define how requirements will be represented, how these **representations** will be organized and **related** to each other.
	   o Viewpoints provide templates for addressing the **concerns** of stakeholders. They include standards and guidelines for model types used for requirements, attributes that are included and used in models, model notations that are used and analytical approaches used to identify and maintain relationships among models.
	   o **No single viewpoint alone can form an entire architecture**. Each viewpoint has different model notations and techniques, and each is important from solution perspective. Examples of viewpoints include:
	      ▪ Business process models,
	      ▪ Data models and information,
	      ▪ User interactions, including use cases and user experience,
	      ▪ Audit and security and
	      ▪ Business models.
	   o The actual requirements and design for a solution from a chosen viewpoint are referred to as a **view**. A collection of views makes up the **requirements architecture** for a specific solution. The set of

coordinated, complementary views provides a basis for assessing the completeness and coherence of requirements.

- o Overall, viewpoints tell what **information** they should provide for each stakeholder group to address their concerns, while views describe the actual requirements and designs that are produced.

➢ **Template Architectures** – An **architectural framework** is a collection of viewpoints that is standard across an industry, sector, or organization. They can be treated as **predefined templates**. The framework can be populated with domain-specific information to form a collection of views if it is having accurate information populated in it.

➢ **Completeness** – An architecture helps ensure that a set of requirements is **complete**, **cohesive** and tells a **full story**. No requirements should be missing from the set, inconsistent with others, or contradictory to one another. All the **dependencies** between requirements need to be considered.

- o Structuring requirements according to **viewpoints** ensure this completeness. Iterations of elicitation, specification and analysis activities can help identify gaps.

➢ **Relate and Verify Requirements Relationships** – Each relationship between requirements is examined by tracing requirements and to ensure that the relationships satisfy the following quality criteria:

- o **Defined** – There is a relationship and the type are described.
- o **Necessary** – The relationship is necessary for understanding the requirements holistically.
- o **Correct** – Elements do not have the relationship described.
- o **Unambiguous** – There are no relationships that link elements in two different and conflicting ways.
- o **Consistent** – Relationships are described in the same way using the standard descriptions as defined in the viewpoints.

➢ **Business Analysis Information Architecture** – The information architecture is a **component** of the requirements architecture because it describes **how** all of the business analysis information for a change relates.

- o It defines **relationships** for types of information such as requirements, designs, types of models and elicitation results.
- o Understanding this type of information structure helps to ensure that the full set of requirements is **complete** by verifying the relationships are complete.

Guidelines & Tools	➢ Architecture Management Software – Helps to manage the volume, complexity, and versions of the relationships within the requirements architecture. ➢ Legal / Regulatory Information – Describes legislative rules or regulations that must be followed. They may impact requirements architecture or its outputs. ➢ Methodologies and Frameworks – A predetermined set of models and relationships between them to be used to represent different viewpoints.
Techniques	➢ **Data Modelling** – Describe the requirements structure as it relates to data. ➢ **Functional Decomposition** – Used to break down an organizational unit, product scope into its component parts. ➢ **Interviews** – Used to define the requirements structure collaboratively ➢ **Organizational Modelling** – Used to understand the various organizational units, stakeholders and their relationships which might help define relevant viewpoints.

	➢ **Scope Modelling** – Used to identify the elements and boundaries of the requirements architecture. ➢ **Workshops** – Used to define the requirements structure collaboratively.
Stakeholders	➢ Domain Subject Matter Expert, Implementation Subject Matter Expert, Project Manager, Sponsor, Tester – May assist in defining and confirming the architecture for requirements. ➢ Any stakeholder
Output	➢ **Requirements Architecture** – Requirements and interrelationships among them, as well as any contextual information that is recorded.

Task 5: Define Design Options

Purpose	To define the solution approach, identify opportunities to improve the business, allocate requirements across solution components, and represent design options that achieve the desired future state.
Description	➤ When designing a solution, there may be one or more **design options** identified which represent a way to satisfy a set of requirements and would be **tactical** rather than strategic. ➤ Trade-offs are made among design alternatives and the effect of them on the delivery of value to stakeholders needs to be assessed.
Inputs	➤ **Change Strategy** – Describes the approach that will be followed to transition to the future state. This may have some impact on design decisions in terms of what is feasible or possible. ➤ **Requirements (validated, prioritized)** – Only validated requirements are considered in design options. Requirements with the highest priorities might deserve more weight in choosing solution components to best meet them as compared to lower priority requirements. ➤ **Requirements Architecture** – A full set of requirements along with relationships is used in defining design options that can address the holistic set of requirements.

Elements	➤ **Define Solution Approaches** – The solution approach describes whether solution components will be created or purchased, or some combination of both. Proposed integration of components is considered in all the below design options. Solution approaches include:
	   o **Create** – Solution components are newly constructed, assembled or developed by experts as a response to the requirements set. This option includes **modifying** an existing solution.
	   o **Purchase** – Solution components are selected from a set of offerings that fulfil requirements. These offerings are usually products or services **owned** and **maintained** by third parties. It is also referred to as **COTS** (Commercial off the shelf) solution.
	   o **Combination of both** – Design options may include a combination of both creation and purchase of components.
	➤ **Identify Improvement Opportunities** – As part of the process, several opportunities to improve the operation of the business may occur and are compared. Some common examples are:
	   o **Increase Efficiencies** – Automate or simplify the work people perform which can increase consistency of behaviour thus reducing the likelihood of repetitive tasks by different stakeholders.
	   o **Increase Access to Information** – Open up the gates for accessing information to staff who interact with customers and thus reducing the need for specialists.
	   o **Identify Additional Capabilities** – Highlight capabilities that have the potential to provide future value and can be supported by the solution.
	➤ **Requirements Allocation** – Requirements allocation is the process of **assigning** requirements to solution components and releases to best achieve the **objectives** to maximize the **value** and **benefits** as well as to minimize **costs**.
	   o The value of solutions might vary depending on how requirements are implemented and when solution becomes **available** to stakeholders.

	o Requirements allocation typically starts when a **solution approach** has been determined and continues until all requirements are allocated which is throughout the design and implementation of a solution.
	
	➢ **Describe Design Options** – Design options are investigated and developed while considering the **desired future state**, and in order to ensure the design option is valid. **Solution performance measures** are defined for each design option. Design elements make up design components that contribute to the design option. Design elements may describe:
	  o Business policies and business rules,
	  o Business processes to be performed and managed,
	  o People who operate and maintain the solution,
	  o Operational business decisions to be made,
	  o Software applications used in solution, and
	  o Organizational structures

Guidelines & Tools	➢ Existing Solutions – Existing products or services that are considered as a component of a design option. ➢ Future State Description – Identifies the desired state of the enterprise that design options will be part of and helps to ensure design options are viable. ➢ Requirements (traced) – Define the design options that best fulfil known requirements ➢ Solution Scope – Defines the boundaries when selecting viable design options.
Techniques	➢ **Benchmarking and Market Analysis** – Used to identify and analyze existing solutions and market trends. ➢ **Brainstorming** – Used to help identify improvement opportunities and design options. ➢ **Document Analysis** – Used to provide information needed to describe design options and elements. ➢ **Interviews** – Used to help identify improvement opportunities and design options. ➢ **Lessons Learned** – Used to help identify improvement opportunities. ➢ **Mind Mapping** – Used to identify and explore possible design options. ➢ **Root Cause Analysis** – Used to understand the underlying cause of the problems being addressed in the change to propose solutions to address them. ➢ **Survey or Questionnaire** – Used to help identify improvement opportunities and design options. ➢ **Vendor Assessment** – Used to couple the assessment of a third-party solution with an assessment of the vendor to ensure the solution is viable. ➢ **Workshops** – Used to help identify improvement opportunities and design options.
Stakeholders	➢ Domain Subject Matter Expert – Provides the expertise within the business to provide **input** and **feedback** for the potential benefits of a solution. ➢ Implementation Subject Matter Expert - Provides inputs about the **constraints** of a solution and its **costs**. ➢ Operational Support ➢ Project Manager ➢ Supplier – Provides information on the **functionality** associated with a design option.

Output	➤ **Design Options** – Describe various ways to satisfy one or more needs in a context. They may include solution approach, improvement opportunities, and the components that define the option.

Task 6: Analyze Potential Value and Recommend Solution

Purpose	To estimate the potential value for each design option and to establish which one is most appropriate to meet the enterprise's requirements.
Description	➤ This task describes how to **estimate** and **model** the potential value delivered by a set of requirements, design, or design options. ➤ **Potential value** is analyzed many times over course of change. This includes considering that there is uncertainty in the estimates. The analysis may be a planned event, or it may be triggered by a modification to the context or scope of the change. ➤ Design options are evaluated by comparing the potential value of each option to other options. There may be no best option to recommend or there may be a clear best choice. ➤ In some cases, this means to develop a **proof of concept** and measure performance whereas in some cases, all proposed designs may be **rejected,** and more analysis may be needed to define a suitable design. At times, the best recommendation is to **do nothing**.
Inputs	➤ **Potential Value** – Can be used as a benchmark against which the value delivered by a design can be evaluated. ➤ **Design Options** – Need to be evaluated and compared to one another to recommend one option for the solution.

Elements	➤ **Expected Benefits** – Expected benefits describe the **positive value** that a solution is intended to deliver to stakeholders. Value can be any positive outcome such as benefits, reduced risk, compliance with business policies or an improved user experience.
	  o Benefits are determined based on the **analysis** of the benefit that stakeholders **desire** and the benefit that is possible to **attain**.
	  o The total expected benefit is the net benefit of **all the requirements** a particular design option address. They are realized over a **period**.
	➤ **Expected Costs** – Expected costs include any potential **negative value** associated with a solution, including the cost to acquire the solution, any negative impacts it may have on stakeholders and the cost to maintain it over time.
	  o Expected costs can include timeline, effort, operating costs, purchase/implementation costs, maintenance costs, physical resources, information, and human resources.
	  o **Opportunity cost** is considered when estimating the expected cost of change. Opportunity cost of any design option is equal to the value of the best alternative not selected.
	➤ **Determine Value** – The potential value of a solution to a stakeholder is based on the **benefits** delivered by that solution and the associated **costs**. Value can be positive or negative.
	  o Business analysts consider **potential value** from the points of view of stakeholders. Value to the **enterprise** is more heavily weighted than value for any individual group. An overall positive increase in value for the enterprise as a whole justifies proceeding with the change.

	- o Potential value is **uncertain value**. Many changes are proposed in terms of intangible or uncertain benefits, while costs are described as tangible, absolute and might grow. Complete estimate is defined by comparing tangible and intangible costs alongside the tangible and intangible benefits. This should consider the **degree of uncertainty** pertaining at the time the estimates are made.
	➤ **Assess Design Options and Recommend Solution** – Each design option is assessed based on the potential value it is expected to deliver.
	   o There could be a need to re-evaluate design options to include a better understanding of the **cost of implementation** and to determine the best **cost-to-benefit** ratio.
	   o The best option(s) deemed to be the most **valuable** solution to address the need is deemed. In many cases, best recommendation could be to do nothing if none of the design options are worthwhile. Various factors taken into consideration to assess each design option are:
	      ■ **Available Resources** – Limitations regarding the number of requirements that can be implemented based on the allocated resources.
	      ■ **Constraints on Solution** – Regulatory requirements or business decisions may require that certain requirements be handled manually or automatically, or that certain requirements be prioritized above all others.
	      ■ **Dependencies between Requirements** – Some requirements could have limited value but are needed to be delivered as they support high level requirements.

Guidelines & Tools	➤ Business Objectives – Used to calculate expected benefit ➤ Current State Description – Provides the context within which the work needs to be completed and can be used to identify and quantify the value to be delivered from a potential solution. ➤ Future State Description – Describes the desired future state that the solution will be part of in order to ensure design options are appropriate. ➤ Risk Analysis Results – Potential value of design options includes the assessment of the level of risk associated with design options ➤ Solution Scope – Defines the scope of the solution that is being delivered
Techniques	➤ **Acceptance and Evaluation Criteria** – Used to express requirements in the form of acceptance criteria when assessing proposed solutions and determining whether a solution meets the defined business needs. ➤ **Backlog Management** – Used to sequence the potential value. ➤ **Brainstorming** – Used to identify potential benefits of requirements in a collaborative manner. ➤ **Business Cases** – Used to assess recommendations against business goals and objectives. ➤ **Business Model Canvas** – Used as a tool to help understand strategy and initiatives. ➤ **Decision Analysis** – Used to support assessment and ranking of design options. ➤ **Estimation** – Used to forecast the costs and efforts of meeting the requirements as a step towards estimating the value. ➤ **Financial Analysis** – Used to evaluate the financial return of different options and choose the best possible return on investment.

	➢ **Focus Groups** – Used to get stakeholder input on which design options best meet the requirements.
	➢ **Interviews** – Used to get stakeholder input on which design options meet the requirements.
	➢ **Metric and Key Performance Indicators (KPIs)** – Used to create and evaluate the measurements used in defining value.
	➢ **Risk Analysis and Management** – Used to identify and manage the risks that could affect the potential value of requirements.
	➢ **Survey or Questionnaire** – Used to get stakeholder input on which design options best meet the requirements
	➢ **SWOT Analysis** – Used to identify areas of strengths and weaknesses that will impact the solution.
	➢ **Workshops** – Used to get stakeholder input on which design options best meet the requirements
Stakeholders	➢ Customer – Represents the market segments affected by the requirements and solutions and will be involved in **analyzing the benefits and costs** for the same.
	➢ Domain Subject Matter Expert
	➢ End User – Provides an **insight** into the potential value of change.
	➢ Implementation Subject Matter Expert
	➢ Project Manager
	➢ Regulator
	➢ Sponsor – **Approves** the expenditure of resources to purchase or develop a solution and approve its final recommendation.
Output	➢ **Solution Recommendation** – Identifies the suggested, most appropriate solution based on an evaluation of all defined design options. The recommended solution should maximize the value provided to the enterprise.

Glossary

- **Opportunity Cost** – Opportunity costs are alternative results that might have been achieved if the resources, time, and funds devoted to one design option had been allocated to another design option. It refers to the benefits that could have been achieved by selecting an alternative change strategy.
- **COTS** – Commercial off the Shelf. COTS refer to the solution components purchased from the market or shared from a partner to achieve the goal within solution space.
- **Validation** - Testing against the business requirements. Always done against a business problem or opportunity. User Acceptance Test is about validating the solution.
- **Verification** - Testing to check the quality of the documented requirements. Attempts to improve the quality of the requirements and the solution.
- **Design -** They represent a way of satisfying the set of requirements. Design includes the details of requirements
- **Requirements allocation -** The process of assigning requirements to solution components and releases in order to best achieve the business objectives.
- **Viewpoints** - This describes what information should be provided to each stakeholder group
- **Release planning -** Allocation of requirements to phases and iterations and the plan to achieve the business goals considering priorities

Case Study

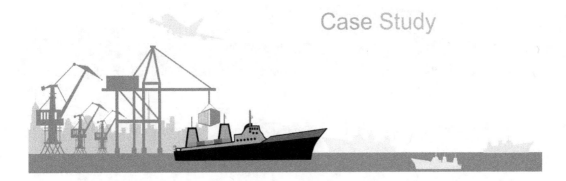

Case Study

A youth fashion apparel brand *Below25.com* has retail stores in all the major cities catering to the young fashion-conscious population. The sales team wanted to monitor and track the sales trend across the stores and regions as its competitors have been growing faster. This was a matter of concern for the company.

The company hired BACS Consulting to develop the software application to help them achieve their goal.

BACS sent its team to study the requirements. The team gathered the requirements and identified design options for the requirements. Here is an extract from the Requirements register listing the requirements and design options.

Requirements	Design options
Sales data store wise, region wise as well as country wise	A dashboard prototype developed internally or get a pre-designed dashboard (part of a reporting system)
Facility to sort data in all the reports	Buy/Build a grid to support the functionality
Facility to filter data in all the reports	Buy/Build a grid to support the functionality
Facility to edit data in all the reports	Buy/Build a grid to support the functionality

Table 7.2: Design Options

Evaluating Design options

The design options for the grid functionality were to either build it from scratch or buy a ready to use grid component. The team used a build vs buy decision analysis to come up with the correct one. Here is the matrix used by the BACS team:

Criteria	Weight	Develop grid internally	Buy a grid
Features	5	5	5
Ease of customization	4	5	3
Product support	4	5	4
Cost	5	3	4
Implementation duration	5	2	5
Total		XX	YY

Table 7.3: Decision matrix for Design Options

Case Study Questions

Q1. Table 2 shows the decision matrix prepared by the BACS Consulting team. What are the total scores for Developing a grid internally and buying a grid respectively?

A. 88, 90
B. 90, 88
C. 20, 21
D. 460, 483

Q2. The build option had a better score. However, the company took a decision to buy the ready-to-use grid. What could be the possible reason for this trade-off?

A. Ease of implementation
B. Implementation duration
C. Product support
D. Sponsor's decision

Q3. The BACS team used the following to define the design options. Without using these, the design options would not have been appropriate in the given context.

1. Change Strategy
2. Existing Solutions
3. Validated Requirements
4. Verified Requirements

Choose the correct option from below:

A. All four
B. 1, 2 and 3
C. 1, 2 and 4
D. 1, 3 and 4

Case Study Answers

Answer – Q1. The total score is calculated by adding the product of weightage and the points for each design option. For design option 1, the score = 5*5 + 4*5 + 4*5 + 5*3 + 5*2 = 90. Similarly, the score for option 2 comes to be 88. The correct answer is B.

Answer - Q2. The trade-off is made for a less dominant option (In this case Buy a grid) when the less dominant option is better in a criterion than the dominant one. In this case, the company, *Below25.com,* is worried about its competitor so a faster implementation is a priority. As the Buy option is having a much higher score for this (Means it can be implemented much faster), the organization decided to go for it even though it was not the dominant choice. Section **7.5.2 of BABOK.**

Answer – Q3. Options 1, 2, and 4 are correct. These are the inputs to the task – Define design options. Section 7.5.3 of BABOK.

Exercises and Drills

Question 1: Match the following requirements characteristics with their description.

1. Design options	A. Requirements are possible, reasonable to implement given all assumptions and constraints
2. Concise	B. Requirements must not be open to multiple interpretations
3. Feasible	C. Describe various ways to satisfy the business needs
4. Unambiguous	D. Two requirements describe the same feature but produce different results.
5. Inconsistent	E. Contains no extraneous and unnecessary content

Question 2: Match the following relationships quality criteria with their meaning.

1. Defined	A. The relationship is necessary for understanding the requirements holistically
2. Necessary	B. There are no relationships that link elements in two different and conflicting ways
3. Correct	C. Relationships are described in the same way using the same set of standards
4. Unambiguous	D. There is a relationship and the type of relationship is described
5. Consistent	E. The elements do have the relationship described

Question 3: Match the following.

1. Create solution approach	A. Simplify or automate the work that people perform
2. Purchase solution approach	B. Approach where solution components are assembled, constructed, or developed by experts
3. Increase efficiencies	C. Highlight capabilities that have the potential to provide value in the future
4. Improve access to information	D. Approach in which solution components are selected from a set of already developed offerings fulfilling the requirements
5. Identify additional capabilities	E. Reduce the need of specialists by providing more information to staff interfacing with customers

Question 4: Complete the crossword:

Across	Down
2. A collection of views makes up the requirement _____ for a solution (12)	1. A set of conventions that define how requirements will be represented, organized and related (9)
3. The actual requirements and designs for a solution from a chosen viewpoint (4)	
	4. A customer chooses an inferior design option rather than the best one (8)
	5. If Assumptions are not identified in the project, it may have unmitigated _____ (4)

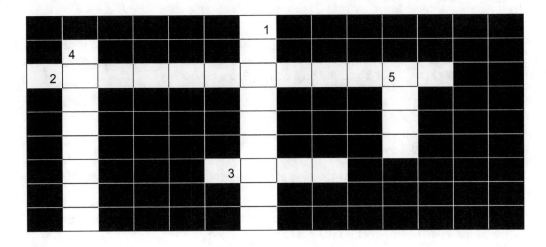

ANSWERS:

Answer 1: 1 – C, 2 – E, 3 – A, 4 – B, 5 – D

Answer 2: 1 – D, 2 – A, 3 – E, 4 – B, 5 – C

Answer 3: 1 – B, 2 – D, 3 – A, 4 – E, 5 – C

Answer 4:

						1V							
	4T					I							
2A	R	C	H	I	T	E	C	T	U	5R	E		
	A					W				I			
	D					P				S			
	E					O				K			
	O			3V	I	E	W						
	F					N							
	F					T							

Mock Questions

Q1. Miranda is a business analyst and is conducting requirements elicitation. As she is gathering the requirements, she needs to analyze and model the requirements so that developers can use this for developing the application. What would she be modelling?

    A. Requirements and solutions
    B. Requirements and designs
    C. Needs and requirements
    D. Needs and solutions

Q2. A business analyst has completed modelling of requirements and designs, what would be the next task for the BA?

    A. Ensuring that requirements are designed and approved by implementation SMEs
    B. Ensuring that requirements are verified and validated
    C. Ensuring that requirements are verified and documented
    D. Ensuring that requirements are verified and traced

Q3. Where do we capture the requirements metadata?

A) System Requirements Specification (SRS)
B) Requirements Traceability Table (RTT)
C) Design Document
Choose the right option.

    A. Only A
    B. Only A & B
    C. All the options
    D. Only A & C

Q4. Requirement architecture represents the structure of all the requirements pertaining to a change. Choose the best option from the following, which is also TRUE about requirements architecture.

    A. Requirement architecture is used for tracing the requirements
    B. It is used to show how solution functions work together as a whole to achieve value for business
    C. Even though stakeholders have different viewpoints, requirements architecture standardizes the representation
    D. None of these

Q5. Ronit Sharma has compared multiple options for implementing a financial accounting system for his customer. Solution A scored max score overall, however, the sponsor decided to go with Solution B, even though its score was less than solution A. What could have been the reason?

    A. As sponsor was the decision-maker, he made a choice, as he wished
    B. The sponsor did not like the solution A, even though it has the max score
    C. The sponsor preferred to go for a solution, which had the min implementation time
    D. The decision was taken because of risks involved

Q6. A business analyst is documenting the solution requirements for a proposed e-commerce application. The application will be developed in multiple phases. The services offered to the Asian Pacific countries is scheduled for Phase-III, whereas the Phase-I and II will launch the services in India. Which of the following is TRUE about the acceptance criteria for this project?

A. All the acceptance criteria will get developed by the stakeholders and not by the Business analyst
B. The acceptance criteria for a phase will be typically done separately for each phase
C. The acceptance criteria for Phase-I, II and III will typically be done in parallel while the execution of Phase-I is happening
D. The acceptance criteria for the entire project will be the same and will be decided at the beginning of the project

Q7. Which of the following is TRUE about the involvement of stakeholders in the validation of requirements?

A. Only Domain Expert SME and Implementation SME can validate the requirements
B. Any relevant Stakeholder can validate the requirements
C. Requirements validation is primarily self-review and peer review process within Business Analyst group only
D. Only Domain SME, Subject matter experts, Sponsor, and Project manager validate the requirements

Q8. A business analyst is assessing a few design options. The requirement is critical to the proposed solution. One of the design options has the most favourable cost-benefit analysis. However, the sponsor suggests the BA to evaluate outcomes if other design options are used. What are the outcomes of choosing other design options known?

A. Total Cost of Ownership
B. Opportunity Cost
C. Sunk Cost
D. Operational Cost

Q9. Within the first few weeks of the launch of a new web-based application, a critical workflow failed due to an unhandled exception. An investigation demonstrated that a programmer had used a numeric data type for a text field. Which of the following techniques could have caused this defect?

A. Prototyping and document analysis
B. Business process modelling
C. Use cases and Prototyping
D. Prototyping and Data modelling

Q10. What type of use case relationships does the following scenario represent?

For a case management system for attorneys, several features needed search feature. So, a search use case was created to represent search functionality. This use case was then shown to be used by any use case needing it.

Choose the best option from the four options.
A. Include
B. Extend
C. Expanded
D. Generalization

ANSWERS:

Q1. Answer B: The question intentionally mentions that the modelling is to be done to develop the solution requirements, which developers use. This means that Miranda must model not only requirements (use cases/user stories) but also design (like prototypes). Therefore, the correct answer is B. This answer requires an overall understanding of the RADD knowledge area. Chapter 7.

Q2. Answer B: Correct answer, Option B. Once the requirements are specified and modelled, the next task would be to get these verified and validated. The specified and modelled requirements are used as inputs to these two tasks. Refer to the inputs of task 7.2 and 7.3. Thus, the correct answer is option b.

Q3. Answer B: The requirements metadata can be captured in SRS or RTT (or any other requirements artefact where requirements details are presented). Examples of Metadata are a type of requirements, source of requirements, etc. Section 7.1.4.1 mentions Matrices as one of the ways to capture attributes or metadata and RTT, as well as SRS, can contain matrices. So, option b is correct.

Q4. Answer B: (Section 7.4.2 of BABOK) - Requirements architecture is not intended to demonstrate traceability, so option 1 is incorrect.

Option 3 is also incorrect as requirement architecture actually structures requirements in different ways to align them with the viewpoints of different stakeholders. Whereas it ensures the requirements form a single whole that supports the overall business objectives and produces a useful outcome for stakeholders to achieve the business objective. Thus, Option B is correct. (Refer to the third paragraph of Section 7.4.2.)

Q5. Answer C: Trade-offs involve taking a tactical or strategic choice. In this case, the sponsor made a trade-off and decided to go for a solution, which was taking minimum time to implement, even though it was not the best solution option as per decision analysis. So, the correct answer is option c whereas option D is incorrect as the question does not mention risk factors. (Section 7.5.2)

Q6. Answer B: Acceptance criteria are defined in the form of value attributes as explained in section 10.1.3.1. One of the value attributes is about specific situations and contexts. This means that value attributes will differ for India or Asia pacific geographies and so the acceptance criteria. This implies that acceptance criteria need to be defined separately for each phase. Acceptance criteria are typically defined while finalizing the requirements. Thus, option b is the correct answer.

Q7. Answer B: Section 7.3.7. As per this section, all stakeholders can participate in the validation of requirements however the business analyst, in conjunction with the customer, end users, and sponsors, has the primary responsibility for determining whether requirements are validated? Thus, option b is the right answer.

Q8. Answer B: Section 7.6.4.2. Opportunity cost is the expected outcome or result if an alternative design option would have been chosen.

What would be the value achieved if an organization invests in option B instead of option A. In this case, the opportunity cost of option A is equal to the value produced by investing in option B. This is what is described in the question, so the correct answer is B.

Q9. Answer D: Data modelling helps in defining the data types for individual fields in a process and its steps. Data models are created in line with the prototypes. These two should be completely aligned. Anyone of them not aligned with the other can produce data mismatch defects. None of the other options include data modelling so they are not correct.

This question is formed using the concepts of data modelling and prototyping. No specific reference available.

Q10. Answer A: Include relationship is used to showcase common or shared behaviour between the use cases. As per BABOK, this relationship is most often used either when some shared functionality is required by several use cases or to abstract out a complex piece of logic. (Refer to Section 10.47.3.1 of BABOK)

In this question search use case is shared by several use cases. This is represented as INCLUDE relationship. Thus, option a is the correct answer.

Solution Evaluation

The Solution Evaluation knowledge area describes the tasks that business analysts perform to **assess the performance** and **value delivered** by the solution in use by the enterprise and to recommend the removal of **barriers** or **constraints** that prevent the full realization of the value.

Solution Evaluation knowledge area focuses on an **existing solution**. This could only be a partial solution, but the solution or solution component has already been **implemented** and is **operating** in some form.

Solution Evaluation tasks that support the realization of benefits may occur before a change is initiated, while the current value is assessed after a solution has been implemented.

Solution Evaluation tasks can be performed on solution components such as:

- **Prototypes or Proofs of Concept** – Working but limited versions of a solution that demonstrates value.
- **Pilot or Beta Releases** – Limited implementations or versions of a solution used to work through problems and understand how well it delivers value before fully releasing the solution.
- **Operational Releases** – Full versions of a partial or completed solution used to achieve business objectives, execute a process, or fulfil a desired outcome.

Solution Evaluation describes the tasks that analyze the actual value being delivered, identifies limitations preventing the value to be realized and makes recommendations to increase the value of the solution. It focuses generally on a **component of an enterprise** rather than an entire enterprise. Solution evaluation process comprises of 5 steps as shown below:

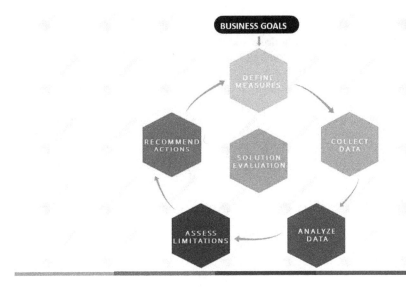

Usage and application of core concepts within the context of Requirements Analysis and Design Definition are as follows:

- o **Change** – Recommend a change to either a solution or the enterprise in order to realize the potential value of the solution.
- o **Need** – Evaluate how a solution is fulfilling the need.
- o **Solution** – Assess the performance of the solution, examine if it is delivering the potential value and analyze why value may not be realized by the solution.
- o **Stakeholder** – Elicit information from the stakeholders about solution performance and value delivery.
- o **Value** – Determine if the solution is delivering the potential value and examine why value may not be realized.
- o **Context** – Consider the context in determining the solution performance measures and any limitations within the context that may prohibit the value from being realized.

Solution Evaluation Tasks

01 **Measure Solution Performance**

02 **Analyze Performance Measures**

03 **Assess Solution Limitations**

04 **Assess Enterprise Limitations**

05 **Recommend Actions To Increase Solution Value**

Task 1: Measure Solution Performance

Purpose	To define the performance measures and use the data collected to evaluate the effectiveness of a solution in relation to the value it brings.
Description	➢ Performance measures determine the **value** of a newly deployed or existing solution. ➢ The measures used depend on the **solution** itself, the **context** and how the organization defines **value**. ➢ Performance may be assessed through **key performance indicators** aligned with enterprise measures, goals and objectives for a project, process performance targets, or tests for a software application.
Inputs	➢ **Business Objectives** – The measurable results that the enterprise wants to achieve. It provides a benchmark against which solution performance can be assessed. ➢ **Implemented Solution (external)** – A solution that exists in some form.

Elements	➢ **Define Solution Performance Measures** – Business analysts ensure that any existing performance measures are **accurate**, **relevant** and elicit any additional performance measures identified by stakeholders. The type and nature of measurements are considered when choosing the **elicitation method**.
	    ○ Business goals, objectives and business processes are influenced by third parties such as solution vendors, government bodies or other regulatory organizations and are common sources of measures.
	    ○ Solution measures may be **quantitative** (numerical, countable) or **qualitative** (can include attitudes, perceptions) or **both**, depending on the value being measured.
	➢ **Validate Performance Measures** – Validating performance measures helps to **ensure** that the assessment of solution performance is useful. Business analysts validate performance measures and any influencing criteria with **stakeholders**. Decisions about which **measures** are used to evaluate solution performance often reside with the **sponsor** but may be made by any stakeholder with decision-making authority.
	➢ **Collect Performance Measures** – Business analyst consider the following factors when collecting performance measures:
	    ○ **Volume or Sample Size** – A volume or sample size appropriate to the initiative is selected. A small sample size may lead to inaccurate conclusions whereas a large sample size may not be practical to obtain.
	    ○ **Frequency or Timing** – This may have an effect on the outcome
	    ○ **Currency** – Most recent measurements represent correctly than older data.

Guidelines & Tools	➢ Change Strategy – Change strategy in use or used to implement the potential value. ➢ Future State Description – Boundaries of proposed new, removed, or modified components of enterprise along with potential value expected from future state. ➢ Requirements (validated) – A set of requirements that have been analyzed and appraised to determine their value. ➢ Solution Scope – The solution boundaries to measure and evaluate.
Techniques	➢ **Acceptance and Evaluation Criteria** – Used to define acceptable solution performance.

	➤ **Benchmarking and Market Analysis** – Used to define measures and their acceptable levels.
	➤ **Business Cases** – Used to define business objectives and performance measures for a proposed solution.
	➤ **Data Mining** – Used to collect and analyze large amounts of data regarding solution performance.
	➤ **Decision Analysis** – Used to assist stakeholders in deciding on suitable ways to measure solution performance and acceptable levels of performance.
	➤ **Focus Groups** – Used to provide subjective assessments, insights, and impressions of a solution's performance.
	➤ **Metrics and Key Performance Indicators (KPIs)** – Used to measure solution performance.
	➤ **Non-Functional Requirements Analysis** – Used to define the expected characteristics of a solution.
	➤ **Observation** – Used either to provide feedback on perceptions of solution performance or to reconcile contradictory results.
	➤ **Prototyping** – Used to simulate a new solution so that performance measures can be determined and collected.
	➤ **Survey or Questionnaire** – Used to gather opinions and attitudes about solution performance.
	➤ **Use Cases and Scenarios** – Used to define the expected outcomes of a solution.
	➤ **Vendor Assessment** – Used to assess which of the vendor's performance measures should be included in the solution's performance assessment.
Stakeholders	➤ Customer
	➤ Domain Subject Matter Expert
	➤ End User – Contributes to the actual value realized by the solution in terms of solution performance. They may be consulted to provide reviews and feedback on areas such as workload and job satisfaction.
	➤ Project Manager
	➤ Sponsor
	➤ Regulator
Output	➤ **Solution Performance Measures** – Measures that provide information on how well the solution is performing or potentially could perform.

Task 2: Analyze Performance Measures

Purpose	To provide insights into the performance of a solution in relation to the value it brings.
Description	➢ The measures collected in the task 'Measure Solution Performance' require interpretation and synthesis to derive **meaning** and to have **actionable items**. Performance measures rarely trigger a decision about the **value** of a solution. ➢ In order to conduct meaningful analysis, business analysts require an understanding of potential value as well as need to consider variables such as goals and objectives of an enterprise, key performance indicators (KPIs), the level of risk of the solution, the risk tolerance of stakeholders and an enterprise.
Inputs	➢ **Potential Value** – Describes the value that may be realized by implementing the proposed future state. It can be used as a benchmark against which solution performance can be evaluated. ➢ **Solution Performance Measures** – Measures and provides information on how well the solution is performing or potentially could perform.
Elements	➢ **Solution Performance versus Desired Value** – A solution might be providing high performance, but less value is generated whereas there could be some solutions having low performance but generating potential great value. In such cases, other measurements are collected, and a **solution risk** is raised. ➢ **Risks** – New risks may be uncovered towards solution performance and to the enterprise. ➢ **Trends** – Time period is considered to guard against **anomalies** and **skewed trends**. Accurate depiction of solution performance to make decisions can be provided by analyzing a large enough sample size. ➢ **Accuracy** – The accuracy of performance measures is essential to the validity of their analysis. To be considered accurate and reliable, the results of performance measures should be reproducible and repeatable. ➢ **Performance Variances** – Difference between **expected** and **actual** performance represents a **variance** that is considered when analyzing solution performance. **Root cause analysis** may be necessary to determine the underlying causes of significant variances within a solution.
Guidelines & Tools	➢ Change Strategy – Change strategy in use or used to implement the potential value. ➢ Future State Description – Boundaries of proposed new, removed or modified components of enterprise along with potential value expected from future state. ➢ Risk Analysis Results – Overall level of risk and the planned approach to modifying individual risks. ➢ Solution Scope – The solution boundaries to measure and evaluate.
Techniques	➢ **Acceptance and Evaluation Criteria** – Used to define the acceptable solution performance through acceptance criteria. The degree of variance from these criteria will guide the analysis of that performance. ➢ **Benchmarking and Market Analysis** – Used to observe the results of other organizations employing similar solutions. ➢ **Data Mining** – Used to collect data regarding performance, trends, and variances from expected performance levels and understand patterns and meaning in that data.

	> **Interviews** – Used to determine the expected value of a solution and its perceived performance from a group > **Metrics and Key Performance Indicators (KPIs)** – Used to analyze solution performance on judging how well a solution contributes to achieving goals. > **Observation** – Used to observe a solution in action. > **Risk Analysis and Management** – Used to identify, analyze, develop plans to modify risks and to manage risks on an ongoing basis. > **Root Cause Analysis** – Used to determine the underlying cause of performance variance. > **Survey or Questionnaire** – Used to determine the expected value of solution and its perceived performance.
Stakeholders	> Domain Subject Matter Expert > Project Manager > Sponsor – Can identify **risks**, provide **insights** into data and potential value of a solution. Makes **decision** about the significance of expected versus actual solution performance.
Output	> **Solution Performance Analysis** – Results of analysis of measurements collected and recommendations to solve performance gaps and leverage opportunities to improve value.

Task 3: Assess Solution Limitations

Purpose	To determine the factors internal to the solution that restricts the full realization of value.
Description	> Assessing solution limitations identifies the **root causes** for under-performing and ineffective solutions and solution components. > Assess Solution Limitations are closely **linked** to the task to **Assess Enterprise Limitations**. > These tasks may be performed concurrently, and internal and external factors are to be identified which will limit the value. Assessment of such factors internal to the solution is focused via this task. > Assessment is performed at **any time** during the solution life cycle. It may occur on a solution component during its development, on a completed solution prior to full implementation or on an existing solution that is currently working within an organization.
Inputs	> **Implemented Solution (external)** – A solution that exists. The solution should be in some form, may not be in operational use, or it may be a prototype. > **Solution Performance Analysis** – Results of the analysis of measurements collected and recommendations to solve for performance gaps and leverage opportunities to improve value.
Elements	> **Identify Internal Solution Component Dependencies** – Solutions often have internal dependencies that limit the performance of the entire solution to the performance of the least effective component. Business Analysts identify dependencies about solution components and determine if there is anything about those dependencies that limit solution performance and value realization. > **Investigate Solution Problems** – **Problem analysis** is conducted to identify the source of the problem if the solution is consistently producing outputs that are not effective.

TECHCANVASS

	o Problems are identified in a solution or solution component by examining instances where the outputs are below an **acceptable level of quality** or where the **potential value** is not being realized. Problems may be indicated by an inability to meet a stated goal, objective, or requirement or may be a failure to realize a benefit that was projected to increase solution value.
	 ➤ **Impact Assessment** – All the identified problems are reviewed in order to assess the **effect** they have on the operation of an organization or the ability of the solution to **deliver** its potential value.
	     o Above action requires determining the **severity** of the problem, the probability of **re-occurrence** of the problem, the **impact** on the business operations and the **capacity** of the business to absorb the impact.
	     o Business analysts identify which problems must be resolved, mitigated through actions, or which can be accepted as well as assess risks to the solution and potential limitations of the solution. This risk assessment is specific to the solution and its limitations.

Guidelines & Tools	➤ Change Strategy – Change strategy in use or used to implement the potential value. ➤ Risk Analysis Results – The overall level of risk and the planned approach to modify the individual risks. ➤ Solution Scope – The solution boundaries to measure and evaluate.
Techniques	➤ **Acceptance and Evaluation Criteria** – Used both to indicate the level at which acceptance criteria are met or anticipated to be met or not met by the solution. ➤ **Benchmarking and Market Analysis** – Used to assess if other organizations are experiencing the same solution challenges and determine how they are addressing it. ➤ **Business Rules Analysis** – Used to illustrate current business rules and the changes required to achieve the potential value of the change. ➤ **Data Mining** – Used to identify factors constraining the performance of the solution. ➤ **Decision Analysis** – Used to illustrate the current business decisions and the changes required to achieve the potential value of the change. ➤ **Interviews** – Used to help perform problem analysis. ➤ **Item Tracking** – Used to record and manage stakeholder issues related to why the solution is not meeting the potential value. ➤ **Lessons Learned** – Used to determine what can be learned from the inception, definition and construction of the solution to have been impacted its ability to deliver value ➤ **Risk Analysis and Management** – Used to identify, analyze and manage risks to a solution and potential limitations restricting the realization of the potential value. ➤ **Root Cause Analysis** – Used to identify and understand the combination of factors and their underlying causes that led to a solution being unable to deliver its potential value. ➤ **Survey or Questionnaire** – Used to help perform problem analysis.
Stakeholders	➤ Customer ➤ Domain Subject Matter Expert ➤ End User – Contributes to the **actual value** realized by the solution in terms of solution performance. They may be consulted to provide **reviews** and **feedback** on areas such as workload and job satisfaction.

	> Tester > Sponsor – Responsible for **approving** the potential **value** of the solution as well as approving a **change** to the potential value. > Regulator
Output	> **Solution Limitations** – A description of the current limitations of the solution including constraints and defects.

Task 4: Assess Enterprise Limitations

Purpose	To determine how factors external to the solution are restricting value realization.
Description	> Solutions may depend on environmental factors that are within an enterprise or external to the enterprise. Enterprise limitations may include factors such as culture, operations, technical components, stakeholder interests or reporting structures. > Assessing enterprise limitations identifies **root causes** and describes how enterprise factors **limit** the value realization. > This assessment may be performed at any time during solution life cycle on a solution component during development, on a completed solution prior to implementation or on an existing solution.
Inputs	> **Current State Description** – The current internal environment of the solution including environmental, cultural, and internal factors influencing the solution limitations. > **Implemented (or Constructed) Solution (external)** – A solution that exists. The solution should be in some form, may not be in operational use, or it may be a prototype. > **Solution Performance Analysis** – Results of the analysis of measurements collected and recommendations to solve for performance gaps and leverage opportunities to improve value.

Elements	> **Enterprise Culture Assessment** – The beliefs, norms, and values shared by the members of an enterprise define the enterprise culture.
	  o Cultural assessment is performed to:
	    ▪ Identify whether stakeholders understand the reasons why a solution exists,
	    ▪ Find out if the solution is going to be providing beneficial value to stakeholders
	    ▪ Identify cultural changes that are required to realize the value of the solution
	  o Enterprise culture assessment helps to identify, evaluate the acceptance of solution is used to identify, evaluate the extent to which culture can accept a solution. It also shows readiness for enterprise to judge its ability and willingness to adapt to these cultural changes. Internal and external stakeholders are evaluated to:
	    ▪ Identify the depth of understanding and willingness to accept the solution,
	    ▪ assess cost-benefit analysis along with potential value from the solution and
	    ▪ determine the activities that are needed to ensure awareness and understanding of the solution.
	> **Stakeholder Impact Analysis** – This is conducted to find out how the solution is going to affect a stakeholder group. Following factors are considered during stakeholder impact analysis:

	o **Functions** – Processes performed by stakeholder which includes usage of solution in the form of input provided by a stakeholder to a process, usage of the solution to execute the process and outputs received from the process o **Locations** – Stakeholders may be in disparate locations which will impact the way they will use the solution and their ability to realize the value of the solution. o **Concerns** – Issues, risks, and overall concerns the stakeholders have with the solution. ➢ **Organizational Structure Changes** – This refers to organizational changes and their structure that is impacted by a solution. The use of a solution and the ability to adopt a change can be enabled or blocked by **relationships** among stakeholders, **reporting** structure to allow a solution to perform effectively, assessment of organizational **hierarchy** to support the solution, informal relationships within an organization and impact of the ability of a solution to deliver potential value. ➢ **Operational Assessment** – This identifies which **processes** and **tools** within the enterprise are adequately equipped to benefit from the solution and if assets are in place to support it. Following factors are considered while conducting an operational assessment: o policies and procedures o capabilities and processes that enable other capabilities o skill and training needs, o HR practices, o risk tolerance and management approaches and o tools and technology that support a solution.
Guidelines & Tools	➢ Business Objectives – Considered when measuring and determining solution performance. ➢ Change Strategy – Used or in use to implement the potential value. ➢ Future State Descriptions – Boundaries of proposed new, removed, or modified components as well as potential value expected from future state. ➢ Risk Analysis Results – Overall level of risk and planned approach to modify individual risks. ➢ Solution Scope – Solution boundaries to measure and evaluate.
Techniques	➢ **Benchmarking and Market Analysis** – Used to identify existing solutions and enterprise interactions. ➢ **Brainstorming** – Used to identify organizational gaps or stakeholder concerns. ➢ **Data Mining** – Used to identify factors constraining the performance of the solution. ➢ **Decision Analysis** – Used to assist in making an optimal decision under conditions of uncertainty. ➢ **Document Analysis** – Used to gain an understanding of the culture, operations, and structure of the organization. ➢ **Interviews** – Used to identify organizational gaps or stakeholder concerns. ➢ **Item Tracking** – Used to ensure that issues are not neglected or lost and that issues identified by the assessment are resolved. ➢ **Lessons Learned** – Used to analyze previous initiatives and how the enterprise interacted with the solution. ➢ **Observation** – Used to witness the enterprise and solution interactions to identify impacts.

	➢ **Organizational Modelling** – Used to ensure the identification of any changes to organizational structure that need to be addressed.
	➢ **Process Analysis** – Used to identify possible opportunities to improve performance.
	➢ **Process Modelling** – Illustrate the current business processes or changes that must be made to achieve the potential value of the solution.
	➢ **Risk Analysis and Management** – Used to consider risks in areas of technology, finance, and business.
	➢ **Roles and Permissions Matrix** – Used to determine roles and associated permissions to stakeholders as well as stability of end users.
	➢ **Root Cause Analysis** – Used to determine if the underlying cause may be related to enterprise limitations.
	➢ **Survey or Questionnaire** – Used to identify organizational gaps or stakeholder concerns.
	➢ **SWOT Analysis** – Used to demonstrate how a change will help the organization maximize strengths and minimize weaknesses and to assess strategies developed to respond to identified issues.
	➢ **Workshops** – Used to identify organizational gaps or stakeholder concerns.
Stakeholders	➢ Customer
	➢ Domain Subject Matter Expert
	➢ End User
	➢ Regulator
	➢ Sponsor – **Authorizes** and ensures **funding** for solution delivery. Act as a **champion** to resolve problems identified as part of organizational assessment.
Output	➢ **Enterprise Limitation** – Current limitations of the enterprise including the impact of solution performance on enterprise.

Task 5: Recommend Actions to Increase Solution Value

Purpose	To understand the potential value and future value, differences between them, factors that create that difference and to provide recommendations on action plan to align both values.
Description	➢ The goal of the task is to **improve solution performance** and **increase value realization**.
	➢ It focuses on understanding the performed assessments, understand common patterns and identify alternatives and actions to achieve above mentioned goal.
	➢ Recommendations identify how a solution can be **replaced**, **changed** via enhancements or **retired** after a particular time. This includes long term effects and contributions of the solution to stakeholders and may include recommendations to adjust the organization to achieve the above goal.
Inputs	➢ **Enterprise Limitation** – A description of current limitations of enterprise including how the solution performance is impacting the enterprise.
	➢ **Solution Limitation** – A description of current limitations of the solution including constraints and defects.
Elements	➢ **Adjust Solution Performance Measures** – Appropriate measures need to be identified in order to identify and define more appropriate measures to tune the performance of the solution in order to support the fulfilment of **business goals** and **objectives**.

> **Recommendations** – Recommendations are provided for the situation where solution performance is lower than expected. Some common examples of the same are as follows:

- o **Do Nothing** – In case of the situation where the change is not possible with the **resources** available or in the allotted **time frame**, **value** of the change is relatively low than the effort that is put in for the change, or when the **risk** around change is significantly high, it is recommended to do nothing.

- o **Organizational Change** – Organizational change management generally refers to a **process** and set of **tools** for managing change at an organizational level. These changes could be around providing recommendations for changes to **organizational structure**, making new **information** available to stakeholders and create new **skills** required to operate the solution. Possible recommendations include:
  - ▪ **Automating or simplifying work people perform** – Identifying tasks that can be automated, work activities and business rules that can be reviewed and analyzed for re-engineering, outsourcing or changes in responsibilities.
  - ▪ **Improving access to information** – Greater amount and better quality of information available to decision makers and regular staff.

- o **Reduce the Complexity of Interfaces** – Reducing the complexity of interfaces that come into picture due to the transfer of work between systems or between people can enhance better understanding. This can be achieved by better analyzing **API interfaces**.

- o **Eliminate Redundancy** – Reduce the cost of solution implementation by identifying common needs that can be met by a single solution. This can be achieved by conducting process re-engineering via **lean principles**.

- o **Avoid Waste** – Change processes to completely remove those activities that do not add value or that do not contribute to the final product directly. Again, this can be achieved via applying **lean** principles.

- o **Identify Additional Capabilities** – Solution options may be providing certain capabilities that are not providing immediate potential value but will provide future value for sure. Solution can support rapid development and implementation of the same. This can be achieved via performing **Capability Gap Analysis**.

- o **Retire the Solution** – Replacement of the solution may be needed because **technology** has reached the end of its life, **services** are being insourced or outsourced, or the solution is not fulfilling the **goals** for which it was created. Additional factors that may impact the decision include:
  - ▪ **Ongoing costs versus initial investment** – Ongoing cost for an existing solution increases over time whereas newer alternatives will have higher investment cost and less maintenance cost over time.
  - ▪ **Opportunity Cost** – Potential value that can be realized and achieved by pursuing alternative courses of action.
  - ▪ **Necessity** – It is feasible to maintain the solution component until it is providing appropriate value. At a certain point, it becomes impractical to maintain and continue with it.

	• **Sunk Cost** – Describes the money and effort already committed to an initiative. While deciding on future action, this investment is effectively irrelevant as it cannot be recovered. Decisions should be based on **future investment** required and **future benefits** that can be gained.
Guidelines & Tools	➢ Business Objectives – Considered in evaluating, measuring and determining solution performance. ➢ Current State Description – Provides the context within which work needs to be completed. ➢ Solution Scope – Solution boundaries to measure and evaluate.
Techniques	➢ **Data Mining** – Used to generate predictive estimates of solution performance. ➢ **Decision Analysis** – Used to determine the impact of acting on any of the potential value or performance issues. ➢ **Financial Analysis** – Used to assess the potential costs and benefits of a change. ➢ **Focus Groups** – Used to determine if solution performance measures need to be adjusted and use to identify potential opportunities to improve performance. ➢ **Organizational Modelling** – Used to demonstrate potential change within the organization's structure. ➢ **Prioritization** – Used to identify the relative value of different actions to improve solution performance. ➢ **Process Analysis** – Used to identify opportunities within related processes. ➢ **Risk Analysis and Management** – Used to evaluate different outcomes under specific conditions. ➢ **Survey or Questionnaire** – Used to gather feedback from a wide variety of stakeholders to determine if the value has been met or exceeded.
Stakeholders	➢ Customer ➢ Domain Subject Matter Expert ➢ End User ➢ Regulator ➢ Sponsor – Authorizes and ensures funding for the implementation of any recommended actions.
Output	➢ **Recommended Actions** – Recommendation of what should be done to improve the value of the solution within the enterprise.

Glossary

- **API** – Refers to an application programming interface. It is a set of functions that allows the creation of applications that access the features or data of other systems. In short, it acts as a communication medium for two software programs.
- **Capability Gap Analysis** – It is referred to as change management. Due to a given change in an organization, capability gap analysis helps to identify the differences between the current state and desired future state in the area of capabilities owned by individuals.
- **Lean**– This refers to the creation of perfect value for customers by using a perfect process and having zero waste.
- **Solution performance metrics** - These are the criteria (qualitative or quantifiable) by which the performance of the solution will be measured.
- **Proof of concept (POC)** - A working but limited version of a solution that demonstrate value.
- **Operational Release** - Full versions of a partial or completed solution used to achieve business objectives, execute a process, or fulfil a desired outcome.
- **Implementation** - Implementation refers to post-sales process of guiding a client from purchase to use of the software or hardware that was purchased. This includes requirements analysis, scope analysis, customizations, systems integrations, user policies, user training, and delivery.
- **Key Performance Indicators (KPIs)** - A Key Performance Indicator is a measurable value that demonstrates how effectively a company is achieving key business objectives. Organizations use KPIs at multiple levels to evaluate their success at reaching targets.
- **Scope** - Scope of work defines the extent of work in a software project e.g. what is in scope (to be done) and what's out-of-scope. Scope is not the same as requirements
- **online transaction processing system (OLTP)** - OLTP systems record business interactions as they occur in the day-to-day operation of the organization, and support querying of this data to make inferences.
- **Environmental Factors** - In business analysis, the word 'environmental' can sometimes be used to refer all external factors that affect a business (just like in environmental analysis) from Political to Legal, and everything in between.
- **Sunk Cost** - A sunk cost is a cost that has already been incurred and cannot be recovered. A sunk cost differs from future costs that a business may face, such as decisions about inventory purchase costs or product pricing.

Case Study

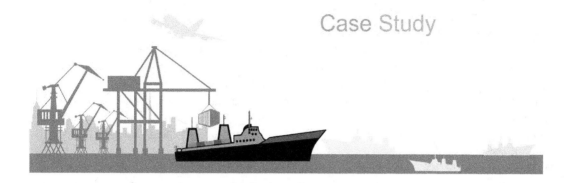

Cavalier group LLC is a medical equipment manufacturer. The company is seeing a surge in demand. The company board in its quarterly review raised concerns regarding the advertising and marketing spend. The board has passed a resolution to take steps to improve this as the cost is increasing rapidly but not the Sales. The board passed a resolution to retain BACS Consulting to help them develop a strategy and a roadmap.

BACS Consulting sent a team led by Nikhil Jain, the lead business analyst. We discussed this case study in the Strategy Analysis chapter to explain the current and future states and the change strategy proposed by the BACS team. Microsoft Dynamics 365 implementation was proposed to integrate all the disparate systems and have a unified view of data across the departments.

The business goal was to optimize the marketing and advertising spend. The team defined the following Key Performance Indicators (KPIs) to track the solution performance.

Lead Acquisition Cost: Lead Acquisition cost (LAC) is the target lead acquisition cost based on the revenue target for the coming year. The formula to calculate it is as follows:

Revenue Target X Closing Rate (Historical)

The closing rate (historical) is calculated by calculating the ratio of opportunities and closed deals for the past years.

PERFORMANCE MEASURES – CRM at Cavalier Group LLC

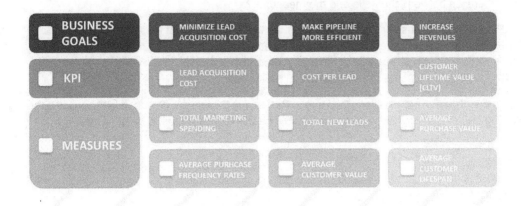

Fig 8.1: Solution Evaluation at Cavalier

Funnel Conversion Rate: It measures the rate at which leads move through the marketing funnel. The Funnel Conversion Rate metric helps the team understand and monitor how effective their efforts are in prompting leads to complete goals and move through to the end of the funnel. It is calculated by the formula:

(Number of leads that have moved to the next stage in the funnel/Leads in funnel stage) x100

Customer Lifetime Value (CLV): Customer lifetime value (CLV) is one of the most important metrics to measure at any growing company. By measuring CLTV in relation to the cost of customer acquisition (CAC), companies can measure how long it takes to recoup the investment required to earn a new customer -- such as the cost of sales and marketing. To compute the CLV, we use the following formula:

(Customer revenue for a period – Gross margin) / Churn percentage

To know how it is calculated, you can visit the following URL:

https://blog.hubspot.com/service/how-to-calculate-customer-lifetime-value

Case Study Questions

Q1. BACS consulting has identified KPIs and measures for the solution. Whom should Nikhil contact to get these validated?

1. Sponsor
2. Any stakeholder as per governance approach
3. Any stakeholder as per information management approach
4. Any Stakeholder as per business analysis approach

Choose the correct answer from below:

A. All the Four
B. 1 and 3

C. 1 and 4

D. 1 and 2

Q2. Key performance Indicator and measures are shown in Fig 1 as defined by BACS consulting. What is the difference between the KPIs and the measures?

A. KPIs indicate the business objectives and measures are values of these

B. KPIs indicate the achievement of goals and measures track these

C. KPIs indicate the achievement of the performance of measures

D. KPIs indicate the degree of achievement of measures

Q3. The historical data of the cavalier group suggests that 1 in 5 deals are closed. If the group is targeting USD 500,000 as the revenue target, what should be the value of leads to be generated?

A. USD 100,000

B. USD 50,000

C. USD 2,500,000

D. USD 2,000,000

Case Study Answers

Answer – Q1. The performance measures are validated by the Sponsor or any stakeholder who has decision-making authority as per the Business analysis governance approach. **Option D is correct.** Section 8.1.4.2 of BABOK.

Answer – Q2. Performance measures are created to track KPIs. The KPIs are indicators to track if the solution can achieve the goals. The solution is developed to help an organization achieve the goals. **So, option B is correct.** Section 10.28.2 BABOK.

Answer – Q3. The question states that 1 in 5 deals are closed which means that the closing rate is 1/5. Cavalier group had set the revenue target as $500,000. So, the company should target to generate leads worth $2,500,000 in the year to reach the revenue target of $500,000. **So, the correct answer is C.**

Exercises and Drills

Question 1: Match the following tasks with their respective description.

1. Measure solution performance	A. Determines factors internal to the solution that restrict the full realization of value
2. Analyze performance measures	B. Identifies and defines actions an enterprise can take to increase the value that can be delivered by a solution
3. Assess solution limitations	C. Provides insights into the performance of a solution in relation to the value it brings
4. Assess enterprise limitations	D. Determines the most appropriate way to assess the performance of a solution
5. Recommend actions to increase solution value	E. Determines factors external to the solution that restrict the full realization of value

Question 2: Match the following stages of development with their description.

1. Prototypes or Proof of Concept (POC)	A. limited implementations/ versions of a solution before fully releasing the solution
2. Pilot or Beta releases	B. Full versions of a partial/ completed solution used to achieve business objectives, execute a process, or fulfil a desired outcome
3. Operational releases	C. Working but limited versions of a solution that demonstrate value

Question 3: Match the following.

1. Sunk cost	A. Common needs of different stakeholders that can be met with a single solution
2. Opportunity cost	B. Potential value that could be realized by pursuing alternative initiatives
3. Avoid waste	C. Value of a change is low vis-a-vis the effort required to make the change
4. Eliminate redundancy	D. Money and effort already committed to an initiative
5. Do nothing	E. Remove those activities completely which do not add value to the final product

Question 4: Match the following.

1. Acceptance and Evaluation Criteria	A. To understand the solution boundaries to measure and evaluate.
2. Solution Scope	B. Used to find performance variances
3. Root Cause Analysis	C. Provides data to measure performance variances
4. Measure Solution performance	D. Used to evaluate and determine performance measure
5. Business Objectives	E. It is used to define acceptable solution performance

ANSWERS:

Answer 1: 1 – D, 2 – C, 3 – A, 4 – E, 5 – B

Answer 2: 1 – C, 2 – A, 3 – B

Answer 3: 1 – D, 2 – B, 3 – E, 4 – A, 5 – C

Answer 4: 1 – E (Section 8.1.6 BABOK), 2 – A (Section 8.2.5 BABOK), 3 – B (Section 8.2.4.5), 4 – C (Section 8.2.2 BABOK), 5 – D (Section 8.5.5)

Mock Questions

Q1. When it is determined that the solution is consistently producing incorrect outputs, which of these is performed to identify the source of the problem?

    A. Root cause Analysis
    B. Solution performance Analysis
    C. Performance Variance Analysis
    D. Cost Benefit Analysis

Q2. The difference between expected and actual performance represents a variance that is considered when analysing solution performance. How do we discover the variance?

    A. Sponsors provide this information
    B. Implementation SME provides this info
    C. Charts on Organizational dashboard
    D. Project team provides this info

Q3. A leads management system is not successful in a product company and a business analyst has been asked to analyze it. The BA finds that most of the employees have dual reporting leading to delays in the lead's approval and allocation. Which of the following correctly represents the discovered issue?

    A. A limitation of the software
    B. Enterprise limitation
    C. Solution scalability issue
    D. None of these

Q4. The sponsor is evaluating whether to continue with the project, so he asks the project team to check and to confirm the money already spent on the project. What is this spent money referred to as?

    A. Sunk Cost
    B. Project Cost
    C. Opportunity Cost
    D. Ongoing Cost

Q5. When solutions do not have built-in performance measures, how is the solution performance measured?

    A. Using the industry-standard measures
    B. The solution performance cannot be measured
    C. The project manager decides the performance measurement KPIs
    D. Sponsor can be contacted to understand the performance expectations

Q6. A Business Analyst is assessing the impact of a solution on stakeholders. Which of the following factors does not have any impact on the Stakeholders?

    A. Stakeholders using the solution to participate in a process
    B. Locations of the stakeholders
    C. The risk profile of the Stakeholders
    D. The concerns of the stakeholders about the solution

Q7. A Business Analyst has defined the performance measures for a proposed solution. Before collecting data for these measures, the BA wanted to ensure the validity of these measures. How can the BA validate the measures?

    A. The BA can validate it by conducting document analysis
    B. The BA can validate it by talking to the stakeholders

C. The BA can validate by using Organizational metrics
D. None of these

Q8. The Business analyst determines the severity of the issues with a solution so that appropriate remedial actions can be taken. Which of the following remedial actions/approaches can be taken?

A) Address the issues
B) Mitigate the issues
C) Do Nothing with the issues
D) Implement additional quality control measures

Select the most appropriate answer.

    A. All the Four
    B. A, B, and C
    C. B, C, and D
    D. A, C, and D

Q9. A team is tasked to assess the limitations of a recently implemented solution. What is this team going to look for?

    A. The technical limitations of the software application
    B. Overall limitations of the software application
    C. Overall limitations of the software application and the organization
    D. Overall limitations of the software application and the team going to use it

Q10. A Business analyst is assessing the performance of a solution. The BA has identified certain variances in actual vs planned goals. However, the BA wants to confirm the goals before submitting the findings. Where should he look for finding the goals?

    A. Current State analysis report
    B. Change Strategy Document
    C. Performance Analysis report
    D. System Requirements document

Answers

Q1. Answer A: Root cause analysis is a technique that is used to investigate solution problems. Thus, the correct answer is option a. (Refer to BABOK Section 8.3.6 and 8.3.4.2 - Investigate solution problems)

Q2.Answer D: Performance measurement is a process that starts by defining the performance measures or metrics. The actual data is collected and then compared with expected data. The difference in values is the variance. These activities are conducted by Project teams; hence option D is correct.

Option A is incorrect. Sponsor does not provide the variance.
Option B is incorrect. Implementation SME does not do that as well.
Option C is incorrect. Organization dashboard is simply a tool and can just help in automating the task of calculating the variance based on actual data collection. (BABOK - Section 8.1.4)

Q3. Answer B: This seems to be an enterprise issue as most of the people have dual reporting. Dual reporting is not good for teams as it causes approval delays and other issues. (Section 8.4.2 describes enterprise limitations)

Q4. Answer A: Money spent in the past on a project is known as Sunk Cost, therefore choice A is correct. (Refer to BABOK 8.5.4.2 Sunk cost section - The last bullet point)

Q5. Answer D: When solutions don't have built-in performance measures, it has to be decided in consultation with the stakeholders. However, there is no option stating that. So, in this case, we need to contact the Sponsor to understand performance expectations. The measures can then be created with those inputs. Refer to the stakeholder's section 8.1.7. Hence the correct answer is D. (Section 8.1.2 of BABOK)

Q6. Answer C: The risk profile of the stakeholders is NOT a factor that is considered by the Business analyst when conducting stakeholder impact analysis whereas their function, concerns and, location do.

The solution will impact the stakeholders the same way irrespective of their risk profile. However, stakeholders react differently to the solution based on their risk profile. But that was not the question. So, the answer is C. (Section 8.4.4.2 of BABOK)

Q7. Answer B: The best way to validate the performance measures is to discuss and get it validated by Stakeholders. (Section 8.1.4.2 of BABOK)

Option A is not correct as historical data may not provide any help as performance measures depend on the project context.
Option C is incorrect as Organizational metrics can only help if it is relevant to the project context. Thus, option b is the right answer.

Q8. Answer A: BA's are responsible to assess the risks associated with a solution. They may employ several approaches such as assessing the severity of the risk, chances of reoccurrence, etc. All the given points A, B, C, and D are valid in this case as issues can be resolved or mitigated whereas they may also be left unresolved as the impact of these issues is minimal. (Section 8.3.4.3)

Q9. Answer B: Assessing a solution for issues and limitations mean finding any limitation in the software application. It is not restricted to only Technical issues. It is related to the task "Assess solution limitation" and it looks for the internal factors restricting full realization of the expected value. Option B is the correct answer, but option A is incorrect.

Options C and D are incorrect because the assessment of solution limitations does not include assessment of enterprise limitations. (Section 8.3.1 of BABOK)

Q10. Answer B: The goals and expectations of a solution are defined in the change strategy document. So, when the BA wants to verify the goals, change strategy is the document to look for. So, the correct answer is B. (Section 8.3.4.2 of BABOK)

Option A is incorrect, as Current state analysis does not include the business goals.
Option C is incorrect as performance analysis report is prepared to highlight the variances in the actual vs expected goals report.
Option D is incorrect as System requirements document includes the requirements and not goals.

Techniques

Acceptance and Evaluation Criteria

Purpose

Acceptance Criteria define the minimum set of requirements or outcomes that must be met for a solution to be regarded as acceptable to the stakeholders.

Evaluation Criteria define a set of measures to evaluate solutions and designs to choose the one which provides maximum value to the stakeholders.

Description

- Acceptance and Evaluation criteria are measurable & testable in nature and hence provide for objective and consistent assessment of solutions and designs.
- This assessment technique is applicable at all levels of a project/initiative.
- Typically, acceptance criteria technique is used when one possible solution is being assessed while evaluation criteria are used when multiple solutions are being evaluated to select the one that provides maximum value to stakeholders.
- Evaluation criteria measure specific solution attributes such as cost, performance, usability, functionality on a continuous or discrete scale to select the best solution or design option. Unmeasurable attributes can be measured using expert judgement and various scoring techniques.
- Evaluation and acceptance criteria may be defined with the same value attributes. During the evaluation, the value attributes help select the best solution and during acceptance, the same value attributes can be used to make decisions on whether a solution is accepted or not.

Elements

- Value Attributes
  - Value Attributes are the characteristics that the solution must possess or avoid that determine or influence its value to stakeholders.
  - Value attributes typically include the ability to provide information or perform an operation, possess specific capabilities as well as non-functional characteristics like performance, usability, security, scalability, and reliability.
  - These attributes should be valid & relevant to stakeholders' needs and should be approved by the stakeholders.
- Assessment
  - Testability – Acceptance criteria must be stated in the form of test cases to verify the solution against them. These test cases are mostly executed during user acceptance testing (UAT) and result in true or false.
  - Measures – Evaluation criteria are expressed as parameters that can be measured against a continuous or discrete scale through various methods such as benchmarking or expert judgment. Tools may have to be designed to perform the evaluation, record as well as process the outcomes.

Usage Considerations

Strengths - Acceptance Criteria

- A useful technique in agile ways of working as all requirements are expressed as testable acceptance criteria.
- Effective in scenarios where requirements express contractual obligations.

- Provide criteria based on shared understanding to assess the requirements.

Strengths - Evaluation Criteria

- Provide the ability to assess key-value attributes of interest to the stakeholders.
- Assist in the delivery of an expected return on investment or other potential value.
- Assists in defining priorities.

Limitations - Acceptance Criteria

- May be difficult to alter if tied to contractual obligations.

Evaluation Criteria - Attaining stakeholder agreement on evaluation criteria is not an easy task.

Example

Acceptance Criteria

A business analyst is working on creating a mobile application for a private bank. The objective of the project is to create a mobile application that will enable the relationship managers to maintain their profile and performance specific information, their customers' information, and view all products provided by banks and many more. He has been asked by the product owner to create user stories and define acceptance criteria that should be met for the story to be considered as acceptable. Below is an example of a user story and some of the associated acceptance criteria for the login functionality.

User Story

Title: As a Bank Relationship Manager, I should be able to log into the application so that I can view my information, my customers' information, and banks' products.

Acceptance Criteria

Given: Relationship manager has installed the mobile application

When: He/she opens the mobile application

Then: Login Screen of the mobile application appears with fields to enter the username & password, Eye icon, "Sign-In" button and "Forgot password" link

Given: Login screen of the mobile application is opened

When: No character/numeral is entered in Username or Password

Then: "Sign-In" button is disabled

Given: Login screen of the mobile application is opened

When: One or more character/numeral is entered in Username or Password

Then: "Sign-In" button is enabled

Given: Login screen of the mobile application is opened

When: Password is entered, and 'Eye' icon is selected while entering the password

Then: Characters entered in Password are displayed instead of asterisk characters

Given: Username and Password are entered

When: Credentials entered are correct and "Sign-In" is tapped

Then: Relationship manager successfully signs in to the application and 'Dashboard' screen is opened

Given: Username and Password are entered

When: Credentials entered are invalid/incorrect and "Sign-In" is tapped

Then: Login is unsuccessful and error validation is shown "Couldn't sign you in. Please check your username and password"

Given: Username is entered

When: Password is left blank and "Sign-In" is tapped

Then: Login is unsuccessful and error validation is shown "Couldn't sign you in. Please check your username and password".

Given: Password is entered

When: Username is left blank and "Sign-In" is tapped

Then: Login is unsuccessful and error validation is shown "Couldn't find your account. Please check your username and password".

Evaluation Criteria

A business analyst is working for a publishing company that is looking to purchase a commercial-off-the-shelf software solution to fulfil its royalty management business needs. With the cost, installation time, licensing, and ease of use for all the solutions being similar, the stakeholders decide to build the evaluation criteria as key essential system features.

The business analyst builds the list of required system features/capabilities in shared understanding with business stakeholders and assesses the solutions based on the devised features list to reach the conclusion that Solution 2 satisfies most of the feature requirements (as shown below).

S No.	Essential System Features	Solution 1	Solution 2	Solution 3	Solution 4	Solution 5
1	Royal repository with data insertion, validation, and maintenance	Y	Y	Y	Y	Y
2	Royalties calculations capability	Y	Y	Y	Y	Y

3	Royalties workflow management capability	Y	Y	Y	Y	Y
4	Multi-product handling capability	Y	Y	Y	Y	Y
5	Multi-channel handling capability	Y	Y	N	N	N
6	Report generation capability and download PDF or Excel	N	Y	Y	N	N
7	Administrative tools to manage security settings	Y	Y	Y	N	N
8	Creation and maintenance of templates	Y	Y	N	Y	N
9	Accommodation of new business models	Y	Y	Y	Y	Y
10	Real-time addition of new fields	N	Y	Y	Y	Y
11	Automated email reminders for critical process workflows	N	Y	Y	Y	N
12	Extensive search, sort and filter capabilities	Y	Y	Y	Y	Y
13	Integration with upstream and downstream systems	Y	Y	Y	Y	Y
14	Generate contractual documents	N	Y	N	N	N
15	Productivity tools to limit data entry like wizards	Y	Y	N	N	N
16	Generate contracts and deal documents	N	Y	Y	Y	Y
17	Accounting of invoices and payments	N	N	Y	Y	Y
18	Performance measurement capability	N	Y	N	Y	N
19	Multiple payment types handling capability	N	N	Y	N	Y
20	Distribution of statements in PDF or Excel	N	N	Y	Y	N
21	Compliance with SOX and other audit standards	Y	Y	Y	Y	Y
22	Data auditing / History maintenance	Y	Y	N	N	N
	Total	**13**	**19**	**16**	**15**	**12**

Backlog Management

Purpose

A backlog is used to record, track, and prioritize work items when the volume of work items goes beyond the capacity to complete them. Backlog management refers to an organized approach to manage the backlog.

Description

- Backlog Management deals with determining which work items should be included in the backlog, the attributes to consider to describe them, tracking mechanism, periodic review & prioritization approach to be employed, determining factors for their selection for execution and removal from the backlog.
- Work items at the top of a managed backlog have the highest business value and the highest priority and these are generally selected as next items for implementation.
- Backlog should be reviewed at periodic intervals since stakeholders' needs might change resulting in priorities of work items getting impacted.
- An eye should be kept on the number of work items in the backlog. Growing backlog would mean an increased demand or reduced supply while a declining backlog would mean a reduced demand or enhanced supply.
- Some large projects/initiatives may have more than one backlog. One backlog will have the complete set of global work items whereas other one will include work items that are expected to be taken up for execution within a short time.

Elements

- Items in the backlog
  - Backlog items are the ones that have business value and work associated with it
  - Typical backlog items include (but not limited to) use cases, user stories, Functional/Non-functional requirements, designs, customer orders, risk items, change requests, defects, planned rework, maintenance.
  - A single person/role (product owner or business analyst) may hold the authority and responsibility to add new work items in the backlog or in some cases, a committee carries out this task based on a shared agreement.
- Prioritization
  - Work items in a backlog are prioritized relative to each other. In most cases, work items are numerically ranked based on the specific measure(s) while in some cases, a multi-phased prioritization approach can be used. In a multi-phased approach, prioritization may be at a broad level (high, medium, low) initially and later high priority items are taken up to be ranked relative to each other numerically.
  - Priorities of backlog items may change based on stakeholders' needs, work items dependencies, or backlog management rules.
- Estimation
  - When a work item is added to a backlog, very little details are included and hence only high-level estimates are provided. As the relative priority of an item increases, it is reviewed and elaborated further for more accurate effort and cost estimates.
  - Feedback from the production process may also refine the estimates of work items.
- Managing changes to the backlog
  - New/changed requirements added to the backlog are ordered relative to the other items in the backlog.

- o Items are selected based on the available capacity, dependencies between items, current understanding of the size, and complexity.
- o Items are removed from the backlog when completed, or if no longer required to be work upon as decided by decision making stakeholders.
- o Removed items may be re-added to the backlog if stakeholders' needs change, removed items or other priority items could be more time-consuming than expected or resulting work product has defects.

Usage Considerations

Strengths

- Effective in aligning work as per stakeholders' priorities and even responding to changes in priorities.
- Focus and efforts are streamlined since only items near the top are elaborated and estimated in detail while other items receive less attention.
- Effective communication mode for stakeholders to understand the delivery plan of backlog work items.

Limitations

- Some backlogs may become very large and gets difficult to manage.
- Detailing of work to be done for accurate estimation requires experience.
- Lack of sufficient detail in backlog items may lead to loss of information over time.

Example

Finsley bank has hired MobTech Solutions to develop the mobile banking app to allow anytime and anywhere banking to its customers. Rohit Khatri is the business analyst for the project. The stakeholders and the IT team decided to use adaptive approach.

A snapshot of the product backlog is presented on the next page:

Epic Names	Parent Story ID	Story	As a/an	I want to...	so that.	Notes	Iteration / Sprint
Balance Enquiry		Balance Enquiry	User	want to check the available balance as on time	Available balance will display on the screen	Balance checking function	1
Cheque book request		Cheque book request	User	Want to send request for new cheque book	Request will send to bank for new cheque book	Cheque book request	1
Pin number change		Pin number change	User	Want to change pin number	New password will be updated	*New passwords should not be the last five used passwords. **Min * Characters *** One spl character should be there	1
Mini statement		Mini statement	User	To know last ten transactions, I made from my account	User can view last ten transactions		1
ATM Locator		ATM Locator	User	Know all the available ATMs within the city premises	List of all ATMs in the city		
Branch Locator		Branch Locator	User	Know all the available branch details within the city premises	List of branches in the city		
Fund transfer to same bank		Fund transfer to same bank	User	Want to transfer money to another bank account number	My balance will get debited and the receiver account balance will get credited		

TECHCANVASS

Balanced Scorecard

Purpose

Balanced scorecard is a strategy planning tool used to measure organizational performance on four dimensions – learning & growth, business process, customer, and financial. It is used to manage performance in a business model, organizational structure, or business process.

Description

- Business scorecard is outcome-focused and is based on the foundation that value creation drivers are understood, measured, and optimized to create a consistent performance.
- It allows the organization to monitor and measure progress against objectives and to adapt the strategy as needed.
- Balanced scorecard comprises of four dimensions:
  o Learning and Growth (To achieve their vision, how will an enterprise sustain its ability to change and improve?)
  o Business Process (To satisfy their shareholders and customers, what business processes must an enterprise excel at?)
  o Customer (To achieve their vision, how should an enterprise appear to their customers?)
  o Financial (To succeed financially, how should an enterprise appear to their shareholders?)
- Balanced scorecards can be used at multiple levels within an enterprise –
  o Enterprise-wide level
  o Department/Function level
  o Project/Initiative level
- It includes quantifiable objectives, specific performance measures, and targets derived from an organization's vision/strategy.

Elements

The four dimensions of the Business scorecard are explained below –

- Learning and Growth dimension
  o It includes measures regarding employee training and learning, product and service innovation, and corporate culture.
  o Metrics capture training funds, mentoring, knowledge sharing, and technology improvements.
- Business Process dimension
  o Metrics are related to the enterprise's operational performance and customer needs are met by the products.
- Customer dimension
  o Metrics pertains to how well products and services meet customer's needs to the desired satisfaction level, whether the delivery of products and services meet customer's quality expectations and customer's overall experience with the enterprise.
- Financial dimension
  o It includes measures like profitability, revenue growth, and economic value-added.
- Measures or Indicators
  o Two basic types of indicators include lagging indicators (provide results of actions already taken) and leading indicators (provide information about future performance).
  o Measures should be quantitative, linked to strategy, and easily understandable.
  o It needs to be ensured while defining or changing measures that existing measures are not impacted adversely.

Usage Considerations

Strengths

- Fosters balanced planning and thinking.
- Regardless of time span, goals can be synchronized into programs with incremental measures.
- Aligns the work of strategic, tactical, and operational teams.
- Promote forward-thinking and competitive spirit.

Limitations

- Aligning dimensions get difficult in case of an obscure strategy.
- Only available strategy planning tool rather than just one of the tools in a suite.
- May be misapprehended as a substitute for strategic planning, execution, and measurement.

Real Life Example

Mercury healthcare operates several hospitals and its vision is to become the best healthcare provider and to be the best employer. The business consultant has prepared the following balanced scorecard to define a balanced set of measures to help it track its progress towards achieving its vision.

This balanced scorecard is based on the smartsheet healthcare example available at: https://www.smartsheet.com/balanced-scorecard-examples-and-templates

		STRATEGIC OBJECTIVES	KEY PERFORMANCE INDICATORS	TARGETS	INITIATIVES
FINANCIAL	To sustain our mission financially, what should our focus be?	Demonstrate accountability and efficiency	% Utilization of OPD consultant hours	> 85%	
			% Nursing hours utilization	> 80%	
			Absenteeism rate	<5%	
STAKEHOLDERS	How should we appear to our stakeholders?	Overall patient satisfaction	Overall rating of care	85% good or better rating	Management staff leadership initiative
		Patient perception of quality index	% Family physicians that receive discharge summaries	90%	
			Employee and physician engagement	As per survey, >50%	Develop charter for community group
			Community consultation measures	Meet 8 of 10	
INTERNAL PROCESSES	At which internal processes should we excel to better serve our patients?	Processes are patient cantered, focused on quality and patient safety	% Medication reconciliation on admission	95%	Revamp infection-reporting process
			Rate of inpatient falls	<5%	
			Surgical safety compliance checklist	98% completed	
			% Compliance to ICU procedures	95% compliant	Converge report form review group
			# ICU infections	5 per month	

TECHCANVASS

LEARNING	**How should we better develop our systems to serve our patients?**	Enhance and maintain a healthy work environment	Attrition Rate	< 8%	Hire new HR lead
		% Performance development plans completed	# Skills development training	5 per quarter	
			Performance improvement post-training (Average score %)	> 75%	

Benchmarking and Market Analysis

Purpose

Benchmarking is conducted to compare organizational practices against the best-in-class practices to ensure that it is performing effectively. Market analysis, on the other hand, is a research conducted on the customers to understand their needs, wants, preferences, decision-influencing factors, and competition in the market.

Benchmarking and market analysis may lead to some key decisions specific to change initiatives to improve organizational operations, increase customer satisfaction, and increase value to stakeholders.

Description

- Best-in-class practices against which organizational practices are compared in benchmarking may be found in competitor organizations, in government, or industry associations.
- Benchmarking may also be carried out against compliance standards to validate whether an organization is meeting them or not.
- Market analysis or research carried out on customers helps draw out significant information on customers' needs and preferences and drive key business decisions.
- Market analysis also helps an organization takes decisions on partnering, merging, divesting, or exiting a market.

Elements

- Benchmarking – Benchmarking includes carrying out the below activities –
  - o Identifying the relevant areas to be studied.
  - o Identifying leading enterprises (including competitors) in the sector.
  - o Conducting a survey, using request for information (RFI) or paying visits to selected enterprises to understand their practices & capabilities.
  - o Identifying gaps between current and best practices.
  - o Developing a plan to implement best practices.

- Market Analysis – Market analysis includes carrying out the below activities –
  - o Identify customers to be analyzed to understand their needs and preferences.
  - o Identify opportunities that may increase value to stakeholders.
  - o Identify competitors in the market to delve into their operations.
  - o Discover market trends, anticipate growth rates to estimate potential profitability.
  - o Gather market data.
  - o Use existing resources to gather information and clarify questions at hand.
  - o Review data to determine trends and draw conclusions.
  - o Define appropriate business strategies.

Usage Considerations

Strengths - Benchmarking

- Provides organizations with useful information to improve their performance.
- Helps combat competition by identifying best practices followed by competitors.
- Helps identify reasons behind an organization's success.

Strengths - Market Analysis

- Can be tailored to specific target groups with specific questions.
- May expose weaknesses within an organization or industry.
- Assist organizations to identify differences between their products/services and those offered by customers.

Limitations - Benchmarking

- Time consuming and may not yield insightful results if organizations don't possess the required expertise to conduct the analysis.
- May not produce creative and forward-looking solutions as the solutions being assessed are only the ones that are working well in the present state of affairs.

Limitations - Market Analysis

- Maybe a time-consuming and costly process.
- Results may not be readily available.
- May not provide expected and correct results without market segmentation.

Example

In an aim to launch an online grocery store, a business analyst is engaged in a benchmark study. He is doing an investigation on the enterprises that are leaders in this space. Below are the best practices identified by him that needs to be present in the B2C platforms to live up to the expected standards –

- Seamless registration process
- Simple design with effortless navigation and appealing user interface
- Immediate confirmation of receipt of orders
- Rapid search / filter solutions to find the desired products with ease
- Various modes of online payment like internet banking, credit/debit card, wallets, UPI, cash on delivery
- Security in online transactions
- Unlimited Categories and products of various brands across all categories
- Delivery Scheduling to select the desired slots
- User-friendly Return and exchange policies
- Referrals and rewards programs
- Membership option for extra benefits related to discounts and delivery

In addition, he has decided to carry out market analysis in order to understand the needs, preferences & decision-influencing factors of the prospective customers and come out with a solution that enhances customer satisfaction and also provides a competitive advantage.

Below are the needs & preferences he has identified that, if present in the B2C platforms, can provide enhanced value to customers –

- Deliver offline features to enable browsing without internet connectivity
- Share cart with the family to form a common cart before moving to the checkout
- Real-time order tracking
- Live Chat (Support)
- Update on out-of-stock items when available
- Product comparisons

Brainstorming

Purpose

Brainstorming is a technique that fosters creative thinking of a group to generate numerous ideas in a very short period. It enables the derivation of themes from these ideas for further analysis. It is commonly used to identify a list of stakeholders, risks, or solutions to solve a problem.

Description

- Brainstorming is intended to produce a broad set of ideas to solve a problem, analyse the root cause of problems, identify risks, identify stakeholders, provide product launch ideas.
- It draws on the experience and creativity of a group to generate many ideas in a fun & engaging environment. Participants feed off on each other's ideas to generate more ideas.
- Facilitator takes up the task of ensuring that there is no judgement/criticism of ideas and to prevent the discussion to go into a heated debate/argument.

Elements

Below is the step-by-step process is carried out to conduct brainstorming –

1) Preparation – It involves defining a clear area of interest, determining a time limit, identify facilitator and relevant participants, setting expectations & getting their buy-in, and establishing evaluation/rating criteria.

2) Session – It includes conducting the brainstorming session, sharing ideas, recording the ideas visibly, encourage participation, build on other participant's ideas, share as many ideas as possible.

3) Wrap Up – It comprises of evaluation of ideas based on pre-determined criteria, creation of a condensed list of ideas by combining or removing ideas as applicable, rate the ideas, and distribute to the appropriate parties.

Usage Considerations

Strengths

- Elicit many requirements in a short span of time
- Non-judgemental environment fosters creative thinking & complete participation
- Create an environment where tension is reduced between participants

Limitations

- Participation depends on creativity & willingness
- Organization & interpersonal politics may limit participation
- Participants must reduce the temptation to initiate a debate or criticize ideas

Business Capability Analysis

Purpose

Business Capability Analysis is a valuable tool that describes the capabilities of an enterprise or part of an enterprise. It provides a shared understanding and demonstration of outcome, strategy, and performance.

Business Capability Analysis provides a framework for scoping, planning, and prioritization work in an initiative and useful in assessing an organization's ability to offer new products and services.

Description

- Capabilities of an enterprise may be assessed for performance and risks to identify specific performance gaps and prioritize investments.
- With an aim to fill the performance gaps of an existing capability or create a new capability altogether, product development efforts are planned.
- The capabilities required by the enterprise should remain constant if it continues to perform similar functions regardless of whether the execution method undergoes a change of any capacity.

Elements

- Capabilities
  - Capabilities are the abilities of an enterprise to perform or transform something that helps achieve a business goal or objective.
  - Describes the purpose or outcome of the performance or transformation rather than the way(s) through which performance or transformation is carried out.
  - A capability may be possessed by more than one business unit but displayed only once on a capability map.
- Using capabilities
  - Capabilities impact value in an enterprise through increasing or protecting revenue, reducing, or preventing cost, improving service, achieving compliance, or positioning for the future.
  - Capabilities do not necessarily have the same level of value.
  - Several tools exist that can be used to make value explicit in a capability assessment.
- Performance expectations
  - Capabilities can be assessed to identify explicit performance expectations.
  - When a performance gap analysis for a capability is performed, a specific performance gap can be identified which is essentially the difference between the current performance and the desired performance for a business strategy.
- Risk model
  - Risk of a capability pertains to risk(s) in the performance of the capability, or a lack of it thereof.
  - Risks can be categorized as business risk, technology risk, organizational risk, and market risk.
- Strategic planning
  - Business capabilities for the current state & future state of an enterprise can be a guiding force to accomplish its strategy and help establish & maintain a sustainable competitive advantage as well as a distinct value proposition.
  - A business capability assessment can produce a set of recommendations or proposals for solutions that forms the basis for product roadmap creation and release planning.
- Capability Maps
  - Provide a graphical view of elements involved in business capability analysis.
  - There is no set standard for the notation of capabilities maps.

<u>Usage Considerations</u>

Strengths

- Helps create focus and aligned initiatives through shared understanding and demonstration of outcome, strategy, and performance.
- Assist in aligning business initiatives across various organizational aspects.
- Useful in assessing an organization's capability to offer new products and services.

Limitations

- Requires broad and cross-functional collaboration among various teams/functions /departments/units of an organization which might be challenging.
- Fails to provide the desired outcome on alignment and shared understanding when created in isolation rather than in unison.

Business Cases

Purpose

A business case captures the reasoning for undertaking a change initiative. It provides justification for taking up an initiative based on the anticipated benefits and value to be realized by the organization compared to the cost, effort, and other considerations to acquire, implement and/or operate the proposed solution.

Description

- A business case is used to define the need, determine the desired outcomes, assess constraints, assumptions, and risks, and recommend a solution.
- Time and effort spent on creating a business case should be based on the size of the initiative and anticipated value.
- A business case provides adequate detail for seeking a decision without providing any specifics on the implementation approach for the proposed solution.
- A scribe may also be appointed to record the decisions and outstanding issues.

Elements

- Need Assessment
  - Need refers to a business goal or objective linked to one or more strategies of an enterprise.
  - Need assessment assists in identifying a problem or an opportunity. Different alternatives to solve the problem or make use of the opportunity are assessed in a business case.
- Desired Outcomes
  - Desired outcome describes the future state that is reached when the need is met.
  - These are best described as measurable so that they can effectively evaluate the success of a business case or solution.
  - Different solution options are evaluated on their ability to achieve the desired outcomes to determine the most suitable option for a recommendation. Desired outcomes should be independent of the recommended solution.
- Assess Alternatives
  Various solution alternatives should be evaluated for the below factors –

  - Scope
    - Defined using organizational boundaries, system boundaries, business processes, product lines, or geographic regions.
    - Clearly outlines the in-scope and out-of-scope items and maybe similar or different for different solution alternatives.
  - Feasibility
    - Feasibility check should be carried out from an organizational and technical perspective.
    - Organizational feasibility checks assess an organization's knowledge, skills, and resources whereas technical feasibility is from the point of view of experience in the proposed solution's technology stack.
  - Assumptions, Risks, and Constraints
    - Assumptions are known, understood, and accepted facts that may affect an initiative.
    - Constraints are limitations that may restrict a solution alternative.
    - Risks are potential problems that may negatively impact a solution.
    - A shared understanding and agreement on these factors help set practical expectations.
  - Financial Analysis and Value Assessment

- Includes a cost estimate to implement and operate the alternative and quantified financial benefit derived from its implementation.
- Non-financial benefits such as improved employee morale, increased flexibility in change response, improved customer satisfaction, and reduced risk add significant value to the organization and hence must be considered.

- Recommended Solution
  - Recommended solution is the most suitable solution out of all the alternatives to solve the problem or leverage the opportunity.
  - Solution must be detailed enough to include estimated costs, estimated duration, and measurable benefits for the stakeholders to determine whether to go ahead with its implementation or not.

Considerations

Strengths

- Provides relevant information to decide about a change initiative.
- Provides a detailed financial analysis of cost and benefits.
- Facilitates decision making throughout the initiative.

Limitations

- May be determined by author bias.
- Information not updated once the funding is secured and the initiative starts off.
- Cost and benefit estimations may turn out to be invalid upon further investigation.

Real Life Example

An e-commerce organization has been expanding its operations in various parts of India and because of its decentralized employee management systems, it has started facing issues in administering the workforce. The systems are based on obsolete technology and are increasingly becoming ineffective leading to high costs being incurred on the organization. It has been discussed among the strategic team that in order to more effectively manage employee administration at reduced costs, the organization must implement a web-based application that will provide a centralized platform to manage all required administrative activities. The strategic team has decided to create a business case to capture the detailed reasoning for undertaking a change initiative that can be demonstrated to the business heads/sponsors to take their go-ahead.

It has been decided among the strategic team that the business analyst, who is a key member of the strategic team, will work on creating the business case. The BA decides to include the below sections in the business case to make it detailed enough for stakeholders to determine whether to go ahead with its implementation or not.

Section	Objective
Executive Summary	Outlines the purpose of writing the business case. Also, it summarizes the current situation, problem statement, and the project objectives.

Need		Describes the business problem that the change initiative and recommended solution will address.
Desired Outcomes		Describes the anticipated outcome for the change initiative. Should include how the initiative will benefit the business and describe the measurable future state.
Solution Alternatives	Cost-Benefit Analysis	Illustrates the costs of the project and compare them with the quantified benefits and savings to determine if the initiative is worth pursuing.
	Assumptions	Cover initial assumptions for the proposed solution.
	Constraints	Cover initial constraints for the proposed solution.
	Risks	Covers initially identified risks for the proposed solution.
Recommended Solution		Summarizes the most suitable solution approach for addressing the business problem including its estimated costs, estimated duration, and measurable benefits.

TECHCANVASS

Business Model Canvas

Purpose

A business model canvas is a framework that illustrates how an enterprise creates, delivers, and captures value for and from its customers.

It provides a holistic view of the business as a whole and serves as a blueprint for implementing a strategy. It provides for mapping of programs, projects, and other initiatives to the strategy of the enterprise and demonstrates where the enterprise is investing, where a particular initiative fits, and any related initiatives.

Description

- A business model canvas is made up of nine building blocks that explain how an enterprise creates, delivers, and captures value –
  - Key Partnerships
  - Key Activities
  - Key Resources
  - Value Proposition
  - Customer Relationships
  - Channels
  - Customer Segments
  - Cost Structure
  - Revenue Streams

- Depicts the relationship between an enterprise's operations, finance, customers, and products/service offerings.
- It can be used as a diagnostic tool in the sense that it can investigate the current state of business in terms of resources (time, cost, effort) that organization is currently spending in various areas.
- It can also work as a planning and monitoring tool as it provides a framework for understanding inter-dependencies and priorities among groups and initiatives.

Elements

- Key Partnerships
  - Refers to partners and suppliers with whom the enterprise gets into a strategic relationship.
  - Partnerships can be in the form of mergers & acquisitions, joint ventures, relationships with buyers & suppliers.
  - Benefits from indulging in partnerships include optimization & economy, risk reduction, acquisition of resources & activities, and lack of internal capabilities.
- Key Activities
  - Refers to critical activities that lead to creation, delivery, and maintenance of value, as well as support the operation of the enterprise.
  - Key activities can be classified as –
    - Value-add – Aspects & activities for which customer is willing to pay
    - Non-value-add – Aspects & activities for which customer is not willing to pay
    - Business non-value-add - Aspects & activities for which customer is not willing to pay but must be performed like regulatory activities & cost of doing business.

- Key Resources
  - Assets that are central to execute a business model. Resources can be classified as –

- - Physical – Applications, locations, and machines
  - Financial – Monetary aspects such as cash and lines of credit
  - Intellectual – Proprietary aspects such as knowledge, patents and copyrights, customer databases, and branding
  - Human – People needed to execute a particular business model
- Value Proposition
  - Fundamental offering an enterprise is trying to give its customers.
  - Maybe a single product or service or set of goods and services that are bundled together to address needs or solve problems of a customer or customer segment.
- Customer Relationships
  - Classified as customer acquisition and customer retention.
  - Methods used in establishing and maintaining customer relationships are chosen based on the level of interaction desired and the method of communication.
- Channels
  - Different ways through which an enterprise interacts with and delivers value to its customers.
  - Common channels include marketing channels, distribution channels, sales channels, partnering channels.
  - Typically, channels are used to market offerings, enable customers to evaluate the value proposition, let customers purchase a good or service, help the enterprise deliver on the value proposition, and provide support.
- Customer Segments
  - Group customers with common needs and attributes so that their needs can be addressed in a more effective manner.
  - For efficient targeting, segments can be defined based on different needs, varying profitability, different distribution channels, formation & maintenance of customer relationships.
- Cost Structure
  - Includes the type of business models, the differences in the types of costs and their impact, and where the enterprise is focusing its efforts to reduce costs.
- Revenue Streams
  - Methods by which enterprises generate value from each customer segment in exchange for the realization of a value proposition.
  - Revenue can be generated from a one-time purchase of a good or service or as recurring revenue from periodic payments for a good, service, or ongoing support.
  - Common revenue streams include –
    - Licensing or Subscription fees – The customer pays for the right to access a particular asset.
    - Transaction or Usage fees – The customer pays each time they use an asset.
    - Sales – The customer has ownership rights to use an asset.
    - Lending, Renting, or Leasing – The customer has temporary rights to use an asset.

Usage Considerations

Strengths

- Simple and straightforward tool to understand and put to use.
- Effective framework to understand and optimize business models.

Limitations

- Does not consider social and environmental impacts.
- Focuses more on value propositions as compared to business strategy.

A business analyst has been assigned to perform an analysis of the current state of an online grocery store. The strategy team wants a holistic view of the business that will enable them to utilize it as a blueprint for implementing a major strategic initiative.

In order to investigate the current state of business in terms of resources (time, cost, effort) that organization is currently spending in various areas and illustrate how an enterprise creates, delivers, and captures value for its customers, the business analyst decides to create a business model canvas with all required components - key partnerships, key activities, key resources, value proposition, customer relationships, channels, customer segments, cost structure, and revenue streams.

Below is the business model canvas created by the business analyst for the online grocery store:

The Business Model Canvas

Key Partners	Key Activities	Value Propositions	Customer Relationships	Customer Segments
Suppliers **Wholesalers** **Market Stores** **Technology Partners** **Legal Partners** **Payment Gateway** **Merchants** **Food Safety and Standards** **Transportation Partners**	Processing Orders Managing Warehouse Inventory Managing Supply Chain Managing Transportations and Logistics Creating and Managing Partners Introducing New Product Lines and Products Managing Customer Relationships Technology (web and app) Upgrades **Key Resources** Human Resources (Operations Team, Marketing and Sales Team, Research and Development Team, Customer Support Team) Physical Resources (Office, Office Materials, Delivery Vehicles, Packaging Materials, In-House Inventory) Technological Resources (Web and Database Servers, Broadband Routers, Printers, Photocopiers, Scanners)	Quick Delivery of Multiple Items at the Doorstep Saving of Time and Effort Easy Accessibility Through Online Modes Economical (Items can be purchased at price lower than brick and mortar stores) Multiple Modes of Payment Permitted Exclusive Promotional Offers and Discounts	Customer Support Email/SMS Membership Programmes Referral Programmes Feedback (reviews and ratings) Live Chat **Channels** Web Application Mobile Application Delivery Vehicles Advertising Channels	Corporate Professionals with Hectic Work Schedule Elder People People with Physical Disabilities Young Tech Savvy People Restaurants

Cost Structure	Revenue Streams
Cost of Developing and Maintaining Web and Mobile Application **Human Resources Cost** **Technology Cost** **Physical Resources Cost** **Transportation Cost** **Marketing and Promotions Cost**	Sale of Grocery Items On-Page and On-App Advertisements Customer Membership Programme Fees

Business Rules Analysis

Purpose

Business rules analysis is a technique used to capture business rules from sources, express them clearly, validate them with key business stakeholders, refine them to align with business goals, and organize them so that they can be effectively managed and reused. It is used for shaping and guiding regular business behaviour and operational decision making.

Description

- A business rule is a specific and testable form of business policy that guides business behaviour and operational business decisions.
- There may be varied sources of business rules. Some sources may be explicit like documented business policies, regulations, or contracts or implicit like undocumented stakeholder knowledge, generally accepted business practices, or cultural norms.
- Business rules should be practicable, explicit, specific, and accessible as a single version of truth source under the control of the business.
- Basic principles for business rules include defining them using business vocabulary to facilitate validation, articulating & maintaining them separately from their enforcement and processes they affect, mapping them to the decisions that they influence, defining them at the atomic level, and maintaining them in a way so that amendments can be done.

Elements

- Definitional Rules
  - Outline concepts produce knowledge or provide information.
  - Represent operational knowledge of an organization that cannot be violated but can be misapplied.
  - Lay down how information may be derived, inferred, or calculated based that may be inferred, or calculated from one or more other rules.
- Behavioural Rules
  - People rules that shape day-to-day business activities by placing some obligation or prohibition on conduct, action, practice, or procedure.
  - Direct actions of people in terms of necessitating them to perform actions in a certain way, prevent them from carrying out actions or stipulate the conditions for some actions.
  - There is a possibility that behavioural rules can be violated despite taking extraordinary precautions.
  - Additional analysis required to determine how strictly the rule needs to be enforced, sanctions to be imposed if violated, and any additional responses. Various enforcement levels include strict enforcement, override by an authorized party, or with an explanation or no active enforcement.

Usage Considerations

Strengths

- If managed as a centralized repository across the enterprise, modifications, and re-use of business rules is hassle-free.
- Provide structure to govern business behaviours.

- Clear and well-managed business rules allow policy changes without altering processes or systems.

Limitations

- May produce a long list of ambiguous business rules.
- If not validated against one another, business rules can generate unexpected results or contradict each other when combined.
- Business rules may be inappropriate or contradictory if the vocabulary used to create them is poorly defined.

Real Life Example

A business analyst is carrying out an elicitation exercise with critical business stakeholders to extract business and stakeholder requirements for creating an e-grocery platform. As a first step, they work towards identifying the key business rules that would govern key decisions and define, constrain, or enable the operations.

They amass a set of business rules as the elicitation session concludes. Below is an excerpt from the complete list:

BR ID	Business Rule Category	Business Tule Title	Business Rule Description
BR_01	Definitional	Adding amount to user's wallet	The amount corresponding to undelivered items or refunds will be added to user's wallet for future purchases
BR_02	Definitional	Total order value computation	Total amount for an order is computed by adding price of all items, delivery fee and GST and deducting the coupon code or e-voucher
BR_03	Definitional	Credit for non-delivery of order	If the order is not delivered in a specified time period, 10% of the total order amount will be credited into user's wallet
BR_04	Definitional	Variation in product price for weight change	In case weight of a product is more or less than the weight ordered, the maximum variation in product's price will be 10%
BR_05	Definitional	Delivery charges wave off for big order amount	Delivery charge will be waived off for an order with total order amount above Rs. 1000
BR_06	Definitional	One account per email and mobile number	A user should not be permitted to create multiple accounts with the same email address and phone number
BR_07	Definitional	One delivery address per order	A user should only be allowed to get a single order delivered at one address and not multiple addresses at once
BR_08	Definitional	No delivery slot changes after placing order	Once an order has been placed, user will not be able to change the delivery slot that was selected while placing the order
BR_09	Definitional	No item modifications after placing order	Once an order has been placed, user will not be able to make any modifications in the selected items and will need to contact customer support for any changes

Collaborative Games

Purpose

Collaborative Games is essentially an elicitation & stakeholder collaboration activity that encourages the participants to work together in developing a shared understanding of a problem or a solution.

Description

- Collaborative games are organized techniques that are designed to facilitate collaboration by eliciting and exploring information that may not occur through regular elicitation methods.
- Different games are used to encourage the participants to share their knowledge and experience on a given topic, identify hidden assumptions, and explore that knowledge.
- It facilitates stakeholder groups with different viewpoints to work together and develop a shared understanding because of the relaxed environment in which discussions are held.
- It is benefitted by having a facilitator who explains and enforces the rules of the game. The facilitator also ensures that the game progresses ahead and all participants play a role.
- It also involves visual elements like sticky notes, whiteboards, etc which promotes creative and logical thinking.
- A few examples of collaborative games –
  - Product Box – It involves building a product box as if it was being sold in a retail outlet and is used to discover features that would help arouse interest for it in the market.
  - Affinity Map – This game is about writing features on sticky notes, pasting notes on a wall, and then moving them closer to features that appear to be related and are used to identify similar features.
  - Fishbowl – Two participant groups are formed. One group speaks and other documents observations and then roles are reversed. The purpose is to identify hidden assumptions/perspectives.

Elements

Below-mentioned step-by-step process is usually followed to carry out collaborative game's technique –

- Game Purpose – Different collaborative games have different purpose specific to that type of game. Facilitators ensure that the participants understand the purpose so that the discussions carried out are towards the accomplishment of the purpose.
- Process – Collaborative games follow a process that keeps it headed towards its purpose. In general, games typically have at least three steps –
  - Opening – Participants get involved, understand the rules of the game, and start creating ideas.
  - Exploration – Participants engage, look for an association between ideas, test ideas, and try out new ideas.
  - Closing – Ideas are evaluated and participants determine which ideas are beneficial to the purpose at hand.
- Outcome – Facilitator and participants work together in assessing the results and settle on the next actions.

Usage Consideration

Strengths

- May disclose hidden assumptions and perspectives.

- Fosters creative thinking.
- Challenges reserved participants to play an active role.
- May disclose that business needs are not realized.

Limitations

- May be considered as impractical and can make reserved participants uneasy.
- Can be perceived as laborious and inefficient.
- Can lead to a false sense of confidence in the conclusions.

Concept Modelling

Purpose

The primary purpose of a Concept model is to organize the business vocabulary with an aim to be consistent and thorough in domain knowledge understanding and communication. It identifies the correct choice of terms to use in communications, including all business analysis information.

Description

- Concept model starts with a glossary and put together a rich vocabulary that is not data or implementation biased.
- Concept model is a valuable tool in below situations –
  - Enterprise aims to organize, manage, and communicate core domain knowledge.
  - Considerable number of business rules need to be encapsulated.
  - Stakeholders are not at ease with models having technical nomenclature like data models, class diagrams.
  - Business process reengineering initiatives require innovative solutions.
  - Enterprise faces regulatory or compliance challenges.
- Concept models do not intent to unify, codify, and simplify data but rather put together a rich vocabulary of terms expressed as natural language statements.

Elements

- Noun concepts – Most basic concepts and typically considered as 'givens'.
- Verb concepts –
  - Basic structural connections between noun concepts.
  - Expressed in standard phrases to avoid ambiguity.
  - Can possibly be stated as building blocks of statements such as business rules.
  - These concepts can also be derived, inferred, or computed using definitional rules.
- Other connections – Besides verb concepts, other connections types include categorizations, classifications, partitive connections, and roles.

Usage Considerations

Strengths

- Enables communication of clear-cut meanings and subtle distinctions in a business-friendly manner.
- Independent of data design biases and ensure complete business vocabulary coverage.
- Exceedingly useful in domain-heavy and decision-laden business processes.
- Ensures business rules and complex decision tables are unambiguous and fit together in a unified manner.

Limitations

- May set high expectations on how quickly integration can be done based on business semantics.
- Requires specialized skill set to think conceptually and in a non-procedural manner.
- Stakeholders may be unfamiliar with knowledge-and-rule focus
- Requires tools to support real-time use of standard business terminology in writing business rules, requirements, and other forms of business communication.

Data Dictionary

Purpose

A data dictionary (also known as metadata repository) is used to record standard definitions of data elements to enable a common interpretation among stakeholders.

Description

- Data dictionary is used to document definitions, their meanings, and allowable values and provide information on how those elements combine into composite data elements.
- It may be used to provide metadata for data mining and other advanced analytics.
- It is often used in conjunction with the entity-relationship diagram and may be extracted from a data model.
- It can be maintained in the form of a spreadsheet or using automated tools.

Elements

- Data Elements – A data dictionary contains a formal definition of primitive and composite data elements as well as their meanings and allowable values.
- Primitive Data Elements – Information included in data dictionary pertaining to primitive data elements is as follows –
  - Name – Unique name of the data element
  - Aliases – Other names with which the data element is referred
  - Values/Meanings – List of acceptable values for the data element stated in the form of an itemized list or approved format
  - Description – Definition of a data element in the context of the solution
- Composite Data Elements – Information included in data dictionary pertaining to composite data elements is as follows –
  - Sequences – Order of primitive data elements in the composite data element. Plus sign is normally used to show that one element is followed by another.
  - Repetitions – Reoccurrence of one or more primitive data elements in the compositive data element.
  - Optional Elements – A primitive data element that may or may not occur in the composite data element.

Usage Considerations

Strengths

- Provides a shared understanding of the meaning, content, and format of relevant data.
- Promotes consistent understanding and utilization of data throughout the organization.

Limitations

- Metadata could become obsolete in the absence of regular maintenance.
- Significant time and effort required to maintain and sustain its accuracy and completeness.
- May have limited value across the organization unless the metadata is carefully considered for multiple scenarios.

TECHCANVASS

Real Life Example

An automobile company is working on creating an internal employee portal where all required information of employees will be maintained, and any updates can be done by an employee on his/her own instead of the human resources team. The portal would contain personal information (name, DOB, address, marital details, family, education, work experience, PF details, passport/visa details, medical dependant details, etc.), employment information (organizational assignment, working location, reporting manager details, etc.), account information (bank details, PAN, Aadhar, UAN, etc.) and investment information (specific to tax).

As a part of specifying requirements, the business analyst decides to create a data dictionary to standardize the definitions of data elements thereby enabling a common interpretation and preventing the likelihood of any discrepancy. Below is a snippet from the data dictionary prepared by the business analyst:

ID	Business Data Object	Field Name	Alias/ Alternate Name	Description	Unique Values?	Data Type	Length	Valid Values
DD_PS01	Personal	First Name		First Name of the Employee	N	Text	<100 Characters	Contain letters and periods but not digits
DD_PS02	Personal	Last Name	Family Name	Family Name of the Employee	N	Text	<100 Characters	Contain letters and periods but not digits
DD_PS03	Personal	Current Address		Current Residential Address of the Employee	N	Alphanumeric	<500 Characters	Contain letters, digits and special characters like . , -
DD_PS04	Personal	Marital Status		Current Marital Status of the Employee	N	Text	<50 Characters	Acceptable values include Single, Married, Divorced, Widowed
DD_AC01	Account	Bank Name		Name of the Bank where Employee has Salary Account	N	Text	<50 Characters	Contain letters only
DD_AC02	Account	Account Number		Salary Account Number in the Bank	Y	Integer	<20 Characters	Contain digits only with min 9 and max 18 characters
DD_AC03	Account	PAN	Personal Account Number	Personal Account Number of the Employee	Y	Alphanumeric	10 Characters	Contain letters and digits with exactly 10 characters
DD_EM01	Employment	CWL	Current Work Location	Current Work Location at Which Employee is Based	N	Text	<20 Characters	Acceptable values include Delhi, Noida, Gurugram and Chennai
DD_EM02	Employment	Delivery Unit	Line of Business	Current Delivery Unit that Employee is a Part of	N	Alphanumeric	<20 Characters	Acceptable values include Research, Transformation, Delivery

Data Flow Diagrams

Purpose

Data Flow diagrams illustrate the movement and transformation of data between external entities and processes. It visually depicts where data comes from, which process(es) transform the data, and if the output results are stored or utilized by another process or external entity.

Data flow diagrams provide a clear representation of a transaction-based system and boundaries of a physical, logical, or manual system. Furthermore, it can be utilized for verification of functional decompositions or data models and helps define the scope of a system thereby enabling the estimation of work.

Description

- The data represented in a data flow diagram should be described in a data dictionary.
- Data flow diagrams can consist of multiple layers of abstraction. The various levels of a data flow diagram are –
  - Level 0 (Context diagram) – Show the entire system as a transformation engine with externals as the source or consumer of data.
  - Level 1 – Show the transformational processes with input data, transformed output data and data stores.
  - Level 2, 3, or so forth – Show the further decomposition of major processes from level 1 diagram. Externals remain the same while further flows & stores are defined.
- Different data flow diagram types include –
  - Logical data flow diagram – Represents the future state and models transformations that need to occur regardless of the current physical limitations.
  - Physical data flow diagram - Represents current or future state and models all physical aspects like data stores, printers, forms, devices, and other manifestations of data.

Elements

- Externals (Entity, Source, Sink)
  - A person, organization, automated system, or any device that is capable of producing or receiving data.
  - These are outside the system under analysis and are essentially the sources and/or destinations of the data.
  - Must have at least one data flow going to or coming from it.
  - Represented by using a noun inside a rectangle.
- Data Store
  - Data repository from where data may be read repeatedly and can be stored for future use.
  - Must have at least one data flow going to or coming from it.
  - Represented as either two parallel lines or as an open-ended rectangle with a label.
- Process
  - A manual or automated task with a business objective that transforms the data into an output.
  - Named as a verb-noun phrase.
  - Must have at least one data flow going to and coming from it.
  - Represented as a circle or rectangle with rounded corners.
- Data Flow
  - Shows the data flowing into an external process, and a data store.
  - Every data flow will connect to or from a process representing the input to and output from a process, respectively.

 o Named using a noun and represented as a line with an arrow.

Usage Considerations

Strengths

- Useful technique for discovering processes & data and explain the logic behind data flow in a system.
- Can be utilized for verification of functional decompositions or data models.
- Helps define scope or boundary of the system thereby enabling estimation of work.
- Relatively easy to interpret.
- Clearly depicts interfaces to other systems in the landscape.
- Can be an effective component of a system document.

Limitations

- Can be complex and difficult to understand when used for large-scale systems.
- Different modelling notation could create challenges related to documentation.
- Does not represent the sequence in which activities are performed.
- Does not contain much detail on processes and stakeholders.

Real Life Example

A business analyst (BA) is working on building requirements for a medical equipment rental system to be utilized by a major medical equipment institution.

The BA is in the process of specifying and modelling requirements gathered from the stakeholders. He decides to visually represent the data flow as well as the data transformations in order to allow all the stakeholders to easily interpret the flow of data between the external entities, various processes, and data repositories. The data flow diagram created by BA becomes an important constituent of the functional specification document that he creates for capturing the requirements of the said system.

Below is a Level 1 data flow diagram that is created by the BA for the medical equipment rental system:

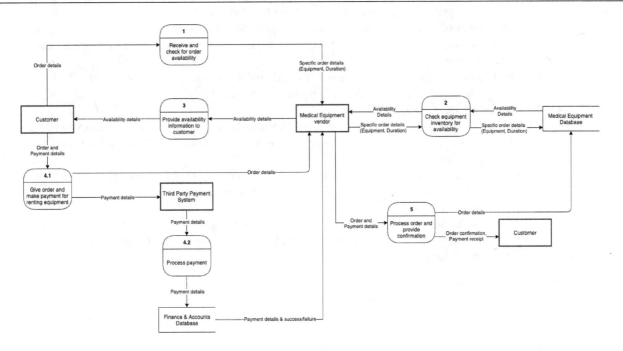

Data Mining

Purpose

Data Mining is an analytics process that investigates huge data sets and summarizes it in such a manner that valuable patterns and insights are discovered. The valuable insights derived from the data mining exercise can have organizations take improved business decisions.

Description

- Data Mining results in mathematical models or equations that describe the data patterns and relationships. These models can be deployed through visual dashboards, business rules management systems, or in a database to facilitate decision making.
- Data mining can be utilized in either supervised or unsupervised investigations.
  - Supervised Investigation – Data is labelled, and a very specific answer can be provided for a question to drive decision making.
  - Unsupervised Investigation – Data is not labelled, and it is more about looking for structure or unusual patterns and then considered for use in decision making.
- Data Mining includes three techniques –
  - Descriptive – Descriptive technique looks at data statistically to describe what has happened in the past. An example is the clustering technique which identifies similar and dissimilar patterns and form clusters.
  - Diagnostic – Diagnostic technique goes a step further and explains why something has happened. An example is decision trees or segmentation technique to show why a pattern exists.
  - Predictive – Predictive technique examines data to predict what will happen in the future. An example is a regression or neural networks that will determine the likelihood that something will occur in the future.

Elements

- Requirements Elicitation –
  - Data Mining's goal can be established in terms of whether top-down or bottom-up strategy is to be followed.
    - Top-down strategy – Devise decision requirements for a business decision and uses formal decision modelling techniques.
    - Bottom-up strategy – Focuses on domain-specific pattern discovery.
  - Top-down versus bottom-up mining strategy facilitates choosing the correct set of data mining techniques.
- Data Preparation: Analytical Dataset –
  - Generally constructed by merging records from multiple tables or sources.
  - Data may be physically extracted into an actual file or it may be a virtual file in the database or data warehouse
  - Data sets may sometimes be huge and hence sample is selected or may need to work-in datastore.
  - Datasets are split into a set to be used for analysis, an independent set for confirming that the model works, and a validation set for final confirmation.
- Data Analysis –
  - This is often the longest and most complex step in data mining and should be automated if possible.

- o Statistical techniques and visualization tools are used to see data distribution, missing data, and calculated characteristics.
- o Analyzing and identifying useful characteristics in data fuels the data mining effort.
- Modelling techniques –
  - o Analytical dataset and calculated data characteristics are fed into supervised or unsupervised statistical algorithms. Multiple techniques may also be used.
  - o Data Mining techniques include classification & regression trees, linear and logistic regression, neural networks, support vector machines, and predictive scorecards.
- Deployment –
  - o Data mining models can be deployed to support human decision making or to support automated decision-making systems.
  - o Data mining results may be presented using visual metaphors or as simple data fields for human decision making.
  - o Data mining identifies business rules that can be deployed using a business rules management system or fitted into a decision model.
  - o In some cases, data mining results can be mathematical formulas that can be deployed as business rules or generated SQL or code.

Usage Considerations

Strengths

- Disclose hidden patterns and insights.
- Data accuracy can be enhanced by integrating data mining results into system design.
- Can reduce or even eradicate human bias through the use of data.

Limitations

- Application of data mining techniques without complete knowledge can result in inaccurate correlations and insights.
- Access to cutting-edge tools/software may lead to accidental misuse.
- Many techniques require specialized knowledge.
- Lack of transparency pertaining to the use of advanced mathematics and direct insights into results can lead to resistance from stakeholders.
- Hard to deploy if the aimed decision making is not well understood.

Data Modelling

Purpose

A data model visually represents the elements (people, places, things, and business transactions) in the form of entities, classes or data objects that are relevant to a business domain, the attributes that are used to describe them, and the relationships among them.

Data models provide a consistent vocabulary for requirements elicitation, requirements analysis and design. In addition, they also support implementation and continuous improvement.

Description

- Different variations of data models include –
  - o Conceptual data model – Describes business information as well as relationships within that information and is independent of any solution or technology.
  - o Logical data model - Abstraction of the conceptual data model that formally manage the integrity of the data & relationships and is associated with the solution design.
  - o Physical data model – Describes physical organization of a database and addresses non-functional requirements like performance, concurrency, and security.
- Different data modelling notations include entity-relationship diagram (ERD) and class diagram. At the conceptual model, both these data modelling notations are likely to produce broadly similar results. However, at the logical and physical level, entity-relationship diagrams would be used to implement a relational database whereas class diagram would be used to aid software development in object-oriented environment.

Elements

- Entity or Class
  - o An entity or class in a data model represent something physical (e.g. Warehouse), organizational (e.g. Sales Area), abstract (e.g. Product Line), or an event (e.g. Appointment).
  - o In an entity-relationship diagram, an entity is identified with a unique identifier and contains attributes and has relationships to other entities in the model.
  - o In a class diagram, a class is identified with a unique identifier and contains attributes and has relationships with other classes. In addition, a class also contains operations or functions that describe what can be done with the class.

- Attribute
  - o Defines information associated with an entity like allowable values, type of information it represents and how much information it can capture.
  - o Attributes can be described in a data dictionary and its allowable values may be specified through business rules.
  - o Attributes include the below values –
    - Name – Unique name of the attribute or any aliases.
    - Values/Meanings – List of acceptable values which may be allowable list of values or data formats.
    - Description – Definition of the attribute within the solution context.

- Relationship or Association
  - o A relationship in an entity-relationship diagram (referred as association in class diagram) that indicate connections between the entities by specifying number of minimum and maximum occurrences allowed on each side of that relationship.

- o Cardinality in an entity-relationship diagram (referred as multiplicity in class diagram) that denotes the minimum and maximum number of occurrences to which an entity may be related. Cardinality values may be zero, one or many.
- Diagrams
  - o The diagram in a data model is called as an entity-relationship diagram (ERD) whereas the diagram in a class model is called as a class diagram.
- Metadata
  - o Data model may optionally contain metadata that describes what does an entity represent, reason of their creation or change, ways they should be used, frequency of their usage and their users.
  - o Metadata may also describe restrictions on creation or usage of entities as well as any constraints specific to security, privacy or audit.

Usage Considerations

Strengths

- Helps develop a consistent vocabulary to be used across the project/initiative by all business and technical stakeholders.
- Logical data model helps ensure that the logical design of persistent data reflects the business need.
- Provides a consistent approach to analyze & document data and its relationships.
- May incorporate different levels of detail providing just enough information to the relevant stakeholders.
- May identify inconsistencies thereby exposing new requirements.

Limitations

- May turn out to be too technical for non-technical stakeholders.
- May cover information related to multiple functional areas of the organization and hence may not be understood by stakeholders who lack knowledge in those areas.

Real Life Example

A business analyst is working on eliciting requirements for creating a web application for a major Indian multinational banking and financial services company.

During the elicitation activity, business analyst decides to create a data model to visually represent the business entities that are relevant to the business, the attributes that describe these entities and the relationships among them. He creates an entity-relationship model to demonstrate the entities, attributes/characteristics that define the entities including primary key (PK) that uniquely identifies each entity record and cardinality that indicate the relationships between the entities.

Entity Relationship Diagram

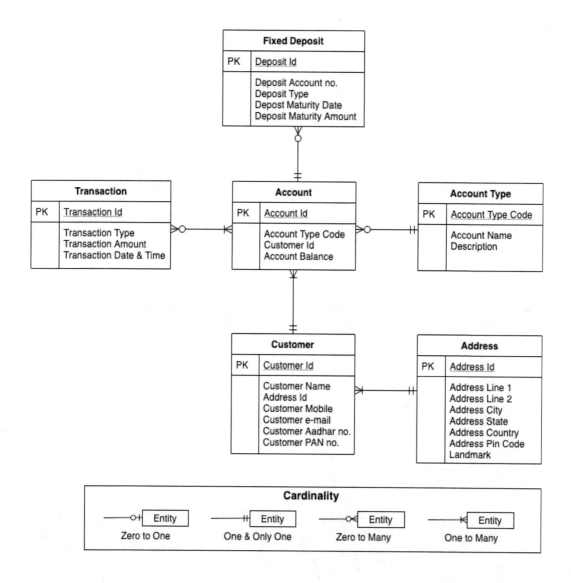

Class Diagram

Below is the corresponding class diagram for the entity-relationship diagram created above.

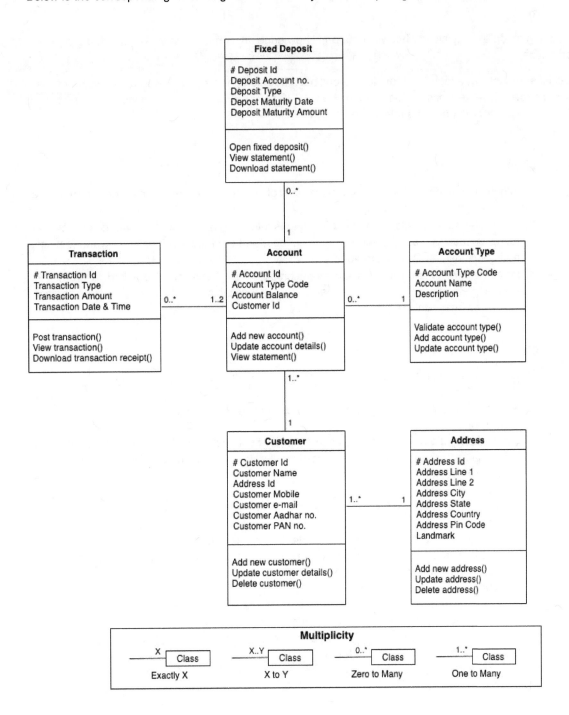

Decision Modelling

Purpose

Decision modelling depicts in what way data and knowledge are combined to make repeatable business decisions.

Decision models, at a high-level, depict the business decisions as they appear in business processes, and the lower level versions can be used to show AS-IS or TO-BE business decisions in sufficient detail to act as a framework for all the relevant business rules.

Description

- Straightforward decision models show how a set of business rules that operate on a common set of data elements combine to decide.
- Complex decision models decompose decisions into their individual components so that each piece of the decision can be separately described, and the model can show how those pieces combine to make an overall decision.
- Comprehensive decision models are all-encompassing models that are linked to processes, performance measures & organizations and show the origin of business rules and represent decisions as analytical insight.

Elements

- Types of Models and Notations. Different decision modelling approaches include –
  - Decision Table
    - Uses a defined set of business rules to determine an outcome and reach a business decision.
    - Represented as a compact table containing a set of business rules. When all the conditions in a rule come out to be true for a set of input data, the outcome or action specified for that rule is selected.
  - Decision Tree
    - Represents specific kinds of business rule set and mainly used in creating customer segments.
    - Each path on a decision tree leaf node represents a single rule, each level in the tree represents a data element and branches represent the different conditions that must be true to continue down that branch.
  - Decision Requirements Diagram
    - Primarily used in complex business decision-making, a decision requirements diagram visually represents information, knowledge, and decision making.
    - Nodes in the diagram are linked together into a network to show how a complex decision can be broken down into simpler building blocks.
    - Key components of a decision requirements diagram are –
      ◊ Decisions – Denoted as a rectangle, it takes a set of inputs and applies rules/logic to select an output from a pre-defined set.
      ◊ Input data – Denoted as an oval, it represents data passed as input to the decision.
      ◊ Business Knowledge Models – Denoted as a rectangle with corners cut off, it represents business rules sets, decision tables, decision trees, predictive models that contain the decision-making logic.
      ◊ Knowledge Sources – Denoted as a document, it represents the original source (people or documents) of decision logic.

Usage Considerations

Strengths

- Helps develop a shared understanding with stakeholders and aid in impact analysis.
- Assists in combining and sharing multiple perspectives.
- Simplifies decision making in complex scenarios.
- Enables grouping of rules by decision thereby allowing managing of a vast set of rules.
- Serves as a useful technique in rules-based automation, data mining, predictive analytics, and business intelligence projects.

Limitations

- May add unnecessary complex business process models when the decision is simple and tightly coupled with the process.
- May limit rules to those required by known decisions thereby limiting the capture of rules not related to a known decision.
- May give a false impression to an organization that it has a standard current-state decision-making process.
- Difficult to collaborate and obtain a sign-off across organizational boundaries.
- May not directly address behavioural business rules.
- Data quality issues may pop-up if business terminology is not clearly defined.

A business analyst is working on specifying and modelling requirements for creating a web application for a major banking and financial services organization.

There are numerous requirements which pertain to repeatable business decisions making. One such requirement is related to identifying the category of customer based on his/her "Saving Bank Balance" and "Total Relationship Value" and it will be one of the inputs for determining the loan amount. In order to represent the required elements of decision making, business analyst creates a decision table which is as shown below:

Decision Table

Saving Bank Balance	Total Relationship Value	Customer Category
<Rs. 25,000	<Rs 5 lakh	Silver
	≥Rs.5 lakh to < Rs. 20 lakh	Silver
	≥Rs. 20 lakh to < Rs. 30 lakh	Silver
	≥Rs 30 lakh	Silver
≥Rs. 25,000 to < Rs. 1 lakh	<Rs 5 lakh	Silver
	≥Rs.5 lakh to < Rs. 20 lakh	Gold
	≥Rs. 20 lakh to < Rs. 30 lakh	Gold
	≥Rs 30 lakh	Gold
≥Rs.1 lakh to < Rs. 2 lakh	<Rs 5 lakh	Silver
	≥Rs.5 lakh to < Rs. 20 lakh	Gold
	≥Rs. 20 lakh to < Rs. 30 lakh	Diamond
	≥Rs 30 lakh	Diamond
≥Rs. 2 lakh	<Rs 5 lakh	Silver
	≥Rs.5 lakh to < Rs. 20 lakh	Gold
	≥Rs. 20 lakh to < Rs. 30 lakh	Diamond
	≥Rs 30 lakh	Platinum

Decision Tree

Below is the corresponding decision tree for the decision table created above.

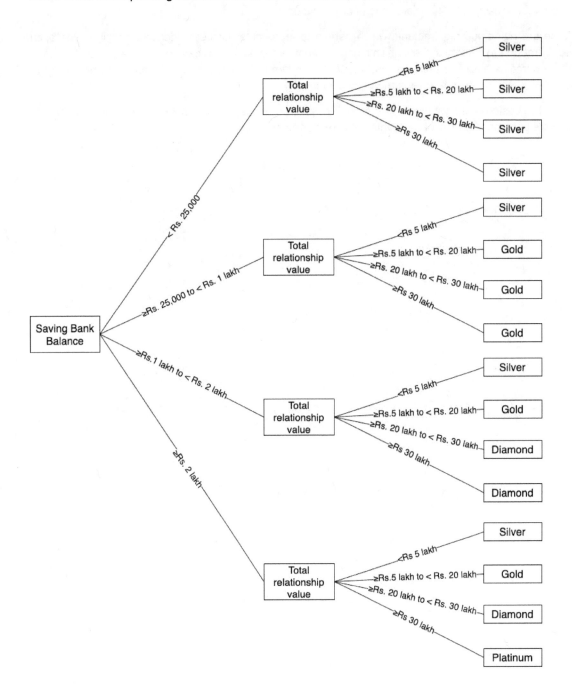

Decision Requirements Diagram

A business analyst is working on specifying and modelling requirements for creating a web application for a major banking and financial services organization.

There are numerous requirements which pertain to repeatable business decisions making. One such requirement is to determine the loan limit or maximum loan amount that can be extended to an applicant. It is a complex business decision that should be broken down into smaller components pertaining to knowledge, information, and separate decision models.

Thus, the business analyst creates a decision requirements diagram to visually represent the complete network of components involved in this complex decision.

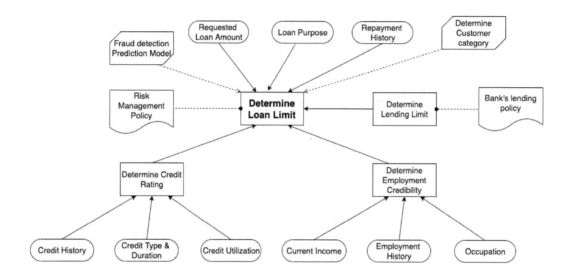

Estimation

Purpose

Estimation is a technique used to forecast the cost and effort involved in taking up a course of action.

It is used to support decision making by forecasting attributes such as cost and effort to carry out a course of action, cost of creating or operating a solution, expected solution benefits or value, business performance, and potential risk impact.

Description

- Estimates may be expressed as a single number or a range. Representing the results of estimation as a range (with minimum values, maximum values, and probabilities).
- Estimation is an iterative process in the sense that estimates are reviewed and revised as more information becomes available.
- Quite a few estimation techniques rely on historical data in order to adjust estimates against prior experience.

Elements

- Common estimation methods include
  - Top-down – Examining the high-level components in a hierarchical breakdown which are fixed and then decomposed into activities. Applicable in a scenario where there is a fixed budget or timeframe.
  - Bottom-up – Examining the lowest-level components in a hierarchical breakdown, estimate the individual cost or effort and then adding all elements to provide an overall estimate.
  - Parametric Estimation – Computes estimate with a calibrated parametric model and works best when there is historical data available. Typically, a unit rate is established and multiplied with the number of units to arrive at the estimate.
  - Rough Order of Magnitude (ROM) – High-level estimate used when there is little or no information available.
  - Rolling Wave – Involves estimating repeatedly throughout an initiative. Generally, it starts with a ROM or top-down estimate and as more information is obtained, detailed estimates are provided for near-term activities.
  - Delphi – Estimation is done using a combination of expert judgment and history. The responsibility holder estimates the tasks and shares the estimates with other experts. Several rounds of estimation are carried out until a consensus is reached with an average of the three estimates being used to determine a final estimate.
  - Project Evaluation and Review Technique (PERT) – Each component of the estimate is given three values - (1) Optimistic value (best-case scenario), (2) Pessimistic value (worst-case scenario), (3) Most Likely value. Then, a PERT value for each component is calculated as a weighted average (Optimistic + Pessimistic + (4 times Most Likely))/6.
- Accuracy of the Estimate
  - Measure of uncertainty that evaluates how close an estimate is to the actual value.
  - In a scenario where little or no information is available, a Rough Order of Magnitude (ROM) estimate is delivered that is expected to have a high level of uncertainty.
  - ROM estimates are often no more than +50% to -50% accurate while definitive estimates that are much more accurate are expected to be within 10% or less.
  - ROM estimates and definitive estimates can be combined throughout a project or initiative using rolling wave estimates.
- Sources of Information

Common sources of information include –

- o Analogous Situations – Using similar past elements (project, initiative, risk, etc.) to estimate an element.
- o Organization History – Makes use of previous experience with similar work within the organization.
- o Expert Judgment – Leverages the expertise of individuals who have performed similar work in the past.
- Precision and Reliability of Estimates
- o In a situation where multiple estimates are made, the precision of estimates is a measure of how close the estimates are to each other and by assessing variation (or standard deviation), an agreement can be reached.
- o Reliability or repeatability of estimates is exhibited in the variation of estimates when different estimation methods are used, or different individuals perform the estimation.
- Contributors to Estimates
- o Generally, estimators are those individuals or teams who are responsible for carrying out the work that they are estimating.
- o Estimates created by the team are usually more accurate than those done by one individual.
- o Some organizations may have a dedicated team(s) that estimate much of its work. In such a scenario, it needs to be made sure that context is not lost.
- o An external expert may be called to perform or review the estimate when a high level of confidence is desired.

Usage Considerations

Strengths

- Provides a rationale for an assigned budget, time frame, or size of a set of elements.
- Teams may be provided an unrealistic budget or schedule if estimations are not done.
- Team of knowledgeable individuals provide more accurate estimates than one individual.
- Updating and refining estimates during the work cycle help ensure success.

Limitations

- Estimations done by the team can differ extensively from the actual values if they do not possess adequate knowledge about the elements being estimated.
- Employing a single estimation method may lead to unrealistic expectations.

- **Top-down Estimation**

A business analyst is working on a fixed bid waterfall project that is time-boxed and has a fixed budget. The overall estimate of the project is 600 hours considering the timeframe that has been provided to the project team. It has been agreed between the business analyst and project manager that business analysis activities will constitute 20% of the overall estimate. Hence, the business analyst provides a business analysis effort of 0.20*600 = 120 hours.

- **Bottom-up Estimation**

A business analyst working on creating a sales dashboard has decent knowledge of the data fields to be incorporated, calculation logics to be built, interfaces for retrieving data, and input/output systems under the impact. In addition, he is aware of the number of stakeholders for requirements elicitation and requirement documents to be produced. Thus, he creates a detailed work breakdown structure of all activities/tasks to be carried out, put efforts against each activity/task, and sum it up to produce a business analysis effort estimate of 500 hours.

- **Parametric Estimation**

It takes a business analyst 20 hours to elicit and document requirements for adding product taxonomies in a retail application. A new project involves adding 15 product taxonomies in the application and hence total business analysis effort will be 20*15 = 300 hours.

- **Rough Order of Magnitude (ROM)**

Depending on the little information available regarding the size of the B2C telecom project, number of modules to be built and high-level knowledge of functionality to be created for each module, the business analysis effort is 400 hours with a buffer of -50% to +50%.

- **Rolling Wave**

In a learning management project that the project team is working on, the business analyst provides detailed and near accurate business analysis estimates for the user stories that are elaborated and high-level estimates for the stories in the backlog that are not yet detailed out. As these stories are elaborated to fine detail, the business analyst will provide more accurate estimations for these stories as well.

- **Delphi**

A business analyst working on a digital asset management application does business analysis estimation and comes out with an effort estimate of 600 hours. He shares the same with two other business analysts who propose effort estimates of 900 hours and 1200 hours in the first meeting that happens among them. They discuss all scenarios, thoughts, ideas, knowledge, and experience that made them come out with this figure. They re-estimate and come out with effort estimates of 900 hours, 1100 hours, and 1300 hours. They again defend their estimates with reasons and decide to re-estimate. They again hold a discussion with their latest estimates as 1000 hours, 1050 hours, and 1150 hours. Ultimately, they conclude on the final effort estimate as 1100 hours.

- **Project Evaluation and Review Technique (PERT)**

A business analyst is estimating the business analysis effort for building critical business KPI reports. The following 3 estimates are provided by the business analyst –

Most likely value (M) = 12 days

Optimistic value (O) = 7 days (best case scenario - assumes stakeholder availability when needed, fewer review cycles, timely sign-off)

Pessimistic value (P) = 17 days (worst case scenario - assumes meeting cancellations, multiple review cycles, delay in sign-off)

Weighted Average = (7 + 17 + (4*11))/6 = 68/6 = 11.33 days (about 11 days)

Business analyst summarizes that the final business analysis effort estimate for the task at hand is 11 days.

Financial Analysis

Purpose

Financial Analysis is one of the most critical techniques used by the business analyst to understand the financial aspects of multiple investment options to be able to recommend the most beneficial solution.

Description

- Financial analysis is the evaluation of the expected financial feasibility, stability, and benefit realization of an investment option. It thereby enables a business analyst to make a solution recommendation in an initiative by comparing one solution or solution approach to others based on the results of the financial analysis. Financial analysis typically includes –
  - Initial costs and when will these costs be incurred.
  - Expected financial benefits and time period of realization.
  - Continuing usage and support costs.
  - Opening and ongoing risks associated with the initiative.
- A combination of various financial analysis techniques is used as each provides a different perspective.
- Not just in the beginning, financial analysis is applied during the course of the initiative to determine if enough business value is being delivered for it to continue. An initiative is likely to be changed or discontinued if the financial analysis results no longer back the initial recommendation.

Elements

- **Cost of the Change**
  - Cost of developing or procuring the solution components and transitioning the enterprise from the current state to the future state.
  - May include (but not limited to) costs for hardware and software, staff and other resources, buying existing contracts, subsidies, penalties, training.
  - These costs may be shared between organizations within the enterprise.
- **Total cost of ownership (TCO)**
  - Cost to acquire, use, and support the solution to understand its potential value.
  - An agreeable time frame is chosen to compute the total cost of ownership in which life expectancy of hardware is generally agreed to while a standard time period is chosen as life expectancy for software and processes.
- **Value Realization**
  - Value is usually realized over a period of time.
  - Value could be stated annually or as a cumulative value over a specific time period.
- **Cost-benefit Analysis/Benefit-cost Analysis**
  - A systematic approach to compute expected net benefit (or planned business value) by measuring expected total costs/expenses against expected total benefits.
  - Expected Net Benefits (Planned business value) = Expected Benefits – Expected Costs
  - Cost-benefit analysis should be carried out when the solution is in full use and the planned value has started getting accomplished in order to understand when costs are getting incurred and expected benefits are getting realized and of which type.

Financial Calculations

- Return on Investment (ROI)

  - ROI is a percentage return on initial project investment and is a widely used metric to compare initiatives, solutions, solution approaches to determine the best one to pursue.
  - Computed using the formula –
    - ROI = (Total Benefits – Cost of investment)/Cost of investment
  - In case of comparisons among investments, the time period should be kept the same.

- Discount Rate

  - Discount rate is the assumed interest rate used in present value calculations.
  - It is the interest rate an organization assumes it would earn if it invested elsewhere.
  - Generally, organizations use standard discount rates for short term investments and bigger discount rates for long term scenarios owning to risk.

- Present Value

  - Compare the different solutions/solution approaches that could realize benefits at a different rate and time period. The higher present value would mean a greater total benefit.
  - Future benefits are reduced by a discount rate to present-day value. Computed using the formula –
    Present Value = Sum of (Net Benefits in that period / (1 + Discount Rate for that period)) for all periods in the cost-benefit analysis.

  - It does not consider the cost of the original investment.

- Net Present Value (NPV)

  - Net present value is the present value of benefits post deduction of original investment costs. Computed using the formula –
    Net Present Value = Present Value – Cost of Investment

  - Enables the selection of the best investment option considering that higher the NPV value, better the investment.

- Internal Rate of Return (IRR)

  - Internal rate of return is the interest rate at which the investment breaks even i.e. the investment cost is balanced off by the derived benefits.
  - Organization defines a minimum threshold that it expects to earn called hurdle rate to which IRR is compared & investment decisions are made.
  - In a scenario where two solutions/solution approaches are compared, the one with higher IRR is recommended.
  - The IRR calculation is based on the interest rate at which the NPV is 0. Computed using the formula –

    Net Present Value = (-1 x Original Investment) + Sum of (net benefit for that period / (1 + IRR) for all periods) = 0.

    (BABOK V3 – Page 251 - 300)

- Payback Period

- Payback period is a time period needed to bring back the investment made on an initiative, expressed in years or years & months.
- It would be safe to assume that when the payback period has passed, the initiative should deliver benefits unless operational cost has arisen.
- It does not take a discount rate into consideration and there is no standard calculation for it.

Usage Considerations

Strengths

- Enables comparison of investments from diverse perspectives.
- Assumptions and estimates are clearly stated.
- Facilitates identification & analysis of investment influencing factors thereby reducing uncertainty about change.
- Allows re-evaluation of a recommended solution in case of a change in context or need.

Limitations

- Not all costs and benefits can be quantified in a straightforward manner.
- Uncertainty about expected costs and benefits is always a risk.
- May provide a deceptive sense of security if certain pieces of information are missed/incomplete.

Real Life Examples

Cost-Benefit Analysis

Below is an example of a Cost-Benefit Analysis of an Enterprise Content Management Software and Infrastructure Project for a Financial Services client. It can be witnessed that the projection here is that the benefits will be achieved only in the third year.

	Year 0	Year 1	Year 2	Year 3
Expected Benefits				
Revenue		7000	7500	8000
Reduced operating costs		3500	3000	2000
Time savings		2500	2000	2500
Reduced process overheads		1500	1500	1000
Other		500	0	500
Total Annual benefits	0	15000	14000	14000
Costs				
Project costs	6000	4000	0	0
Ongoing support	0	1000	1000	1500
New facilities	5500	0	2500	1500
Licensing	0	1500	1500	1500
Infrastructure renewal	4500	0	1000	0
Other	0	500	1000	500
Total Costs	16000	7000	7000	5000
Net Benefits	-16000	8000	7000	9000
Cumulative Net Benefits	-16000	-8000	-1000	8000

Return on Investment (ROI)

An IT organization has invested in upgrading one of its business intelligence products considering its possible use to solve business problems for multiple clients. The organization made an investment of $3500 in upgrading the product and deployed it for multiple clients thereby garnering a benefit of $70000. We can use the below formula to compute ROI -

ROI = (Total Benefits – Cost of investment)/Cost of investment

ROI = (70000-3500)/3500 = 66500/3500 = 19%.

Present Value

A business analyst is evaluating two solutions approaches S1 and S2 for an initiative.

The projected benefit realized for Approach S1 five years from now is $1,50,000 at a rate of 5%.

Present value = Future value/$(1+Rate)^n$ = $150000/(1+.05)^5$ = $1,17,555

The projected benefit for Approach S2 four years from now is $1,80,000 at a rate of 6%. Present value = Future value/(1+Rate)^n = 180000/(1+.06)^4 = $1,42,630

Higher present value means greater total benefit and hence Approach B2 should be pursued with.

Net Present Value

Net Present Value (NPV) calculations are slightly more complex than present value computations. Instead of the lump-sum approach is taken in present value calculations, NPV takes into account benefits derived during each period when the project is in continuation. If a project continues for five years, there would be a return drawn each year instead of just at the end of the project.

Consider a scenario where a business analyst is creating a business case for an e-commerce initiative in which the inventory management system is to be implemented incrementally across different sites/locations. A global system will not work because of different regulatory guidelines, business processes, magnitude of sales, and categories of product line among other factors. The project can begin deriving benefits with each successful increment implementation instead of just at the finishing point of the full initiative.

In solution approach A1, consider an interest rate of 12% and a 5-year time period.

NPV calculation works in the following manner –

1) Calculate the cash flow or anticipated future value for each time period.
2) Convert cash flow/future value of each time period into present value using the formula - Present value = Future value/(1+Rate) ^n.
3) Add the present value of each time period.
4) Deduct the total investment cost for the initiative from the total present value and the result is net present value or NPV.

Below are the data points and calculation results for the example being discussed:

Year	Future Value	Present Value
1	15000	13393
2	20000	15944
3	18000	12857
4	25000	15924
5	18000	10227
Total Present Value		68345
Investment		60000
Net Present Value		$8345

Similar calculations are carried for another solution approach A2 that results in the Net Present Value of $5395. Considering that higher the NPV value better is the investment, solution approach A1 is chosen one.

Internal Rate of Return (IRR)

An organization is planning to purchase a project portfolio management product. Company A is selling the product P1 for $300000, the cash inflows for three years will be $70000, $75000, $60000 and then will sell it to any pertinent customer for near about the same price as what it was purchased for i.e. $295000. Using the hit & trial method in the formula or IRR function in excel, the value of IRR comes out to be 18.25%.

Company B is selling the product P2 for $200000, the cash inflows for three years will be $60000, $75000, $40000 and then will sell it to any pertinent customer for near about the same price as what it was purchased for i.e. $200500. IRR in this case is 25%.

In a scenario where two solutions/solution approaches are compared, the one with higher IRR is recommended and hence organization will go for product P2 from Company B.

Payback Period

The e-learning management system will cost the organization $2,00,000 to create over a period of five years. The expected benefit derived from the project is $10,000 per month. It will take 1 year and 8 months to recover the costs. Hence, the Payback period is 1 year and 8 months.

Focus Groups

Purpose

Focus group is a technique used for obtaining ideas, opinions, attitudes, and preferences about a product, service, or opportunity from a set of pre-qualified participants in an interactive setting. It can be utilized at various stages of an initiative in a below-mentioned manner –

- Ideation/Product roadmap creation – Attitudes and perspectives of potential customers help determine whether to build a product or scrap the idea and also determine future priorities if going ahead with developing it.
- Product under development – Ideas are analyzed in relation to already specified requirements to identify new requirements or update existing requirements.
- Developed product but not yet live – Ideas can possibly facilitate the effective positioning of products in the market.
- Live (already in production) product – Opinions and perspectives can be interpreted as customer feedback on the product. Also, it helps to set the base for product revisions in future releases.

Description

- Focus group is a form of qualitative research in which perspectives are shared and results are analyzed & reported as themes rather than quantitative findings.
- It takes place in a group setting which may cause some participants to re-evaluate their thoughts based on other participants' opinions and perspectives.
- A skilled moderator is employed for selecting participants, do the necessary preparation, facilitate the session, and work with business analysts to analyze & generate results.
- A scribe may also be appointed to record the decisions and outstanding issues.
- A business analyst may perform the role of a facilitator, scribe, or participant in the workshops and there should be complete clarity on his/her role.
- Though the activities are similar, the focus group is different from brainstorming. Focus groups follow a more structured and focused approach.

Elements

- Focus Group Objective – A well-defined objective forms the basis for creating questions and holding the focus group session.
- Focus Group Plan – A focus group plan includes –
  - Purpose – Identifies the key topics & questions to be discussed and use of discussion guide.
  - Location – Identifies the session mode (in-person/online) and meeting place (physical/virtual).
  - Logistics – Identifies the room, transportation & other facilities as well as time of the session.
  - Participants – Identifies the active participants (including their demographics), moderators, recorders, and observers (if required).
  - Budget – Identifies the budget and ensures the right allocation of resources.
  - Timelines – Establishes the schedule of the session(s) and expected timelines for sharing analysis results.
  - Outcomes – Identifies how the results will be analyzed & communicated and any future actions.

- Participants
  - Typically, a focus group has 6-12 participants.
  - Additional participants may be invited to make up for those who fail to attend the session.
  - Multiple focus group sessions will have to be held if a large number of participants are needed.

  o Demographics of the participants are determined based on the focus group objective.
- Discussion Guide
  o Include questions and topics that are in alignment with the session objective.
  o Also include a framework to be followed in the session that typically follows the sequence – participant's introduction, explaining the objectives of the session, the manner in which session will be conducted, and how the feedback will be used.
- Assign a Moderator and Recorder
  o Moderator – Competent in keeping the session on track and engaging participants.
  o Recorder – Take notes to make sure that all opinions and ideas are captured.
  o A business analyst can play the role of either the moderator or the recorder.
- Conduct the Focus Group
  o The moderator guides the session as per the stipulated framework and ensures that objectives are met whereas the recorder continues to take notes.
  o A typical focus group session is 1-2 hours long.
- After the Focus Group
  o Once the focus group session ends, a business analyst summarizes the results in the form of a report to be shared with relevant stakeholders.
  o Participants' agreements, as well as disagreements and trends in the responses, are analyzed for preparing the report.

Usage Considerations

Strengths

- Saves sizable time and cost as compared to interviews as data can be gathered from a group of people in a single session.
- Effective way to understand a person's attitudes, experiences, and wishes.
- Active discussion enables participants to re-evaluate their thoughts based on other participants' opinions and perspectives.
- Session can be conducted online if budget & location constraints exist. It can be recorded easily for playback when needed.

Limitations

- Participants may be reluctant to discuss sensitive topics in a group setting.
- Collected data may not be consistent with people's actual behaviour.
- Homogeneous groups may result in incomplete requirements.
- A skilled moderator is required to regulate group interactions.
- Difficult to schedule as all required participants may not be available during the same time slot.
- In an online focus group, participants' interaction may be limited and their attitude may not be determined as body language cannot be observed.
- A vocal participant could possibly influence the results in a particular direction.

Real Life Example

An insurance company is using a proprietary content management system (CMS) for maintaining critical business contract documents. There has been negative feedback of from various internal departments pertaining to both functional and non-functional aspects and increasing demands to incorporate new features to manage processes more effectively. The business sponsor has assigned a business analyst (BA) to take up the responsibility of understanding the stakeholders' problems and build requirements for revamping the CMS.

With a clear objective to elicit opinions, ideas, and perspectives on improving the CMS, the BA decides to conduct a focus group session. He formulates the questions to be discussed, sets up the required logistics to conduct the session in person, requests the attendees from all concerned departments to join the session at the stipulated time and location. He then works on a discussion guide that encompasses the framework for carrying out focus groups and decides to play the role of a moderator to facilitate the session. Thereafter, the session is held for 2 hours in which all attendees discuss at length and present their views on redesigning the CMS with the recorder taking the notes. Eventually, the BA analyses and documents the participants' agreements and disagreements look for common trends and creates a summarized report to be sent to the business sponsor to review and direct the next steps.

Functional Decomposition

Purpose

Functional decomposition is a technique used to break down large processes, systems, functional areas, or deliverables into their simpler sub-components so that each sub-component can be analyzed independently. The purposes served by functional decomposition include (but not limited to) –

- Help manage the complexity and reduce uncertainty in an analysis.
- Facilitates scaling, tracking, and measuring work effort for simpler sub-components.
- Simplify evaluation of the success of each sub-component relative to other larger or smaller components.

Description

- A few considerations are taken before proceeding with functional decomposition –
  - Large systems, processes, functional areas are a set of collaborating functions or components.
  - Sub-components can completely describe their parent components.
  - Any sub-component can have only one parent component when developing the functional hierarchy.
- The depth of decomposition may vary depending on the objective and nature of components.

Elements

- Decomposition Objectives – The objectives behind decomposition drive the entire process and typically include –
  - Measuring and Managing – Isolate controllable contributing factors and identify key metrics and indicators.
  - Designing – Isolate the object of design to simplify a design problem.
  - Analyzing – Investigate the properties of an artefact or behaviour of an event in isolation from its environment.
  - Estimating and Forecasting – Break down a complex denomination into its smaller constituents to reduce the level of uncertainty.
  - Reusing – Create a building block that can be reused across multiple processes.
  - Optimization – Identify & remove a bottleneck, reduce cost, and improve quality.
  - Substitution – Build a specific component that can be substituted without impacting the system.
  - Encapsulation – Combine multiple elements to make one element.
- Decomposition Subjects – Decomposition applies to varied subjects that include –
  - Business Outcomes – Outcomes include income, profit, expenses, volume of service, or production.
  - Work to be done – Breaks work into phases, milestones, activities, tasks, items, and deliverables. Also known as work breakdown structure or WBS.
  - Business Process – Isolate the constituent parts of a business process for measuring, managing, optimizing, or reusing it.
  - Function – Enable the implementation or optimization of a function.
  - Business Unit – Enable the design or reverse engineering of a business unit.
  - Solution Component - enable the design, implementation, or change of a solution component.
  - Activity – Enable implementation, modification, optimization, measurement, and estimation of an activity.
  - Products and Services – Design, implement or improve products and services.
  - Decisions – Identify inputs, underlying models, dependencies, and outcomes of decision for enabling, improving, or supporting them.

- Decomposition Level
  - Level of decomposition draws a line on the decomposition activity i.e. it defines where and when the decomposition must come to an end.
  - The decomposition ends at a juncture where the actors have just enough understanding and detail to proceed and can apply the results in other tasks.
- Representation of Decomposition Results – Decomposition results can be represented using various diagrams that include –
  - Tree Diagrams – Depicts hierarchical division of work, activities, or deliverables.
  - Nested Diagrams - Represents hierarchical part-to-whole relationships between decomposition results.
  - Use Case Diagrams – Depicts the breakdown of a high-level use case into low-level use cases.
  - Flow Diagrams – Depicts process or function decomposition results.
  - State Transition Diagrams – Illustrates the behaviour of an object inside its composite state.
  - Cause-Effect Diagrams – Depicts all components involved in generating a complex outcome.
  - Decision Trees – Represents the structure of a complex decision and its possible outcomes.
  - Mind Maps – Signifies information in categories.
  - Component Diagrams – Depicts how components are joined to construct larger components or systems.
  - Decision Models – Utilized to analyze business logic.

Usage Considerations

Strengths

- Breaks down complex problems into smaller parts for easy understanding and analysis.
- Builds a shared understanding of complex subjects among diverse stakeholder groups.
- Simplifies measurement and estimation of work to be carried out to achieve an objective.

Limitations

- Missing or incorrect information may lead to revisions later.
- Many complex systems cannot be represented by simple hierarchical relationships.
- Investigating all decomposition alternatives can be cumbersome while selecting a single alternative may result in a substandard outcome.
- Require subject matter expertise and extensive collaboration with diverse stakeholder groups.

Real Life Example

A business analyst is working on a large-scale initiative for a government-sponsored construction organization. The objective of the initiative is to implement a project portfolio management (PPM) system into the software landscape of the organization. Based on the understanding gathered from stakeholders, a business analyst creates a module-wise functional decomposition model to get a shared agreement on the features in each module that must be implemented as a part of the project. Below is the visual representation (Next Page).

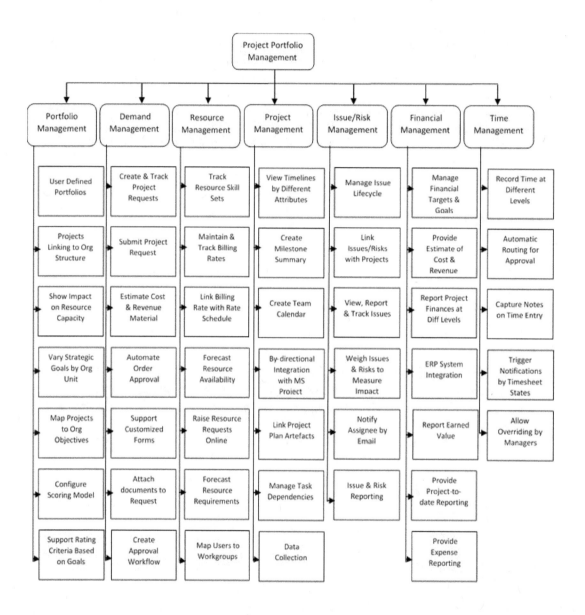

Interface Analysis

Purpose

Interface Analysis is a technique that identifies the interfaces (i.e. connections) between solutions and/or solution components. It identifies all required details of the information that is exchanged between solutions and/or solution components.

Description

- Interfaces are needed to exchange information with other solution components, organizational units, or business processes.
- Interface types include user's direct interaction with solution, people external to the solution, business processes, data interfaces between systems, application programming interfaces (APIs), and hardware devices.
- Interface analysis provide details on users of the interface, details, and volume of information exchanged, timing & frequency of information exchanged, where the information exchange will take place, reason the interface is required and how it is or should be implemented?

Elements

Below step-by-step process is carried out to perform interface analysis –

- Prepare for Identification – It involves utilizing other techniques such as document analysis, interviews, observation, scope modelling, and context diagram to identify the current interfaces as well as any problems that may exist in them.
- Conduct Interface Identification – It includes identifying which interfaces are needed in the future state and illustrate relevant details like the function of interface, usage frequency, assess interface types needed and gather initial details for each interface.
- Define Interfaces – It involves defining the inputs and outputs for the interface, any validation rules, and events that trigger interactions. In addition, interface users, user's workflow, their roles & privileges, and management objective are also determined. Typical interface definition includes name of the interface, its coverage, exchange methods between the entities of interface, message format, and exchange frequency.

Usage Considerations

Strengths

- Ensures increased functional coverage.
- Enables structured allocation of requirements, business rules, and constraints to the solution.
- Its application is imprecise in nature and hence over-analysis is not needed.

Limitations

- Internal components are not assessed and hence this technique doesn't provide any insights in this regard.

Interviews

Purpose

An interview is an organized approach to elicit business analysis information from one or more stakeholders by talking to them, asking applicable questions, and documenting the responses. Interviews can play a significant role in building relationships with stakeholders thereby increasing their involvement and support.

Description

- Interviews can be one-on-one or group in nature. In a group interview (with more than one interviewee), the interviewer is cautious in eliciting responses from the interviewees.
- Interviews are of two basic types –
  - o Structured Interview – Interviewer has a predefined format and order of questions.
  - o Unstructured Interview – Interviewer does not have a predefined format and order of questions. Questions may vary based on how the interviewee responds.
  - o A combination of the two can also be used by adding, removing, and changing the order of questions as needed.
- Successful interviews depend on interviewer's domain knowledge, interviewer's experience & skills in conducting & documenting interviews, interviewee's readiness in providing the required information, interviewee's clarity of goal, and rapport between interviewer & interviewee.

Elements

Below step-by-step process is carried out to perform interview process –

- Interview goal – Defining and clearly expressing the overall purpose of performing interviews with the interviewee.
- Potential Interviewees – Identifying the right set of interviewees with the help of key project stakeholders considering the interview goal.
- Interview Questions – Interview questions are designed based on the purpose of the interview like data collection, understanding stakeholder's thoughts on a change/solution, solution development, or building rapport with stakeholders. Questions fall into two categories –
  - o Open-ended questions – Cannot be answered in a yes, no, or specific manner and a good way to elicit information on subjects which the interviewer is unaware of.
  - o Closed questions – Can be answered in a yes, no, or specific manner and an effective way to clarify or confirm a previous answer.
- Interview Logistics – It involves putting together the required logistics like interview location, schedule, communication mode, scribe (if required), advanced sharing of interview questions, and maintaining the confidentiality of the interviewee (if required).
- Interview Flow –
  - o Opening interview – It includes describing the purpose of the interview, confirming roles, dealing with the interviewee's concerns, and explaining how the information will be managed.
  - o During interview – It involves carrying out the core interview process keeping the goal in mind but adapting based on information provided, solving any interviewee's concerns, practicing active listening, taking notes/recording sessions.
  - o Closing interview – It comprises of asking interviewees for any missed areas, providing contact information for future communication, summarizing session by outlining the usage of interview results, and expressing gratitude to the interviewees.

- Interview Follow-up – Post interview, organize the collected information from the interview, and confirm results with the interviewees who can then review the results, and share feedback.

Usage Considerations

Strengths

- Simple technique is applicable in case of many situations.
- Enables detailed discussions on questions & even observation of non-verbal actions.
- Allows for follow-up questions to confirm understanding & clarify doubts.
- Maintains focus using clear objectives.
- Helps sustain interviewee's confidentiality if required

Limitations

- Considerable time required on the part of interviewers as well as the interviewee.
- Effective interview sessions require training
- Resulting documentation may be subject to the interviewer's interpretation.
- There are chances that the interviewee's responses are unintentionally led by the interviewer.

A business analyst is assigned to elicit requirements for a project which is regarding the revamp of the existing mobile application that allows users to link all plans in one account, pay post-paid, internet and DTH bills, recharge prepaid connection, view detailed usage and many more. He had discussions with project sponsors, project managers & other stakeholders to identify the domain SMEs who are going to be the source of requirements. Since the project is a major face-lift one, it involves detailed discussions to be held and even follow-up discussions to confirm understanding and clarify doubts. Hence, the business analyst decides to go for the Interview technique as it seems most suited to the scenario.

He creates a few open-ended as well as closed questions depending upon whether detailed or specific information is required.

Examples of open-ended questions include –

- What are the key features in the competitor's mobile app that stimulated the decision to revamp the existing app?
- What are the features that are perceived as the most important features from end user's standpoint?
- What are the guidelines that the mobile app layout and screen designs need to confirm to?
- Are there any assumptions or dependencies that need to be considered for building the app?
- What are the possible user personas and user journeys for the app?

Example of closed questions include –

- Should the application work on iOS platform, Android platform, or both?
- What are the payment gateways do you plan to implement to allow end-users to make payment?
- Will the app support offline mode?
- Do you need separate designs for iOS and Android?
- Are APIs of existing apps going to be utilized or new APIs have to be built?

Item Tracking

Purpose

Item tracking is a technique used by business analysts to address stakeholder concerns. It is used to capture stakeholder concerns and assign responsibility to one or more stakeholders who are responsible for its resolution.

Description

- Stakeholders may identify item types as actions, assumptions, constraints, dependencies, defects, enhancements & issues. Item Tracking is an organized approach that addresses these stakeholder concerns.
- Once a stakeholder concern is raised, it is assessed for viability check, classified & tracked to agreed-upon closure.
- Item tracking records may be shared with stakeholders to ensure transparency.

Elements

- Item Record may contain any or all of the below attributes –
  - Item Identifier – A unique identifier for an item
  - Summary – A brief description of the item
  - Category – A grouping of items with similar properties
  - Type – The kind of item raised
  - Date Identified – The date the item was raised as a concern
  - Identified By – The person who initially raised the concern
  - Impact – The possible consequences if the item is not resolved by the resolution due date
  - Priority – The importance of this item to the impacted stakeholders
  - Resolution Date – The date by which the item must be resolved (or closed)
  - Owner – The stakeholder assigned to manage the item to its closure
  - Resolver – The stakeholder assigned to resolve the item
  - Agreed Strategy – An agreed-upon strategy for the item (accept, pursue, ignore, mitigate, avoid)
  - Status – The current status of the item within its life cycle (open, assigned, resolved, cancelled)
  - Resolution Updates – A running log of details about how the item's resolution is proceeding towards closure as well as approval of its completion
  - Escalation Matrix – A level of escalation in case item is not resolved by the given due date
- Item Management – Each item must be tracked to closure and resolution. Also, it needs to be made sure that item resolution efforts pertaining to linked items are not duplicated and are progressing in coordination.
- Metrics – Detailed information is maintained about each item and its progress. Stakeholders can determine how well items are being resolved, the initiative is progressing, and item tracking process is being utilized.

Usage Considerations

Strengths

- Ensures stakeholders concerns are recorded, tracked and resolved.
- Enables stakeholders to rank outstanding items by importance.

Limitations

- There are chances that abundant item data recording might outweigh its benefits.
- Time spent on item tracking details/stats can be better spent on other critical work.

Real Life Example

A business analyst has specified, and modelled requirements and the requirements are now verified for meeting the desired quality standards determined by stakeholders. There are many issues/concerns from stakeholders related to compliance with organizational performance standards, use of modelling notation, templates, or forms, the terminology used in expressing the requirement to stakeholders. Business Analyst uses Item Tracking to ensure that these issues identified during verification are managed and resolved.

Below is an example of an item tracking sheet:

Item Ident ifier	Summary	Categ ory	Date Identified	Identifie d By	Priority	Resolution Date	Owner	Resolved By	Agreed Strategy	Status	Resolution Updates
1	All use case models in the document are not as per the organizational standard template	Standa rds Compli ance	10-April-19	David	High	11-April-19	Manish	Rajeev	Accept	Resolved	More compliant with the standard template
2	Sec 3.2.1 – It is not specified which actor will perform this activity	Requir ements Quality	10-April-19	Renee	Medium	12-April-19	Manish	Ram	Accept	Assigned	
3	Sec 4.3.2 – The phrase 'as needed' is specified. Please explain the requirement clearly	Requir ements Quality	10-April-19	Andrew	High	11-April-19	Manish	Nitin	Accept	Resolved	Requirements decomposed & explained in detail
4	The requirements mentioned in sect 4.3.2 and sec 3.2.2 are not consistent. Please check and update	Requir ements Quality	11-April-19	Andrew	High	12-April-19	Manish	Rajeev	Accept	Assigned	
5	Term counterparty is used for the incorrect role. Please check glossary document	Standa rds Compli ance	12-April-19	David	High	13-April-19	Manish	Ram	Accept	Open	
6	Sec 4.3.3 – Please mention the requirements clearly in terms of acceptance criteria to validate it	Requir ements Quality	12-April-19	Renee	Medium	14-April-19	Manish	Nitin	Accept	Open	

Item Tracking Register

Lessons Learned

Purpose

Lessons Learned, also known as a retrospective, is a technique used by business analysts to collate and document successes, failures, improvement areas of the project or its phases as well as recommendations for improvement for future projects, or its phases.

Description

- Lessons Learned technique can be applied at the end of a project or project milestone or deliverables to identify improvements for the future.
- Lessons Learned sessions do not necessarily follow a standard format but are generally fall into two categories -
  - Formal working sessions with proper agendas and roles
  - Informal working sessions.
- Celebrations can also be included in a lesson learned session to lay emphasis on key learnings that led to achieving success in a project/project iteration.

Elements

- Lessons learned session include carrying out a review of the below items –
  - Business Analysis activities & deliverables
  - Interim or Final solution, service or product
  - Process changes introduced
  - Performance expectations and comparison with results
  - Root causes affecting outcomes

Usage Considerations

Strengths

- Identifying areas for improvement, causes of failure, or factors leading to success.
- Assist in boosting team morale.
- Emphasizes positive outcomes & successes
- Curtails risk for future events
- May provide metrics for evaluating performance

Limitations

- Participants may play blame games in case of a failure outcome.
- Sometimes the participants may be hesitant to document and discuss their problems.
- Meticulous facilitation may be needed for focused discussions.

Metrics and Key Performance Indicators (KPIs)

Purpose

Metrics and key performance indicators (KPIs) measure the performance of a solution or its specific components or any other subjects of stakeholders' interest. Metrics and KPIs help stakeholders understand the extent to which a solution meets a business objective.

Description

- An indicator is a numerical measure that represents the degree of progress towards achieving a goal or objective. A metric is a quantifiable level of an indicator used to measure progress.
- A key performance indicator measures progress towards a strategic goal or objective.
- Monitoring is a continuous data collection process while evaluation is an organized solution assessment process to determine how effectively the solutions meet the desired objectives.
- Reporting is the process of providing regular updates of metrics or indicators to relevant stakeholders as per the predetermined formats and time intervals.
- Metrics and reporting are key components of monitoring and evaluation.

Elements

- Indicators
  - An indicator displays the result of analyzing one or more specific factors related to need, value, activity or output/input.
  - A good indicator should possess the below characteristics –
    - Clear – Must be precise and unambiguous
    - Relevant – Must be applicable to the concern at hand
    - Economical – Must be available at reasonable cost
    - Adequate – Must provide ample details to assess performance
    - Quantifiable – Can be validated independently
    - Trustworthy and Credible – Must be based on evidence and research
  - In a situation where data for direct indicators is not available or when data cannot be collected on a regular basis, a substitute can be used.
  - The source, collection method, collector as well as the cost, frequency, and difficulty of collection should be considered to establish an indicator.
- Metrics
  - Metrics are quantifiable levels of indicators that are measured at a specified point in time.
  - A target metric is the objective to be reached within a specified period. Time to reach target metric can be multi-year, annual, quarterly, or even more regular.
  - The baseline starting point, resources that can improve the factors covered by the indicator, and political environment are considered to set up metric for an indicator.
  - A metric can be a specific point, a limit, or a range.
- Structure
  - Establishing a monitoring and evaluation system requires carrying out the below procedures –
    - Data collection – Specifies sampling procedures, data collection methods, frequency & responsibility.
    - Data analysis – Covers procedures for conducting the analysis and the data consumer.
    - Reporting – Covers the templates, recipients, frequency, and communication mode for reports.

- Baseline data collection – Baseline data provides information on current performance and provides a reference point for measuring progress going further. Needs to be collected, analyzed and reported for each indicator.
  - Key factors in assessing the quality of indicators and their metrics include –
    - Reliability – Relates to stability and consistency of data collection approach.
    - Validity – Extent to which data clearly and directly measures the performance.
    - Timeliness – Aptness of frequency and latency of data to the need.
- Reporting
  - In general, reports compare the baseline data with current metrics, and target metrics with the differences depicted in both absolute and relative terms.
  - Trends are often more reliable and critical than absolute metrics.
  - Visual depiction is more effective than tables, especially in case of qualitative data.

Usage Considerations

Strengths

- Helps assess and understand how well the solution meets the desired business objectives.
- Facilitates organizational alignment, linking goals to objectives, supporting solutions, underlying tasks, and resources.

Limitations

- Excessive data gathering leads to unnecessary spending in collecting, analyzing, and reporting and may take away focus from other key responsibilities.
- Regular and timely feedback need to be provided to individuals in charge of collecting data and generating reports failing which useful reports may not be generated.
- Individuals may start improving their performance on activities specific to a metric even if it results in substandard performance on other activities.

Real Life Example

An IT vendor has revamped the middleware system of a major retail conglomerate by redeveloping it in latest technology available in market. The middleware system connects all major operational systems in the landscape.

As the project has been executed and is now live, there are a few performance metrics and key performance indicators (KPIs) devised by business stakeholders in shared agreement with the IT vendor who is providing post-production operational support for a year. These metrics and KPIs must be reported by IT Operational support team to business every month. Metrics to be created and reported are specific to the performance of the team while KPIs are primarily the service level agreements that have to be complied by the IT Operational support team while also ensuring that the business objectives are met by the solution.

Below are a few KPIs and Metrics that are reported monthly to business –

KPI 1 – System's availability is a major business objective since a downtime would significantly affect all systems and hence business will be severely impacted. As per the agreement, the application availability threshold is 99%. Below is a graph depicting the application availability over the last six months.

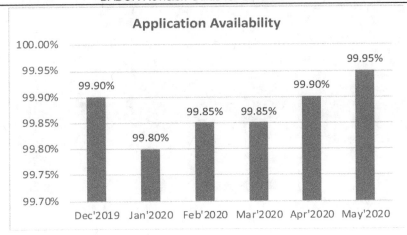

KPI 2 – Resolving issues within stipulated timelines is another major business objective. Mean time to resolve has been defined depending on the priority of the issue (logged as ticket). As per the agreement, mean time to resolve for a priority, 3 ticket is defined as 3 days. Below is a graph depicting the mean time to resolve trend for priority, 3 tickets over the last six months.

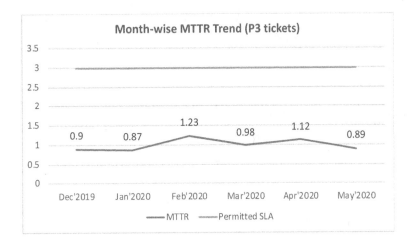

Metric 1 – Another metric of interest to the stakeholders but not a KPI is the ticket volume and backlog trend. Backlog refers to number of tickets remaining to be resolved at the end of a month. This is a good indicator of team's effort and performance on a monthly basis but is not directly related to business objective since ticket volume can increase due to planned system upgrades or any other known major activities and this can also severely affect backlog if such activities are carried out close to month end. This metric can be used to further drill down to areas where ticket count is high to be able to identify the root cause.

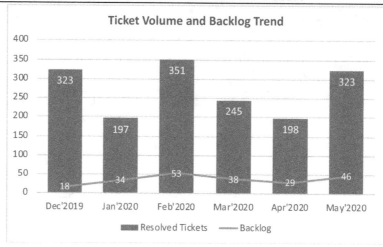

Mind Mapping

Purpose

Mind Mapping is a technique used to capture and articulate ideas and thoughts in a fashion that resembles how our minds process information. It is a very effective collaboration tool that summarizes ideas and thoughts generated on complex concepts or problems in a simplified and consolidated structure thereby facilitating creative problem solving and decision making. It helps explore relationships between the various aspects of a problem in a way that inspires creative and critical thinking.

Description

- Mind mapping involves capturing thoughts and ideas in a non-linear diagram that has no standardized format.
- It uses images, words, colours, and relationships to give a structure to thoughts and ideas.
- A mind map comprises of a central idea (main topic), secondary ideas (topics), multiple layers of ideas (sub-topics), connection between ideas (branches) with an associated keyword that explains the connection. Together, these elements capture and articulate the concept.

Elements

- Main Topic – The main topic of a mind map is the articulated thought or concept. It is positioned in the center of the graphic and is generally expressed as an image.
- Topics – Topics are thoughts or concepts that further articulate the main topic. Association with the main topic is through a branch (connected line) with an associated keyword.
- Sub-topics - Sub-topics are thoughts or concepts that further articulate the topic and directly relate to the main topic. Association with the topic is through a branch (connected line) with an associated keyword.
- Branches - Branches are the associations between the main topic, topics, and sub-topics and include a keyword that articulates the nature of the association.
- Keywords - Keywords are single words that articulate the nature of the association of topics or sub-topics connected by a branch. They categorize topics and triggers additional associations.
- Colour - Colour is normally used to categorize, prioritize, and analyze topics, sub-topics, and their associations.
- Images – Images can be used to express large amounts of information and stimulate creativity and innovation.

Usage Considerations

Strengths

- Summarizes and provides structure to complex thoughts, ideas, and information.
- Facilitates decision making and creative problem-solving.
- Assists in summarizing a large amount of information and hence helps in preparing and delivering presentations.

Limitations

- May be misused as a brainstorming tool and constrain idea generation.
- May be difficult to communicate a shared understanding.

Non-Functional Requirements Analysis

Purpose

Non-functional requirements (also referred to as quality attributes or quality of service requirements) qualities of the system's operations rather than its functional behaviour. They extend the functional requirements of a solution, identify constraints on requirements, or describe quality attributes a solution must possess to be considered as effective.

Non-functional requirements analysis is a technique that deals with identifying the non-functional requirements for a solution.

Description

- Non-functional requirements are not just associated with system solutions, but also apply to process and people aspects of solutions.
- Typically, non-functional requirements are stated in textual formats or in the form of matrices.
- Non-functional requirements described in textual formats as declarative statements will typically have a constraining factor linked to them.

Elements

- Categories
  - Availability – Degree to which the solution is operable and accessible when required
  - Compatibility – Degree to which the solution operates effectively i.e. is compatible with other components.
  - Functionality – Degree to which the solutions' functions meet user needs with respect to suitability, accuracy, and interoperability.
  - Maintainability – Ease with which a solution or its component can be fixed, changed to increase performance, or adapted to a changing environment.
  - Performance Efficiency - Degree to which a solution or its component performs its functions with minimal resource consumption.
  - Portability - Ease with which a solution or its component can be transferred from one environment to another.
  - Reliability – The ability of a solution or its component to perform its required functions without a failure under predefined conditions for a specified time-period.
  - Scalability – Degree to which a solution is able to evolve to handle increased amounts of work.
  - Security – Solution aspects that assure solution and its components will be protected against malware attacks or unauthorized access.
  - Usability – Ease with which a user can learn to start using the solution.
  - Certification – Constraints placed on the solution to meet the required industry standards and principles.
  - Compliance – Constraints placed on the solution to meet regulatory, financial, or legal requirements.
  - Localization – Requirements to be met to work in a localized environment such as language, laws, currencies, cultures, spellings, and user characteristics.
  - Service Level Agreements – Constraints placed on the solution to meet service levels agreed between the provider and the user of the solution.
  - Extensibility – Ability of a solution to be extended to incorporate new functionality.

- Measurement

- o Non-functional requirements must be specified in measurable terms so that they can be verified for acceptance.
- o Instead of describing them vaguely like "easy to learn" and "should respond quickly", they should be quantified as much as possible.
- o Measurement criteria of specific non-functional requirement categories such as certification, compliance, and service level agreement are provided by their source.
- Context
  - o Organizational context should be considered to select the right mix of non-functional requirements while also considering that they may impose contextual pressures on one another.
  - o Context is dynamic in nature and hence its relative stability needs to be considered as it may lead to changes or removal of non-functional requirements.

Usage Considerations

Strengths

- Articulate the constraints imposed on the solution in an unambiguous manner.
- Clearly distinguish itself from functional requirements in that functional requirements define what the solution must do and non-functional requirements provide measurable criteria of how well the functional requirements must perform.

Limitations

- Effectiveness of a non-functional requirement will depend on stakeholders' knowledge of solution needs and their articulation skills.
- Getting agreement on non-functional requirements may be difficult because of conflicting user expectations.
- Different categories of non-functional requirements may have inherent conflicts and require negotiation.
- Exceedingly rigorous non-functional requirements may lead to additional cost and time required to build the solution.
- Many non-functional requirements are qualitative in nature and hence difficult to be measured quantitatively.

A business analyst (BA) is working on creating requirements for a fashion e-commerce mobile application. Based on the understanding that the BA has developed from the business stakeholders pertaining to the essential quality of service attributes that the application should possess, he has specified the quality of service or non-functional requirements in the requirements specification document. Below is an excerpt from the non-functional requirements section –

- Security - The payment processing gateway must be PCI DSS compliant.
- Availability – Application must be available to users with 99.99% uptime.
- Compatibility – Application must be suspended on the event of a call and shall resume from the same position when the call ends.
- Usability – 90% of the users who have completed an order once should be able to place an order in no more than 3 minutes.
- Performance Efficiency – Application should not take more than 5 seconds to load the home screen.
- Reliability – No more than 1 per 1 million order placements should result in a failure if all functional conditions are met.
- Maintainability – Application should be able to be reverted to the previous version if the new version has introduced any functional defects or led to performance degradation or any other issues.
- Portability – Less than 5% of the application implementation should be specific to the operating system.

Observation

Purpose

Observation, also known as job shadowing, is an elicitation technique used for identifying needs and opportunities, understanding business processes, setting performance standards, evaluating solution performance, or supporting training and development by examining & understanding work activities.

Description

- Planning and execution of observation activities is determined by objectives behind it.
- It can be performed in natural work environments or specially constructed laboratory conditions.
- Below approaches can be followed to conduct observation –
  - Active/Noticeable – Observer asks any questions that they have leading to a quick understanding of rationale & hidden processes. They may also intervene strongly by asking actors to perform specific activities to reduce observation time & extract the desired information.
  - Passive/Unnoticeable – Observer doesn't intervene in actors' activities & raise any queries/concerns once the observation is over. The observer may also record videos of the activities and then review it later with the actor to clarify any doubts.

Elements

Below step-by-step process is carried out to perform observation –

- Defining Observation Objectives – It involves defining a clear objective of carrying out an observation session. Typical objectives include understanding an activity, identifying improvement opportunities, creating performance metrics, assessing solutions & validating assumptions.
- Prepare for Observation – It includes identifying stakeholders to be observed including their skill & experience, schedule & frequencies of observations, and whether any existing documentation need to be studied beforehand.
- Conduct Observation session –
  - Before session – Participants need to be explained the purpose behind an observation, reassured that their performance is not being judged, informed that they can stop at any time, recommended to share any concerns/reasoning.
  - During session – Observe the actors performing activities & take any notes on tasks, tools used. Record time taken, quality, process anomalies & concerns/questions. Also, clarify any queries during or after the observation session.
- Confirm and Present Observation Results – Review the notes & recorded data and share with participants to get them validated or fill any knowledge gaps. Results are analysed against the session objectives and presented to stakeholders.

Usage Considerations

Strengths

- Provides practical insights into the activities within a process.
- Enables identification of informally performed tasks or workarounds.
- Facilitates a realistic comparison of productivity with performance standards.
- Provides quantitative evidence for improvement recommendations.

Limitations

- May cause disruption to participants thereby affecting performance.
- Effective only when there is sufficient time at hand.
- Not applicable for evaluating knowledge-based activities.
- Participants being observed may feel threatened/intruded and may also change their work practices when observed.

Organizational Modelling

Purpose

An organizational model is a visual representation of organizational units. It is created to depict how an organization or organizational unit is structured that comprises of roles, responsibilities, and reporting hierarchy with the purpose of aligning those structures with the organization's goals.

Description

- An organization unit is composed of a group of people that aim towards fulfilling a common objective and possess a common set of skills or knowledge.
- Typically, an organizational model comprises of the below constituents –
  o Boundaries of the group
  o Formal relationships between members i.e. reporting hierarchy
  o Functional role of each member
  o Interfaces with other units or stakeholders

Elements

- Types of Organization Models
  o Functionally oriented
    ▪ Employees are grouped based on skill set or competency areas into functions. Examples include finance, HR, sales, distribution, etc.
    ▪ Enables standardization of processes and tasks to be performed.
    ▪ Advantages include effective cost management & reduced duplication of work.
    ▪ Functional silos may get created leading to communication and co-ordination issues between functions reducing the organization's overall efficiency.
  o Market-oriented
    ▪ Employees are grouped based on particular customer groups, geographical areas, projects, or processes.
    ▪ Enables the organization to aim and meet customer needs better.
    ▪ Susceptible to inconsistent operations and duplication of work.
  o The Matrix Model
    ▪ Employees are structured to report to two managers – line manager who is responsible for the performance of a type of work in a functional area and market/product/service/project manager who manages a product or service or project across multiple functional areas.
    ▪ Managers are focused on different goals and may lead to accountability issues.
- Roles – An organizational unit has well-defined roles with each role corresponding to specific skill set, work profile, responsibilities, and has a relationship with other roles in the organization.
- Interfaces – An organizational unit has interfaces with other organization units with each interface that may either be in the form of communication with people in other roles and work packages exchanged among organizational units.
- Organizational charts – It is the fundamental diagram used in creating an organizational model. There is no formal standard, but conventions followed are as under –
  o Box – A box represents an organizational unit, roles within an organization, and people assigned to the role.
  o Line – A line represents lines or reporting which can be either be a solid line that represents direct reporting or dotted line that represents information transfer or situational authority.
- Influencers – Influencers pertain to informal lines of authority, influence, and communication which may not directly align with the formal organizational chart.

Usage Considerations

Strengths

- One of the most common models in most organizations.
- Future projects may reap benefits from the organizational model by knowing people involved as well as their roles and contact them for support as needed.

Limitations

- May get outdated with time.
- Tough to identify informal lines of authority, influence, and communication not depicted in the organizational model.

Real Life Example

A business analyst is working on a new global project for a retail company that has arms in multiple regions. He obtains an organizational model to identify the key stakeholders who should be contacted to get the stakeholder list to participate in the requirements elicitation process.

Below is the market-oriented organizational model that the business analyst gets to lay his hands-on –

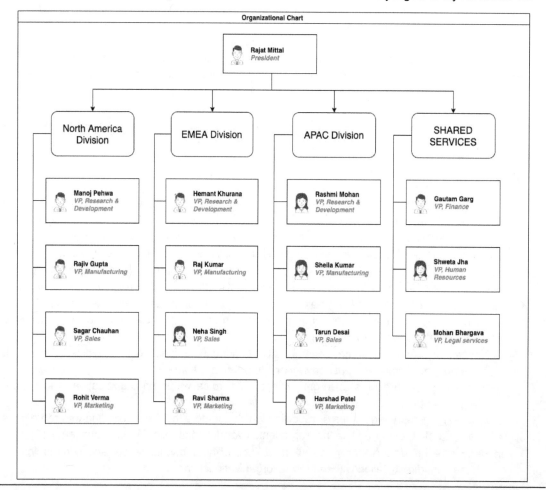

Prioritization

Purpose

Prioritization is a key technique that facilitates stakeholder decisions by determining the relative importance of business analysis information.

Description

- The priority assigned may be based on value, risk, the difficulty of implementation, or other criteria.
- These priorities help decide which business analysis information should be targeted for further analysis, which requirements should be implemented first, or how much time or detail should be allocated to the requirements.
- Common approaches to carry out Prioritization include Grouping, Ranking, Timeboxing/ Budgeting, and Negotiation.
- Selection of a prioritization approach is based on the audience, their needs, and perceived business value.
- Priorities may be re-assessed, and different approaches may be employed if the business environment, stakeholders, or business analysis information change.

Elements

Prototyping Approach – Below are the two common approaches to prototyping –

- Grouping
  - Business analysis information is classified as high, medium, or low priority.
  - Quite a few requirements management tools have priority categories as a requirement attribute.
- Ranking
  - Business analysis information is ordered from most to least important.
  - Certain Adaptive approaches rank requirements in an ordered list (product backlog in Agile scrum).
- Budgeting/Time Boxing
  - Prioritization is based on the allocation of a fixed resource.
  - Timeboxing prioritizes requirements based on the amount of work that can be delivered in a fixed time-period.
  - Budgeting prioritizes requirements based on the amount of work that can be delivered in return for a fixed amount of money.
- Negotiation
  - Involves reaching a shared agreement among stakeholders on which requirements will be prioritized.

Usage Considerations

Strengths

- Facilitates consensus-building among stakeholders.
- Ensures that the anticipated business value is realized.
- Ensures that the estimated timelines are met

Limitations

- Few stakeholders may fail to handle tough choices and understand the importance of trade-offs.
- Prioritization may be intentionally or unintentionally influenced by the solution implementation team.
- Stakeholder's perspective of priority may be subjective if Metrics and KPIs are not available.

Process Analysis

Purpose

Process Analysis is a technique used to assess a process for its efficiency and effectiveness to identify change opportunities for further process improvement. Process analysis can be used with the following objectives –

- Recommending a process that provides increased value
- Identifying gaps between a process's current and future state
- Understanding key considerations for contract negotiation
- Understanding use of data and technology
- Analyzing change impacts

Description

- Process analysis involves analyzing and elaborating the following –
  - o The ways through which the process adds or creates value.
  - o The ways through which the process aligns with organizational goals and strategy.
  - o The degree to which the process is efficient & effective and the desired level of quality.
  - o The ways through which the solution requirements will achieve the future state and meet stakeholder needs.
- Common process improvement specific changes include –
  - o Reducing the time required to complete the process task(s).
  - o Reduction or elimination of bottlenecks mainly related to interfaces between organizational units or people.
  - o Automating steps that are manual and produce expected outcomes.
  - o Increasing the degree of automation in decision making.

Elements

- Identify Gaps and Areas to Improve - Identifying gaps and improvement areas helps identify areas for analysis. Below essential tasks are carried out –
  - o Identify gaps between the current and desired future state.
  - o Identify and classify gaps as value-added and non-value added.
  - o Understand pain points, challenges, and opportunities from diverse perspectives.
  - o Align gaps and improvement areas with strategic direction and changes in the enterprise.
- Identify Root Cause - Identifying the root cause of gaps and improvement areas helps ensure that the solution addresses the actual and core areas. Essential aspects to be acknowledged in identifying root cause include the possibility of multiple root causes, inputs causing a gap or improvement areas, right people for root cause identification and the current measurements & motivators for process's owners/performers.
- Generate and Evaluate Options - Generating solution alternatives that target gaps & improvement areas helps team evaluate different viewpoints for process improvement. It is imperative that impact, feasibility, and value of the proposed solution is identified relative to alternative solution options.
- Common Methods
  - o SIPOC – SIPOC, which stands for suppliers, inputs, process, outputs, and customers, is a process analysis method that originates in the Six Sigma methodology. A SIPOC provides a simple overview of the process by understanding the suppliers, inputs, process, outputs, and customers of the process. It shows who creates inputs to the process, who receives outputs

from the process and initiate information flow on problems, opportunities, gaps, root cause, and options and alternatives.

o Value Stream Mapping (VSM) – Value stream mapping (VSM) is a process analysis method used in Lean methodologies that provides a summarized view of steps involved in the end-to-end process, including both value-adding and non- value-adding or waste elements. It involves monitoring inputs & application points, gauging the wait time for the inputs and the actual processing times at the application points and depicting the logistics or distribution process to the customer.

Usage Considerations

Strengths

- Ensures solutions address the right issues and minimize waste.
- Provide flexibility due to a wide variety of techniques and methodologies.

Limitations

- May be time-consuming at times.
- Challenging to determine which technique to employ and the extent of its use considering there are a multitude of techniques and methodologies at hand.
- May not be effective in knowledge or decision-intensive processes.

A business analyst is working for an e-commerce organization. Lately, the organization has not seen noteworthy sales, and feedback from customers is also a point of apprehension. In addition, increased cost over time is also not improving the situation any further. Key business stakeholders have got the impression that all these adverse outcomes have hidden origins in the overall business processes.

Consequently, the business decision-makers ask the business analyst and key business experts to carry out business process analysis to understand and outline current processes and to identify opportunities for improvement in those processes.

Business analyst decides to put SIPOC business analysis tool to use here since it provides an effective means to understand and represent the suppliers, inputs, process, outputs, and customers of the process and also engage stakeholders in discussions regarding problems, opportunities, gaps, root causes, opportunities for improvement and solution options.

Below is the SIPOC diagram created by the business analyst to sketch out the current process –

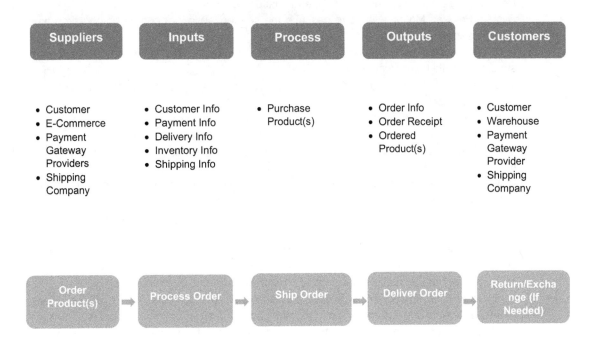

Process Modelling

Purpose

Process modelling is a technique used to produce graphical models to show how work is carried out in an enterprise or part of an enterprise by describing the sequential flow of work across the defined activities and tasks. It acts as a foundation for process analysis.

Process models can be used to illustrate –

- The current and future state of a process
- Context of the solution or solution component
- Sequence of activities in a process
- Visuals to go along with a text description

Description

- Process models fall into various categories –
  - Process Model – Used to document operational procedures.
  - System Process Model – Used to describe the sequential flow of control among programs within a system.
  - Program Process Model – Used to describe the sequential flow of execution of program statements within a software program.
- Process modelling can be done at different levels with each level providing a different degree of detail and precision –
  - High-level (enterprise or context) – Provides a high-level overview of a process and its relationship to other processes.
  - Medium-level (operational) – Provides more detailed activities and identifies all exceptional and alternative paths.
  - Low-level (system) – Provides even further details than medium-level and act as the basis for simulation or execution.
- Process model can be used to define the current or as-is state of a process or a potential future or to-be state.
  - As-is process model provides an understanding and agreement on what is happening at present.
  - To-be process model provides perception of what is desired to happen in the future.
- Typically, a process model includes the participants in the process, the triggering event, sequence of manual and automated activities, the paths & decision points, and the results of the process. Additionally, it may include data/materials, inputs & outputs, and call-out descriptions.

Elements

- Commonly used process modelling notations include –
  - Flowcharts and Value Stream Mapping (VSM) – Used in the business domain.
  - Data Flow diagrams and Unified Modelling Language™ (UML®) diagrams – Used in the information technology domain.
  - Business Process Model and Notation (BPMN) – Used across both business and information technology domains.
  - Integrated Definition (IDEF) notation and Input, Guide, Output, Enabler (IGOE) diagrams – Used for establishing scope.
  - SIPOC and Value Stream Analysis – used for process modelling.
- Typical elements in a process model include the following –

- o Activity – A piece of work that is a part of the business process. It may be a single task or may be further broken down into a sub-process which, like a process, has its own activities, flow, and other process elements.
  - o Event – An occurrence that starts, interrupts, or ends an activity within a process or the process itself. It may be through receipt of a message, passage of time, or occurrence of a condition defined in the business rules.
  - o Directional Flow – A path that indicates the logical sequence of the process workflow.
  - o Decision Point – A juncture where the flow of work splits into two or more flows that may be mutually exclusive or parallel to each other. It can also be used to specify instances where separate flows merge.
  - o Link – A connection to other process maps.
  - o Role – A type of person or group involved in the process.
- Most used process models/notations include –
  - o Flowchart
    - Maybe a simple sequence of activities or complex swimlanes in which activities are segregated by role.
    - Most used in scenarios where the audience is non-technical.
  - o Business Process Model and Notation (BPMN)
    - Provides an industry-standard for modelling business processes that are appropriate for both business and technical stakeholders.
    - Can be used to create both private or public processes and also serve as input to process automation technologies.
    - It can clearly distinguish the activities of different participants/roles in a process with pools and swimlanes where pool represents business entities and swimlane signifies participants/roles.
  - o Activity Diagram
    - Defined in the Unified Modelling Language™ (UML®) that was originally designed to model a single-use case but has now been adopted to model business processes.
    - Use swimlanes to show responsibilities across participants/roles, synchronization bars to show parallel processing, and decision points.

Usage Considerations

Strengths

- Close to how humans understand sequential activities and hence most people get comfortable with the fundamentals of a process model in no time.
- Help identify and accommodate different stakeholder groups as well as their perspectives.
- Effective method of demonstrating many scenarios, sequential flows, and parallel flows.
- Enables highlighting of pain points thereby facilitating identification of potential improvement and also acting as a baseline for continual improvement.
- Can also be beneficial in serving compliance, training, and work-coordination related purposes.
- Provide transparency to all relevant stakeholders on their roles & responsibilities, hand-over of work, and sequence in which work is carried out.
- Ensures labelling consistency across artifacts.

Limitations

- Formal process models are time-consuming and document-heavy these days and hence project teams skip creating process models.

- Can be extremely complex to build and understand if business rules & decisions are also captured in it.
- Can be complex to understand and provide a sign-off if many activities and roles are included.
- High-level model may not provide insights into the actual problems in the process and a more detailed model, as well as stakeholder engagement, may be needed.
- May be difficult to maintain as stakeholders may not update the model when the process is altered and can also become obsolete, especially in a fast-changing environment.

Real Life Example

A business analyst is working on creating a portal to maintain policies for a major insurance organization. One of the key aspects of the initiative is that there will be a two-fold formal approval process to approve and publish policy documents on the portal to be utilized for further business objectives.

Business analyst has created the below activity diagram to demonstrate the document approval process to be put into effect in the portal.

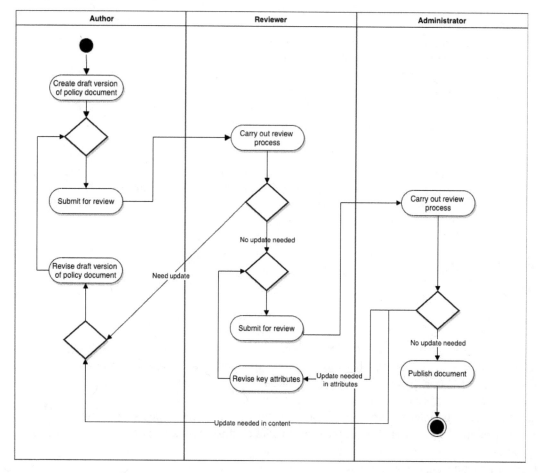

Prototyping

Purpose

In simple words, Prototyping is a technique used to create a design or model of the anticipated solution based on perceived or elicited stakeholder needs. Prototyping is useful in the below scenarios –

- Elicit and validate stakeholder needs/requirements
- Optimize/augment user experience
- Evaluate design options
- Identify missing/incorrect/inadequate requirements timely
- Uncover assumptions and dependencies

Description

- Prototype can be static or non-working, working illustrations, or digital representations.
- It enables the creation of website mock-ups and demonstrates partial/complete product features.
- Business rules prototypes can be used to discover the desired process workflows and business rules.
- Data prototypes can be used for data cleansing and transformation.

Elements

- Prototyping Approach – Below are the two common approaches to prototyping –
  - Throw-away –
    - A simple and inexpensive approach to discover, clarify, confirm requirements specific to user interfaces, processes, business rules, and data.
    - Can be created using simple tools like paper & pencil, whiteboard, or software.
    - May possibly evolve during discussions and development.
    - It never becomes a workable code or sustained as a deliverable and is thrown away as the name suggests.
    - Effective in identifying functionalities that are complex or conflicting in nature and not easily elicited by other techniques.
  - Evolutionary or Functional –
    - Extend initial requirements into a working solution as requirements are further described through usage.
    - Uses a specialized prototyping tool or language to simulate business processes, rules, and data for evaluating a change impact and outcome.
    - These prototypes may be used in the final solution.

- Prototyping Examples – Below can be considered as prototyping forms/examples –
  - Proof of Principle or Proof of Concept –
    - Used for validating the design of the system without exhibiting its appearance.
    - Materials used for creating work used by stakeholders eventually.
  - Form Study Prototype –
    - Explores the size, look, and feel of the desired product without creating actual functionality.
    - May be used to model high-level process workflow or navigation to identify potential gaps in the solution's properties.
    - It is an inexpensive form of a prototype.

  - Usability Prototype –

- Created to test how the end-user interacts with the system.
- Properties like appearance & configuration are not included.
  - Visual Prototype –
    - Created to test the visual facets of the solution.
    - Complete functionality is not modelled.
  - Functional Prototype –
    - Working model created to test a software's functionalities, qualities, and workflows.
    - Used to simulate business processes and business rules and evaluate function calls.

- Prototyping Methods – Common prototyping methods are as follows –
  - Storyboarding –
    - Used to detail different user interactions with solutions, both visually and textually.
  - Paper Prototyping –
    - Used to create an outline of an interface or process with paper and pencil.
  - Workflow Modelling –
    - Used to represent a series of operational workflows pertaining to human aspects.
  - Simulation –
    - Used to exhibit solution and/or its components and it may test various processes, scenarios, business rules, data, and inputs.

Usage Considerations

Strengths

- Visually represent the future state.
- Quick feedback can be solicited from the stakeholders.
- Allows users to be more critical of a throw-away prototype since it is not release-ready.
- Effective technique for technical feasibility investigations, proof of concepts, reveal technology, and process gaps.

Limitations

- May consume enormous time & effort if discussions shift to "how" rather than "what".
- May require an understanding of technology in a few cases.
- Stakeholders may develop unrealistically high expectations related to completion time, performance, reliability, and usability.
- Extensive focus on design instead of requirements may constrain the solution design.

Reviews

Purpose

Reviews are used to assess a work product. It may be used for a wide variety of purposes, but the primary ones are to identify & remove defects and ensure that a work product meets the desired level of quality & confirms to the mandatory standards. It can also be used to reach an agreement on an approach/solution and train reviewers on the work product.

Description

- Different types of reviews are carried out on work products that are customized to the needs of the organization and business analyst.
- Work product may be ongoing or complete (a portion of the deliverable, single deliverable, or package of deliverables). For ongoing work products, review may be conducted to resolve an issue or answer a question while for completed work product, the review is carried out to remove defects or inform the reviewers about the content.
- Typically, peers review an ongoing work product while stakeholders review a completed work product to ensure completeness and correctness.
- A review includes an overview of review objectives & work product, use of checklists & reference materials, review of work products, documentation of findings, and verifying any rework.
- A business analyst plays the role of an essential participant in a review and updates the work product based on reviewers' feedback.

Elements

- Objectives – There may be one or more objectives for a review process that include defect removal, conformance to specifications or standards, completeness and correctness of work product, reaching agreement on approach or solution, answering the question, resolving issues, exploring alternatives, educating reviewers on work products and measurement of work product quality.

- Formal Techniques
  - Inspection – Utilized to create a defect-free work product and includes an overview of the work product, individual review, defect logging & consolidation and follow-up to ensure the required changes were done. It can be performed by peers or stakeholders.
  - Formal Walkthrough/Team Review – Uses the individual review and team consolidation activities often seen in inspection and can be performed by peers or stakeholders.
  - Single Issue Review/Technical Review – Aimed at either one issue or a standard in which reviewers perform a deep investigation of the work product prior to a joint review session held to resolve the matter in focus.

- Informal Techniques

  - Informal Walkthrough – Work product is run through in draft state to seek feedback and does not require intense preparation.
  - Desk Check – Feedback (verbal or written) is provided by a reviewer who had not been involved in work product creation.
  - Pass Around – Feedback (verbal or written) is provided by multiple reviewers. A common copy of the work product may be reviewed or passed from one person to another post individual review.

o Ad hoc – Carried out to solicit informal review or assistance from a peer.

- Participants - Participant roles engaged in a review depending on the objectives, selected technique, and any organizational standards (if exist). Typical review roles include –

  o Author – Creator of the work product who answers questions on the work product and actively listens to the feedback from reviewers. Holds responsibility to incorporate the feedback into work product post review.
  o Reviewer – Peer or stakeholder who examines the work product based on the review objectives.
  o Facilitator – A neutral party who facilitates the review session. He/she keeps participants focused on the review objectives and ensures coverage of relevant work product areas.
  o Scribe – A neutral participant who documents all defects, suggestions, comments, issues, concerns, and outstanding questions raised during the review.

Usage Considerations

Strengths

- Helps detect defects early in project or work product life cycle thereby preventing costly removal caused by late identification.
- All participants involved in review become deeply involved and interested in the quality of outcome.
- Informal reviews like desk checks and pass around can be performed by a reviewer at any fitting time rather than cutting short an ongoing task to attend the review meeting.

Limitations

- Inspection or formal walkthrough gets rigorous often thereby consuming a lot of time and effort.
- Informal reviews provide less assurance of removing all significant defects as compared to a more formal process involving larger teams.
- Difficult to validate that desk checks and pass around reviews have been done.
- Difficult to resolve conflicting feedback in case mode of communication is e-mail.

Real Life Example

Formal review

A business analyst (BA) is working on producing requirements for a retail analytics project for a major retail organization. After specifying the requirements, the next task which the BA plans to perform is to get the requirements verified by business stakeholders to ensure that they meet quality standards and are usable for the purpose they serve. The BA decides to go for the Inspection review approach as this is the most potent formal technique that ensures an intense review and creation of a defect-free work product.

Inspection is carried out by a set of business stakeholders wherein they verify requirement specification work product to ensure that the requirements are atomic, complete, consistent, concise, feasible, unambiguous, testable, prioritized, and understandable. It is also verified whether the requirements are compliant with organizational standards and whether correct modelling notations, templates, forms, and terminologies are used.

The inspection review process is moderated by a neutral facilitator who keeps the participants focused on the review objectives. Defects are logged and tracked to closure to ensure that the requirements specification document is free of defects.

Informal review

A business analyst (BA) is working on a project to implement an enterprise resource planning (ERP) system for a major retail organization. To understand the business process and available system details, BA is using the passive observation (shadowing) technique.

The BA is of the view that instead of getting the elicitation outcome verified at the very end (which may turn out to be costly in terms of time and budget if the elicitation results are majorly incorrect), it would be a good idea to carry out an informal walkthrough with the concerned stakeholder(s) after every observation session. Therefore, he creates a draft of elicitation results post every observation session and does an informal walkthrough with the required participants to make sure that he is on the right path to understand the key processes.

Risk Analysis and Management

Purpose

Risk analysis and management deal with identifying risks (uncertainty areas), analyzing and evaluating those risks, and creating approaches for responding to the risks that are deemed as unacceptable for an initiative.

Failure to identify and address risks may significantly affect the value of a solution in a negative manner. Risk analysis and management involve identifying, analyzing, evaluating, and treating risks to prevent such adverse impacts.

Description

- Business analysts may be required to develop and when required, implement plans for avoiding, reducing, or modifying the risks.
- Risk Management is a continuing activity and regular communication with stakeholders assists in identifying new risks and managing identified risks.

Elements

- Identification
  - o Risks are identified through expertise & experience of stakeholders, experimentation, or historical analysis of similar initiatives.
  - o Risk identification is a continuing activity with a goal of identifying all applicable risks thereby reducing uncertainties.
  - o Risks can be recorded in a risk register that facilitates analysis and addressing those risks.
- Analysis
  - o Risk analysis includes understanding the risk and assessing its probability as well as impact.
  - o Probability can be expressed as a numerical value or as high, medium, or low.
  - o Impact of any risk can be described in terms of cost, duration, scope, quality, or any other factors determined in agreement with stakeholders like reputation, compliance, or social responsibility, etc.
  - o The level of risk may be expressed as a function of the probability of its occurrence and the impact. It may be a simple multiplication of probability and impact. Risk level helps determine its priority relative to other risks.
- Evaluation
  - o Risk analysis results are compared with the potential value of the change initiative or the solution to decide if the level of risk is acceptable or not.
  - o An overall risk level may be determined by summing up all the individual risk levels.
- Treatment
  - o Some risks may be tolerable while some other risks may not be acceptable and need to be addressed.
  - o Possible approaches for addressing risks that can be used independently or in combination include –
    - ▪ Avoid – Ensures that the risk doesn't occur by removing the risk source or adjusting plans.
    - ▪ Transfer – Accountability of dealing with the risk is pushed to or shared with a third party.
    - ▪ Mitigate – Reduces the likelihood of risk occurrence or its negative impacts if the risk does occur.
    - ▪ Accept – Accepts risks and decides that nothing needs to be done about the risk. A workaround will be developed if and when the risk occurs.
    - ▪ Increase – Decides to take on more risk to pursue an opportunity.

- o Once a risk treatment approach is determined, a risk response plan is developed and assigned to the risk owner. In situations where risk cannot be completely eliminated, a risk mitigation plan is created.

Usage Considerations

Strengths

- Applicable to strategic risks, tactical risks, and operational risks.
- Successful risk responses on one initiative can be useful lessons learned for other initiatives.
- Ongoing risk management helps to identify the variation in the risk level of a change or solution allowing re-assessment of risks and effectiveness of risk response.

Limitations

- List of possible risks to most initiatives can easily become cumbersome and difficult to manage.
- Significant risks may not be identified.

Real Life Example

A business analyst is assigned to work on implementing an enterprise resource planning (ERP) system in the environment of a major retail conglomerate.

Business Analyst and Project Manager understand the scale and significance of the initiative and foresee some risks in the requirements elicitation process. They are of the view that failing to identify and address these risks may significantly affect the initiative in meeting the desired business objectives.

The BA carries out risk analysis in association with relevant stakeholders to identify, assess, and manage conditions or situations that could negatively affect the elicitation process or affect the quality of the elicitation outcome. Risk analysis is more important in this large-scale initiative since multiple elicitation techniques are going to be employed. Below is a snippet of a risk register that BA has prepared to record, assess, and address risks.

Table is shown on the next page.

S No.	Risk Event or Condition	Consequence	Probability	Impact	Risk Level	Risk Modification Plan	Risk Owner	Residual Risk		
								Probability	Impact	Risk Level
1	Stakeholders availability & engagement is not as per desired expectations	All requirements will not be captured & solution will not meet the business needs	Medium (2)	High (3)	High (2*3 = 6)	Develop stakeholder engagement plan & obtain agreement on their participation. Escalate to sponsor as the final resort	Roopak	Low (1)	Medium (2)	Low (1*2 =2)
2	Response rate is too low any statistical significance in the survey	Lack of sufficient responses means no insights and inferences from the survey	Medium (2)	High (3)	High (2*3 = 6)	Explore third-party survey management companies & select a suitable one for creating & managing surveys	Roopak	Medium (2)	Medium (2)	Medium (2*2 = 4)
3	Existing business & functional documents are out-of-date & provide incorrect or complete knowledge	Inaccurate know-how on business & functional aspects to establish requirements affecting the project timelines & budget	High (3)	High (3)	High (3*3 = 9)	Before the elicitation begins, stakeholders to put dedicated effort to upgrade and fix documents or provide time slots to brief BAs on the incorrect/incomplete aspects	Roopak	Medium (2)	Medium (2)	Medium (2*2 = 4)

Roles and Permissions Matrix

Purpose

Roles and Permissions Matrix is a useful technique to identify roles, identify solution activities, designating authorities for each role in terms of activities they are authorized to perform. It thereby ensures complete coverage of all identified solution activities, discovers missing roles, and communicate results of a planned change.

Description

- Role and permissions allocation process involves identifying roles, associating these with identified activities, and then assigning authorities to the roles.
- A role is a label for a group of individuals who share common functions with each function portrayed as one or more solution activities.
- An activity can be associated with one or more roles by designating authorities and individuals with that role so that they can perform the associated activity accordingly.
- Project/Initiative level roles and responsibilities may be identified in a RACI (Responsible, Accountable, Consulted, Informed) matrix whereas an IT system roles and responsibilities may be identified in a CRUD (Create, Read, Update, and Delete) matrix.

Elements

- Identifying Role
  - Identifying roles require looking for common functions performed by individuals with similar needs.
  - Reviewing existing documentation like organizational models, job descriptions, procedure manuals, and system user guides aids in identifying roles.
  - Meeting with the stakeholders will ensure that no roles are missed and additional roles that are not specified in documents are captured.
  - Individuals may have same job title but perform different role(s) and may have different job titles but perform same role(s).
- Identifying Activities
  - It can be ensured that all functions are captured and their activities are identified by using the techniques functional decomposition (break down a function into sub-parts), process modelling (familiarize with the workflow and understand the work allotment among users) and use cases & scenarios (understand the activities/tasks carried out by users).
- Identifying Authorities
  - Represent actions that the roles are authorized to perform.
  - Important considerations are the level of security and process workflow.
  - Stakeholder collaboration to validate the identified authorities is essential.
- Refinement
  - Delegations – It includes identifying authorities that can be delegated by one individual to another on a temporary or permanent basis.
  - Inheritances – It pertains to a situation that when an individual is assigned an authority at an organizational level then this authority is limited to only that user's organizational level and any subsidiary organization at unit levels.

Usage Considerations

Strengths

- Provides data security and routine checks by restricting actions based on roles & permissions.
- Fosters capturing and review of transaction history by means of audit logs.
- Provides well-defined and documented roles and responsibilities for activities thereby preventing any discrepancy.

Limitations

- Including too much detail can consume enormous time and effort and provide little or no value.
- Including too little detail might exclude important roles, activities, or authorities.

Real Life Example

Business analyst is working on a Media assets and metadata management project. While carrying out requirements analysis and specifying requirements pertaining to various roles and their authorities, he decides to create a Roles and Permissions matrix to clearly portray each application role and the activities each role is authorized to perform.

Roles and Permissions Matrix / Activity	Internal Stakeholders	Administrator	Manager	Asset Editor	Metadata Editor	Viewer	External Stakeholders	Report Viewer
Create new user accounts		✔						
Modify existing user account		✔						
Delete existing user accounts		✔						
Add Assets into the system		✔	✔	✔				
Delete Assets from the system		✔	✔	✔				
Add Metadata for Assets		✔	✔		✔			
Edit Metadata for Assets		✔	✔		✔			
Delete Metadata for the Assets		✔	✔		✔			
View Assets and associated metadata		✔	✔	✔	✔	✔		
Generate and view metadata reports		✔	✔	✔	✔	✔		✔

Root Cause Analysis

Purpose

Root cause analysis deals with investigating a problem or situation in a systematic and iterative manner to identify and evaluate the underlying causes of the problem. It helps to uncover the real reason why a business problem is occurring thereby facilitating the creation of a viable solution to fix the problem.

Description

- Root cause analysis focuses on the problem's origin as the point of correction rather than dealing only with its effects or symptoms.
- It considers three main types of causes –
  - People (e.g. human error, lack of training)
  - Physical (e.g. equipment failure, poor facility)
  - Organizational (e.g. faulty process design, poor structure)
- Root cause analysis can be used for:
  - Reactive Analysis – Identifies the root cause(s) of an already happening problem for taking appropriate corrective action.
  - Proactive Analysis: Identifies potential problem areas for preventive action.
- Root cause analysis involves carrying out the below four activities –
  - Problem Statement Definition – Defines the problem to be solved.
  - Data Collection – Collects data on nature, magnitude, location & timing of the effect.
  - Cause Identification – Examines the patterns of effects to identify the causes that contribute to the problem.
  - Action Identification – Defines the corrective action that will prevent or minimize the reoccurrence of the problem.

Elements

- Fishbone Diagram or Ishikawa diagram or Cause-and-effect diagram
  - It is used to identify and organize the possible causes of a problem and arrange ideas for further analysis.
  - A fishbone diagram can be created using the below steps –
    - Capture the issue or problem in a box at the top of the diagram.
    - Draw a line from the box to form the spine of the fishbone.
    - Draw diagonal lines from the spine to represent categories (people, processes, tools, policies) of potential causes of the problem.
    - Draw smaller lines to represent deeper causes.
    - Brainstorm potential causes of the problem and capture them under the appropriate category.
    - Analyze and validate the causes.
    - Brainstorm potential solutions once the actual cause has been identified.
- Five Whys
  - It is an approach in which questions are asked repeatedly to identify the root cause of the problem. It can be used independently or together with the Fishbone diagram.
  - Below steps are carried out as part of this approach –
    - Write the problem
    - Ask "Why do you think this problem occurs?" and capture the idea below the problem.
    - Ask "Why?" again and capture that idea below the first idea. Repeat this step until you are satisfied that the primary root cause has been identified.

Usage Considerations

Strengths

- Performed with an objective viewpoint.
- Enables defining an effective solution as a corrective action.

Limitations

- Formal Training may be required to ensure that the actual root causes are identified.
- May not be the best approach to use when the problem is complex in nature.

Real Life Example

Fishbone Diagram

The business analyst (BA) who had worked on implementing a Customer Relationship Management (CRM) system in the IT landscape of a major retail organization has been asked to carry out an analysis to determine the factors internal to the solution that is restricting the full realization of value.

BA carries out an analysis with required stakeholders to identify and organize the possible causes that are potentially leading to a lack of expected performance of the installed solution. Considering there are multiple categories and possible causes in each category, BA captures all causes in a Fishbone diagram for appropriate representation. This will also facilitate an effective analysis & validation of causes and further brainstorming for devising solutions.

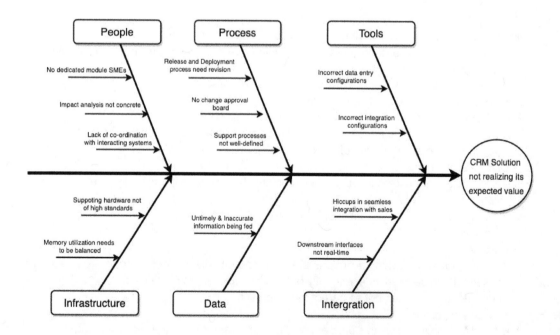

Five Whys

A business analyst has completed his required analysis tasks, created all functional specification artefacts expected from him, and obtained the sign-off for proceeding with a further course of action.

An assessment of business analysis work is carried out by the business stakeholders after it was identified that the requirement sources were not too satisfied with the requirements elicitation and documentation process. After the feedback was provided to the BA, he got in touch with the business stakeholders who carried out the performance review to identify the underlying causes of negative feedback. He decided to use the 'Five whys' approach to get to the root cause of the feedback and identified it as shown below –

Problem: BA has received negative feedback on the business analysis work performed.

Why? Functional specifications were not up to the standards as per the stakeholders.
Why? No. of review cycles to accept functional specifications was beyond set standards.
Why? BA was not aware of any performance measure related to no. of review cycles.
Why? Neither stakeholders communicated to BA nor BA elicited from stakeholders.
Why? Stakeholders did not think it was a priority and no formal document exist.

Scope Modelling

Purpose

A Scope model is a combination of diagrams, matrices, and textual explanations that defines the boundaries of a solution, need, change, or control by placing the applicable elements inside or outside those boundaries.

A scope model provides a basis for defining contractual obligations, estimating work, justifying requirements in-scope/out-of-scope decisions, and assessing the completeness and impact of solutions.

Description

- Scope models enable understanding of the boundaries of:
  - Control – Covers the items being analyzed, roles and responsibilities, and what is internal and external to the organization.
  - Need – Covers stakeholder needs, anticipated value, functional areas, and organizational units to be explored.
  - Solution – Covers requirements met, value delivered, and change impacts.
  - Change – Includes planned actions, stakeholders impacted and events to be controlled.
- The coverage of scope model can be from below perspectives –
  - In-scope – Identifies a boundary as seen from inside and the elements contained by that boundary. Functional decomposition is one of the approaches to show in-scope elements.
  - Out-of-scope – Identifies a boundary as seen from outside and the elements that are not contained by that boundary. A Context diagram is one of the approaches to show out-of-scope elements.
  - Both – Identifies a boundary as seen from both sides and elements on both sides of the boundary. Venn diagram or use case model can be used to depict both in-scope and out-of-scope elements.

Elements

- Objectives
  - Scope models serve the objective of clarifying the span of control, relevance of elements, and areas for applying efforts.
  - Model type to be used is chosen based on actions or stakeholder needs to be supported.
- Scope of Change and Context
  - Business analyst focuses on the elements that are in the scope of the change to establish the ways those elements are modified.
  - In addition, a business analyst is also concerned with the out-of-scope elements but still relevant to establish the interactions between the change, the current and proposed solutions, and the context.
  - In relation to the scope of change & context, the business analyst considers aspects related to business processes, business functions, new or existing capabilities, use cases, technologies, physical assets and external entities (stakeholders, agents, organizations).

- Level of Detail
  - The level of abstraction at which scope elements need to be defined should be proper in the sense that it should neither cause uncertainty nor lead to analysis paralysis.
  - Elements of a scope model can be described by detailing all of them, by referring to a specific level of their decomposition hierarchy, or by grouping them together.

- Relationships - Various diagramming techniques for specifying relationships among elements include –
  - o Parent-Child or Composition-Subset – Relates elements of the same type by way of hierarchical decomposition. Can be depicted on organizational chart, class or entity-relationship diagram, business process model (as subprocesses), state diagram (as composite states).
  - o Function-Responsibility – Relates a function with the stakeholder responsible for its execution. Can be depicted on business process models, collaboration diagrams, sequence diagrams, and use case diagrams.
  - o Supplier-Consumer – Relates elements by way of exchange of information or material objects between them. Can be depicted on data flow diagrams, business process models, collaboration diagrams, sequence diagrams, and robustness diagrams.
  - o Cause-Effect – Relates elements by logical contingency. Can be depicted on a fishbone and other cause-effect diagrams.
  - o Emergent – Several elements can interact to produce results instead of when they are independent.
- Assumptions
  - o Scope model should include critical assumptions and their implications.
  - o Assumptions may include the definition of needs, causality of outcomes, impact of changes, applicability, and feasibility of the solution.
- Scope Modelling Results
  - o Scope model can be represented as textual descriptions, diagrams depicting relationships of elements or matrices describing dependencies between elements.

Usage Considerations

Strengths

- Simplifies agreement process for contractual obligations, effort estimation of an initiative, requirements scoping, solution completeness & impact assessment.

Limitations

- May lack enough detail needed to ensure clear scope identification.
- Revised a scope once created may be difficult owing to political reasons and contractual obligations.
- May not be able to deal with complex boundaries.

A business analyst is working on writing functional requirements for a blogging module of an online learning management system. The objective is to generate relevant content thereby enabling social media promotion to drive search traffic to the website. This will increase the likelihood of generating leads by means of course enrolment.

In addition to specifying and modelling requirements, the business analyst and project manager have mutually decided to visually demonstrate the scope boundary for the first phase to get stakeholder's agreement on the same.

Below is the use case diagram of the blogging module that depicts the use cases to be implemented in the project and captures the in-scope boundary containing the use cases proposed to be implemented in the first phase of the project:

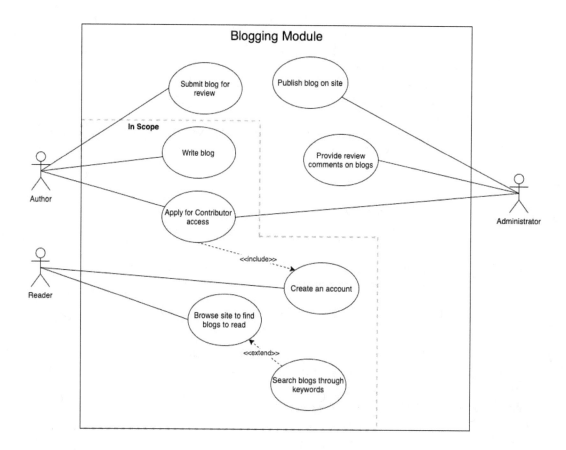

Sequence Diagrams

Purpose

A sequence diagram or event diagram is used to model the interaction of processes or objects during a scenario by showing the information passed between objects in the system through the execution of the scenario. It shows the classes required to execute the scenario and the messages they pass to one another.

It provides a simple and straightforward way to represent the logic in a scenario thereby simplifying stakeholder validation.

Description

- A sequence diagram depicts how objects (typically interface components or software components) used in the scenario interact without showing how these objects are related to each other.
- The objects that exchange messages are represented as boxes arranged at the top of the page from left to right, with a vertical line descending to the bottom of the page.
- Messages exchanged between objects are represented as horizontal arrows with the order of the messages shown in a top-down and left-to-right fashion.

Elements

- Lifeline
  - o Represents the lifespan of an object during the scenario.
  - o Drawn as a dashed line that vertically descends from each object box to the bottom of the page and can be terminated with an X.
- Activation Box
  - o Represents the duration of the execution of an operation.
  - o A call to activate is represented by an arrow (with a solid arrowhead) leading towards the activation box of an object.
- Message
  - o Interaction between two objects takes place through a message.
  - o Represented as an arrow from sender activation box to recipient activation box.
  - o Different message types are –
    - ▪ Synchronous call – Sender object transfers control to the receiver object and cannot perform the next action until a return message is received.
    - ▪ Asynchronous call or signal – Sender object can continue with its own processing after sending a signal to the receiver object. The sender object may send many signals at the same time but may only accept one signal at a time.

<u>**Usage Considerations**</u>

Strengths

- Visually and chronologically represent interaction between objects thereby allowing an easy logic validation by stakeholders.
- Allows for further refinement of use cases to provide a more in-depth understanding of the business process.

Limitations

- Creation of sequence diagrams for all use cases may not be required and may lead to significant time and effort consumption if created.
- Too technical to be utilized in situations other than modelling system flows.

Real Life Example

A business analyst is working on creating requirements for a major government initiative to create a digital wallet platform and online payment system. The platform will enable users to link their bank accounts and make payments directly from their accounts.

In addition, to use cases, the business analyst has been producing associated sequence diagrams as well wherever applicable. One of the many features of the platform is to enable users to check the available balance in the linked bank account. The sequence diagram created for this scenario is as shown below –

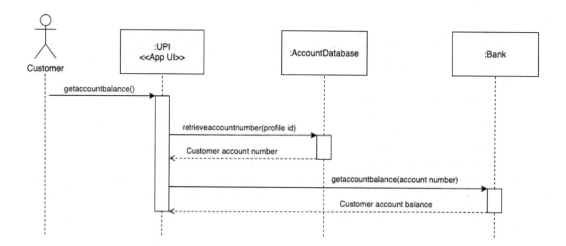

Stakeholder List, Map or Personas

Purpose

Stakeholder lists, maps, and personas are carried out to identify stakeholders affecting or getting affected by a proposed initiative and analyze their various characteristics. This analysis is carried out to ensure –

- All possible sources of requirements for an initiative are identified thereby preventing any likelihood of missed business needs or requirements.
- Stakeholders are fully understood so that decisions can be made regarding stakeholder engagement, collaboration, and communication.

Description

- Stakeholder characteristics that are useful candidates for identification and analysis include –
  - Level of power or influence within the area of change and within the organization
  - Attitudes toward the change
  - Attitudes toward the business analysis work
  - Decision-making authority
- Work done in carrying out a thorough stakeholder analysis include identifying their role, attitudes, decision making authority, and level of influence as well as defining collaboration and communication approaches.
- One or more techniques can be utilized to identify stakeholders and analyze them. Stakeholder lists, maps, and personas are three such techniques to carry out this analysis.

Elements

- Stakeholder Lists
  - Stakeholder List is essential for activities pertaining to stakeholder analysis and the planning to be done for elicitation, collaboration, and communication.
  - Brainstorming and interviews are two common techniques that can be used to generate stakeholder list.
  - It is important to ensure that list is exhaustive i.e. no stakeholders have been overlooked as it can lead to critical business needs or requirements getting missed.
- Stakeholder Map - Stakeholder maps are diagrams that show the relationship of stakeholders to the solution and to one another. Common stakeholder maps are -
  - Stakeholder Matrix – Maps the level of stakeholder influence against the level of stakeholder interest. Matrix is divided into four quadrants –
    - High Influence/High Impact – These stakeholders are critical to the change and business analysts should engage them on a regular basis to ensure that they agree with the change.
    - High Influence/Low Impact – These stakeholders have needs that should be met. Business analysts should engage them to increase their interest in the change and ensure they remain satisfied.
    - Low Influence/High Impact – These stakeholders are supporters of the change but concerned about their lack of influence. Business analysts should show a keen interest in their needs and keep them informed.
    - Low Influence/Low Impact – These stakeholders, if additionally involved, can move into the Low Influence/High Impact quadrant. Business analysts should keep them informed and monitor them regularly to check if their interest or influence change but not spend too much effort.
  - Stakeholder Onion Diagram
    - Onion diagram depicts the level of involvement of stakeholders with the solution.

- It clearly separates out which stakeholders will directly interact with the solution, which are part of the larger organization, and which are outside the organization.
- Responsibility (RACI) Matrix - Responsibility (RACI) Matrix is a well-known stakeholder matrix where RACI stands for Responsible, Accountable, Consulted, and Informed. The RACI roles/designations should be clearly defined for consistent understanding. Common definitions include –
  - Responsible (R) – The person(s) who will be performing the work on the task.
  - Accountable (A) – The only person who is accountable for the task and is the decision-maker.
  - Consulted (C) – The stakeholder (or group) asked to provide an opinion or information on the task. Generally, subject matter experts play this role.
  - Informed (I) – The stakeholder (or group) that is updated regularly on the task and notified of its outcome.
- Personas
  - A persona is defined as a fictional character that illustrates how a typical user interacts with a product and is used to create a group or class of users.
  - Although the user groups are fictional, they are built to represent actual users. Interviews and surveys/questionnaires are two techniques commonly used to elicit information on identifying the user groups.
  - A persona is written in a narrative form that tells the story from the point of view of the stakeholder group.

Usage Considerations

Strengths

- Identifies the stakeholders to be involved in requirements elicitation.
- Assists in planning stakeholder collaboration and communication.
- Helps to understand changes in impacted groups over time.

Limitations

- May not be employed in scenarios where same group of stakeholders is involved in change initiatives.
- Assessing the influence and interest of stakeholders can be a complicated process.

Real Life Example

Below are a few practical examples of various stakeholder analysis representations created by business analyst –

Stakeholder Matrix (Influence/Impact)

High	Bob Taylor		Nicholas Ross
	Joe Edwards	Renee Lodge	
	Keep Satisfied	Engage Closely	
	David Twain	Amanda Jane	
	Andrew Fares		Markus Vera
	Alexa Coriano	Michael Korr	
	Robert Hecker	Dave Richards	Alex Broad
	Monitor	Keep Informed	
	Christy Smith	Mary Allerton	
Low	Steve Taylor		Henry Stone

Influence of stakeholder (vertical axis, High to Low)

Low   **Impact on stakeholder**   **High**

Key
- Green = **Advocate**
- Amber = **Neutral**
- Red = **Blocker**

Stakeholder Onion Diagram

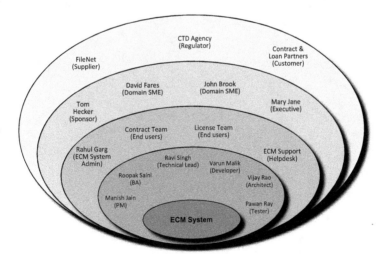

RACI Matrix

Activity / Role	Business Sponsor	Project Manager	Business Analyst	Domain SME	Technical Architect	Technical Lead	Usability Engineer	Database Engineer	Java Engineer	Quality Analyst
Create requirements estimates		A	R	C						
Create design estimates		A			R	C				
Create development estimates		A	C		C	R	C	C	C	
Create QA estimates		A	C							R
Create Project Plan	I	R/A	C			C				
Elicit and document requirements		A	R	C						
Build solution design		A	C		R					
Build solution (UI)		A	C		C	I	R			
Build solution (Database)		A	C		C	I		R		
Build solution (Middleware)		A	C		C	I			R	
Manage overall solution development & integration		A	C		C	R	C	C	C	
Test solution		A	C							R

Key: **R = Responsible**   **A = Accountable**   **C = Consulted**   **I = Informed**

State Modelling

Purpose

State Modelling is a modelling technique used to analyze and illustrate a set of possible states for an entity, its transition from one state to another, and what can happen to an entity in each state.

It is a highly beneficial technique that provides a specific and consistent understanding of an entity that has multiple states and diverse complex business rules associated with it.

Description

- An entity is an object or concept within a system that may be used in several processes and its life cycle has a beginning and an end.
- A state is nothing but a formal representation of the status of an entity.
- State Model or State Transition Model analyses and describes the following –
  o Different possible states of an entity within the system
  o Sequence of states for that entity
  o Transition of an entity from one state to another which may be automatic or conditional
  o Actions that can or must be performed by the entity in each state
- It is dissimilar from a process model in the sense that a process model depicts all the entities that are used in or affected by the process whereas the state model describes states, transitions, and activities pertaining to a single entity across all processes that use it or affect it.

Elements

- State
  o An entity has a finite number of states during its life cycle which may be simple or complex. The complex state may be further decomposed into simple sub-states.
  o Each state has a name and the activities that could be performed in that state which are governed by rules.
  o An entity can be in more than one state at a time.
- State Transition
  o A transition of an entity from one state to another is described in terms of the events and conditions that causes the transition. The events and conditions relate to business processes, business rules, or information content.
  o A transition could be conditional, automatic, recursive, and non-linear in nature.
- State Diagram
  o State diagram represents the entire life cycle of an entity from beginning to end.
  o A state is shown as a rectangle with rounded corners with complex states decomposed into sub-states if required.
  o State transition of an entity is shown with a one-directional arrow pointing from source state to the destination state. It may optionally include an event name that causes the state transition along with conditions and actions.
  o Initial State (indicating the entity's origination) and final state (indicating the end of entity life cycle or that it is discarded) are shown with special circular symbols.
- State Table
  o A two-dimensional matrix showing states and the transitions between them where each row shows a starting state, the transition, and the end state.

    ○ Can be utilized as a predecessor to a state diagram as it provides an easy means to elicit the state names and event names from the domain SMEs. Also, it can be used as an alternative or a complement to a state diagram.

Usage Considerations

Strengths

- Helps identify business rules, information attributes, and activities that apply to the entity.
- Effective tool in documenting and communicating different states and their transitions of various entities in a system.

Limitations

- Used only to analyze, document, and communicate states & transitions of entities perceived to be complex.
- Reaching a shared agreement among domain SMEs on details to be captured in the state model may be cumbersome.
- Generally, a high degree of precision is required to build a state model.

A business analyst has been assigned to work on a one-stop internal company portal for an organization that is setting up bases in multiple geographies. The portal will allow its employees to perform key activities like filling timesheets, applying for leaves, raise tickets for IT issues, and go through all company policies.

In relation to company policies, major regulatory policies have been defined but there are quite a few operations specific policies yet to be created. The policy document goes through multiple states from creation to closure and hence the business analyst decides to depict the multiple states and transitions from one state to another by means of a state diagram. This will enable all relevant parties to be on the same page with respect to all possible states that document can be in, the correct sequence of states, and the events which move a document from one state to another.

Below is the state diagram created by the business analyst:

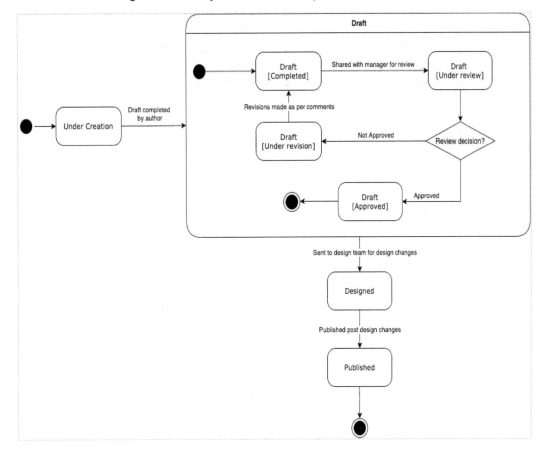

Survey or Questionnaire

Purpose

Survey or Questionnaire is an effective elicitation method to obtain information specific to customers, products, processes, and attitudes. It is a very useful technique when information needs to be gathered from a large group of people who are geographically dispersed in a short period of time.

Description

- Survey or Questionnaire includes preparing a set of questions on the subject matter, sharing it with the relevant stakeholders, collecting their responses, and analyzing in order to develop knowledge on the subject matter.
- Questions can be dispensed in a written form, over the telephone, in person, or through the use of a software that can record the responses.
- Questions should be formulated in a neutral manner and should not influence the stakeholders' response in any manner.
- Survey or Questionnaire includes two types of questions –
  - Close-ended
    - User responses are predefined such as a Yes/No response, a multiple-choice selection, a rank/ order decision, or a statement requiring a level of agreement.
    - Responses are easier to analyze since they can be tied to numerical coefficients.
  - Open-ended
    - User responses are in free-form and more detailed & wider as compared to responses to close-ended questions.
    - Responses are cumbersome to analyze as they are unstructured and in subjective language with incomplete or unnecessary content.

Elements

- Prepare
  - Define the Objective – Establish a clear and specific objective and formulating questions in line with it.
  - Define the target survey group – Identify the target group to be surveyed, its size, and any perceived variations.
  - Choose the appropriate survey or questionnaire type – Determine the right combination of open-ended & close-ended questions to elicit the required information.
  - Select the sample group – If the population is large, select a sample group that is representative of the population so that the survey results can be reliably generalized.
  - Select the distribution and collection methods – Determine the apt communication mode for collecting responses.
  - Set the target level and timeline for a response – Determine the acceptable response rate and timelines for accepting responses.
  - Determine if the survey or questionnaire should be supported with individual interviews – Consider conducting pre- or post-survey or questionnaire interviews if a survey or questionnaire is not intended to provide the depth of information needed.
  - Write the survey questions – Create the survey questions in line with the objective.
  - Test the survey or questionnaire – Perform a usability test to identify errors or scope for improvement
- Distribute the Survey or Questionnaire

- o Communicate the survey's objectives, usage of responses, as well as any confidentiality aspects.
- o Distribution method selection involves factors such as the urgency of obtaining the results, level of security required, and geographic distribution of the respondents.
- Document the Results
  - o Documenting the results include collating & summarizing responses, identifying any emerging themes, devising categories for encoding data, breaking down the data into measurable parts.

Usage Considerations

Strengths

- A quick, simple, and inexpensive elicitation technique.
- Effective method to collect information from large and geographically dispersed stakeholders.
- Surveys using close-ended questions can be effective in gathering quantitative data for statistical analysis.
- Surveys using open-ended questions can be effective in generating insights and opinions in which other elicitation techniques may not turn out to be effective.

Limitations

- Specialized skills in statistical sampling methods are needed when surveying a sample of potential respondents.
- In some cases, the response rate may be too low to be considered statistically significant.
- Responses to open-ended questions need more time to be analyzed.
- Ambiguous questions may be left unanswered or answered incorrectly.
- May not yield the desired outcomes in one go and more follow-up questions or additional surveys may be required.

Real Life Examples

Example 1

An enterprise analyst working with a retail organization is trying to understand the employees' views on the current Customer Relationship Management (CRM) product in use to analyze the issues with it. He decides to conduct a survey considering the users are across the globe and creates a questionnaire of open-ended questions. Below is a snippet of it –

- > How often do you use the ABC CRM product?
- > What tasks do you accomplish by using the product?
- > Which essential features do you use the most?
- > Which key features do you think are missing?
- > How easy is it to use the product?
- > How could the product be improved to better meet your needs?

Example 2

A business analyst is working for an Enterprise Resource Planning (ERP) product company that has recently implemented the ERP product in the environment of a global retail enterprise. In order to measure solution performance, the business analyst creates a questionnaire of close-ended questions to be distributed to the required stakeholders. Below is a snippet of it –

> Are you comfortable to rely on the system information?
> Are you getting up-to-date information from the System?
> Are you getting the required information instantly from the System?
> Does the ERP system aid your decision-making process?
> Are you getting good ERP Technical Support?
> Does the ERP System provide assist in easy decision making?
> Has the ERP system assisted in streamlining your business processes?
> Is the ERP system easy and convenient to use?

SWOT Analysis

Purpose

SWOT Analysis is an effective technique to assess the overall state of an organization in terms of its strengths, weaknesses, opportunities, and threats both internally and externally. SWOT analysis can be carried out to serve the below purposes –

- Assess an organization's current state
- Identify the best options to meet an organization's needs
- Identify potential threats and devise plans to overcome them
- Redefine plans as new needs arise
- Develop criteria for evaluating the success
- Identify strengths to assist in implementing new strategies
- Identify weaknesses that could hinder goals accomplishment
- Develop strategies to deal with threats

Description

- SWOT analysis is defined in a brief, specific & realistic manner and is supported by evidence.
- It can be carried out on a wide-ranging scale ranging from an enterprise as a whole to a division, a business unit, a project, or an individual.
- It provides a clear understanding of the impact of an existing set of conditions on a future set of conditions.
- Beginning SWOT analysis with opportunities and threats sets the context to identify strengths and weaknesses.

Elements

- SWOT stands for Strengths (S), Weaknesses (W), Opportunities (O), and Threats (T) –
  - Strengths (S) – Corresponds to internal factors like experienced personnel, effective processes, IT systems, customer relationships that lead to success.
  - Weaknesses (W) – Pertains to internal factors that perform poorly and likely to lead to failure.
  - Opportunities (O) – External factors including (but not limited to) new markets, new technology, changes in the competitive marketplace that the organization may be able to take advantage of.
  - Threats (T) – External factors including (but not limited to) new competitor, economic downturns that may negatively affect the organization.
- Different strategies can be formulated based on the analysis that answers the below questions –
  - Strengths Opportunities (SO) Strategies
    - How can the strengths be used to make use of potential opportunities?
  - Weaknesses Opportunities (WO) Strategies
    - Can an opportunity be used to eliminate or mitigate a weakness?
    - Does the opportunity to warrant the development of new capabilities?
  - Strengths Threats (ST) Strategies
    - How can strengths be used to avert potential threats?
    - Can the threats be converted into opportunities?
  - Weaknesses Threats (WT) Strategies
    - Can the organization restructure itself to avoid the threat?

- Should the organization consider getting out of this market?

Usage Considerations

Strengths

- Assists in understanding the organization, product, process, or stakeholders.
- Identify critical factors and direct stakeholders' attention to them.

Limitations

- Provides a high-level picture and more detailed analysis is needed in most cases.
- Results may be irrelevant in the absence of a clear context.

Real Life Example

A business analyst is assigned to carry out a SWOT analysis for an e-commerce company because of decreasing sales over the past couple of years. Below is the snippet of the analysis outcome in the form of SWOT Analysis Matrix:

INTERNAL FACTORS STRENGTHS (+)		INTERNAL FACTORS WEAKNESSES (-)	
1	Dominant brand name	1	Ineffective inventory management
2	Strong geographical reach	2	Poor marketing and sales team
3	Effective and widespread distribution channels	3	Mediocre customer service
4	Loyal customer base	4	High cost structure
5	Efficient corporate culture	5	Lack of strong partnerships with retailers

INTERNAL FACTORS OPPORTUNITIES (+)		INTERNAL FACTORS THREATS (-)	
1	New technological innovations related to user experience	1	Strong brand name of competitors
2	Emerging untapped and niche markets	2	Strict laws or regulations in the industry
3	Elimination of international trade barriers	3	Entrance of new competitors on regular basis
4	Merger, joint venture, or strategic alliance to enhance product base	4	Fraudulent activities on web and mobile applications
5	Customer desire for a one-stop shop	5	Ever changing customer needs

Use Cases and Scenarios

Purpose

Use cases and scenarios describe how a person or system interacts with the solution to accomplish a business goal. A scenario describes just one way that an actor can accomplish a particular goal whereas a use case is a combination of multiple scenarios.

Use case diagrams provide a high-level view of the functionalities of a system and facilitates clarification of scope release-wise or for the project. Use case descriptions express the functional requirements and act as significant constituents of functional specification documents.

Description

- Use cases are devised from an actor's perspective and are not intended to describe the internal workings of the solution.
- Use cases describe the interactions between a system and entities external to the system known as actors. An actor may be primary (whose goal is fulfilled by the system) or secondary (who generally provides a service or information to the system). An actor is not necessarily a human user but can also be a software application, hardware, or clock/timer.
- Use cases define primary, alternative and exception flow. The primary flow represents the most basic way to accomplish the goal of the use case. An alternative flow describes a scenario other than the basic flow that results in a user completing the goal of the use case. Exceptions that result in a failure to complete the goal of the use case are expressed as exception flows.
- Use cases may also be classified as business use cases (describe interactions between an actor and process or business function) and system use cases (describe interactions between an actor and a software application).

Elements

Typically, a use case comprises of below constituents –

- Use case diagram – It visually depicts the scope of the solution through the below elements –
  - Actors who interact with the solution.
  - Use cases or functional components of the solution that an actor interacts with.
  - Relationships
    - Relationships between the actors and use cases – Relationships or associations between actors and use cases indicate that an actor has access to the functionality represented by the use case.
    - Relationships between the use cases – Commonly used relationships are –
      - > Extend – Extends the functionality of a use case and is functionally independent of use case it is extending. May be used to show an alternate flow for an existing use case.
      - > Include – Enables usage of the functionality of another use case which may or may not be complete. May be used when a common functionality is required by multiple use cases or to separate out a complex chunk of logic.
- Use case description – It contains the below major components –
  - Name – Each use case has a unique name that commonly includes action taken by the actor and either what is being done or the target of the action.
  - Goal – Summary of the use case that describes its successful result from the primary actor's perspective.

- o Actors – An actor is an entity (human/software system/hardware/timer) external to the system that interacts with the solution. Name of the actor is the role that they play in the solution. Generally, a primary actor starts the use case while a secondary actor plays a supporting role.
- o Pre-conditions – Refers to the fact(s) that must hold true for the use case to begin and is essentially a constraint.
- o Trigger – An event that kicks off the flow of a use case. Common triggers include an action taken by the primary actor or a time-based event.
- o Flow of events – Set of steps carried out by an actor and solution during use case execution. Primary flow is the simplest path to accomplish the actor's goal. Alternative flows describe other paths that can be followed to achieve the same goal. Exception flows describes the solution's response when a goal cannot be achieved.
- o Post-conditions or Guarantees – Refers to the fact(s) that must be true when the use case gets completed. Separate postconditions may exist for successful and unsuccessful execution of a use case which are referred to as "guarantees". Success guarantee describes the post conditions for a successful use case execution while minimal guarantee describes the postconditions for an unsuccessful use case execution.

Usage Considerations

Strengths

- Useful method for clarifying scope.
- Simple and hence understood by stakeholders with no trouble whatsoever.
- Expresses the functional behaviour or high-level functional requirements of the system.
- Business value in terms of desired goal is captured and articulated.

Limitations

- Flexibility of the use case format may result in information being portrayed that would have been elicited and captured better through other techniques. It may also result in capturing unnecessary details.
- Decisions and business rules need to be recorded & managed separately.
- Substantial effort required to map use case steps to solution design.

A business analyst has been assigned to work on writing functional requirements for a blogging module of an online learning management system. The objective is to generate relevant content thereby enabling social media promotion to drive search traffic to the website. This will increase the likelihood of generating leads by means of course enrolment.

He decides to model the desired behaviour of a solution by showing user interactions with the solution through use case diagrams and create thorough descriptions to complement the diagrams.

Below is the use case diagram of the blogging module and description of a use case –

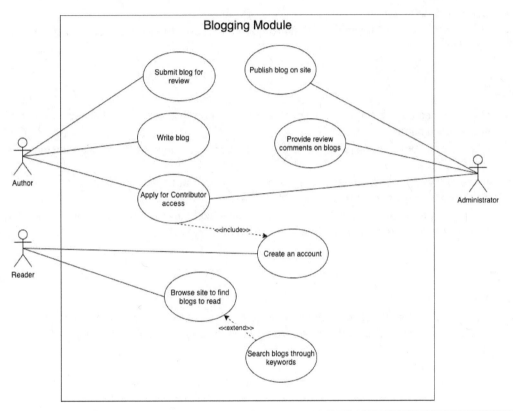

Name	Apply for Contributor Access
Goal	An author requests for a contributor access from Administrator to be able to write blogs
Actors	Author (Primary Actor), Administrator (Secondary Actor)
Pre-conditions	Author applying for contributor access already has an account created with the website
Trigger	Author accesses the contributor access form
Primary Flow	1. Author open the contributor access form.
	2. He/she fills the required details like educational qualifications, primary skills, professional experience.
	3. He/she then selects the relevant subject area(s) to write blogs on.
	4. He/she gives consent to the clauses on payment and plagiarism.
	5. He/she submits the form to send it to the Administrator.
Post-conditions	Administrator Is able to view the contributor access request submitted by the author

User Stories

Purpose

A user story is a concise statement of functionality or quality created for fulfilling one or more of the below objectives –

- Captures stakeholder's needs and prioritizing implementation to generate maximum value.
- Provides a means for estimation, delivery planning, project management, and status reporting.
- Enables generation of user acceptance tests/scenarios for validating the desired implementation of functionalities.
- Used as a metric for measuring the delivery of value.
- Used as a basis for tracing additional requirements and to carry out additional analysis as required.

Description

- User story creates a simplified description of features of value to stakeholders in a short and simple document.
- It is created from the perspective of the stakeholder who wants a feature to be implemented to achieve a goal.
- A user story captures the user who has a need, desired feature, or behaviour that the user wants and benefit or value that the user expects to derive.
- User story promotes additional conversations with stakeholders for refining requirements further and also helps to group the requirements from a delivery perspective.

Elements

- Title
  - In general, it is an optional element that is described as an active-verb goal phrase.
  - Expressed as an activity the stakeholder wants to carry out with the system.
- Statement of Value
  - No mandatory format exists for a user story.
  - Most widely used format is "As a <who>, I need to <what>, so that <why>." where –
    - "who" is a user role or persona
    - "what" is a necessary action, behaviour, feature, or quality
    - "why" is a value that the user expects to achieve
- Conversation
  - User story helps teams explore and understand the feature that it describes and the perceived business value.
  - User story's content is further augmented by teams as more conversations take place and clarity is obtained.
- Acceptance Criteria
  - Define the boundaries of a user story and helps the team understand what the solution needs to provide to deliver value for the stakeholders.
  - Acceptance criteria may be supplemented with other analysis models as needed.

Usage Considerations

Strengths

- Simple and easy to understand.
- Focuses on providing values to stakeholders.
- An array of techniques can be used to create user stories.
- Collaboration on defining and elaborating user stories enhances the domain knowledge of the participating stakeholders.
- Facilitates rapid delivery and frequent customer feedback.

Limitations

- Not an ideal tool for long-term knowledge retention and doesn't provide detailed analysis.
- Teams can be challenged as they do not have detailed specifications.
- Can lose sight of the big picture if stories are not traced back.
- Since the user story is a short and not detailed document, it may not meet the governance needs or act as a baseline for future work.

Real Life Example

A business analyst has been assigned to work on a project to create an online grocery mobile application that will be executed using an adaptive approach. Business Analyst and Product Owners have discussed the key features that constitute the minimum viable product and are in the process of creating user stories to add in the product backlog. Below are a few examples of user stories for the Online grocery mobile application –

> As a first-time visitor, I want to register on the application using my mobile number and password so that I can browse and purchase products.

> As a registered shopper, I can add one or more addresses into my account so that I can get the desired products delivered at the chosen address.

> As a registered shopper, I want to view the different categories of products so that I can select the right category to purchase the desired product.

> As a registered shopper, I should be able to search the products so that I do not have to browse through products and select the desired product easily.

Vendor Assessment

Purpose

Vendor Assessment is a technique to evaluate a potential vendor's ability to meet commitments with respect to the delivery and maintenance of a product or service. It is conducted to ensure that the vendor is reliable, and its product/service fulfils the organization's requirements.

Description

- Vendors need to fulfil certain requirements to be considered/selected for providing the partial/complete solution or become an outsourcing partner. These include (but not limited to) –
  - Financial security of the vendor
  - Capability to maintain specific staffing levels
  - Compliance with required standards
  - Commitment to provide skilled staff to support solution
- Level of formality of vendor assessment is determined based on organizational standards, complexity, and criticality of the initiative or solution. Different formality levels include –
  - Formal through the submission of a Request for Information (RFI), Request for Quote (RFQ), Request for Tender (RFT), or Request for Proposal (RFP).
  - Informal through word of mouth and recommendations.

Elements

- Knowledge and Expertise
  - Vendors and supply Knowledge and Expertise not available with the organization.
  - Desirable to vendors that have the goal of transferring their expertise in methodologies or technologies.
- Licensing and Pricing Models
  - Solutions purchased from or outsourced to a vendor will have licensing or pricing considerations.
  - Since different solutions offering the same functionality may have different licensing models and hence cost-benefit analysis should be carried out to select the best solution option.
- Vendor Market Position
  - Dynamics of vendor's market position need to be evaluated ahead of a long-term partnership.
  - Compare each potential vendor with the competitors to make the best choice.
- Terms and Conditions
  - Terms and conditions pertain to the continuity and integrity of the provided products and services.
  - Below are the important considerations regarding terms and conditions –
    - Challenges in transitioning to any other vendor if needed.
    - Usage and responsibility for protecting the organization's confidential data.
    - Implementation of product customization and availability delivery and regular updates schedules.
- Vendor Experience, Reputation, and Stability
  - Vendors' experience and reputation in terms of meeting contractual & non-contractual obligations and conformance to quality & security standards provide valuable information and facilitate vendor selection.
  - May be necessary to request that it is ensured that the solution will be maintained and enhanced (as required) even if the vendor faces financial difficulties.

Usage Considerations

Strengths

- Reduce the risk of selecting a dependable vendor.
- Enables the creation of a productive and long-term satisfying relationship with the vendor.

Limitations

- Assessing vendors may consume considerable time and effort.
- Does not safeguard against failure as the partnership evolves.
- Evaluation may be biased in some cases.

An enterprise analyst carried out a strategic analysis to solve a business problem and the ultimate decision is to purchase a Commercial-off-the-shelf Project Portfolio Management (PPM) product. After a discussion between the key stakeholders, it was decided that the three best most prominent vendors in the market will be assessed for making the final choice.

The organization plans to float a Request for Proposal (RFP) to the three potential vendors. Once the responses are obtained, the Business Analyst uses a Vendor Assessment scorecard to evaluate the vendors using predefined criteria and a weighted ranking table formulated in consensus with business stakeholders.

As shown below, the scores are given to each criterion based on the response from vendors, and Vendor 2 is chosen based on the best-weighted score among the three vendors.

Vendor Assessment Scorecard				
Scores available from 1 - 5. Basis for scoring must be listed with specific examples.				
1. Adherence to RFP instructions	VENDOR 1	VENDOR 2	VENDOR 3	BASIS FOR SCORE
Timeliness	5	5	5	Arrived by deadline receives all points
Completeness	5	3	2	Completed sections in same order as RFP receives all points
Overall quality & level of Professionalism	2	4	3	Technically compliant & attractive receives all points
Overall Response	5	4	3	Overall qualify very high receives all points
Average Score	4	4	3	
2. Company Information	VENDOR 1	VENDOR 2	VENDOR 3	BASIS FOR SCORE
Financial Stability	5	5	5	Proof of financial stability receives all points
Experience with Similar Companies	2	4	3	Proof of experience with similar companies & initiatives receives all points
Reputation	5	4	3	Positive reputation in the market receives all points
Market Position	2	5	3	High comparative position wrt competitors receives all points
Partnerships	5	4	3	Proven external partnerships receives all points
Average Score	4	4	3	
3. Projects & Requirements Understanding	VENDOR 1	VENDOR 2	VENDOR 3	BASIS FOR SCORE
Overall Comprehension of Project Objectives	5	5	5	Comprehensive & clear elaboration receives all points
Understanding of the Business Requirements	5	3	2	Comprehensive & clear elaboration receives all points
Understanding of the Business Vision	2	4	3	Comprehensive & clear elaboration receives all points
Completeness of Vendor Response	5	5	5	Comprehensive & clear elaboration receives all points
Vendor Ability to Meet Requirements	1	5	4	Comprehensive & clear elaboration receives all points
Average Score	4	4	4	
4. Terms and Conditions	VENDOR 1	VENDOR 2	VENDOR 3	BASIS FOR SCORE
Product Continuity	5	5	5	Most suitable terms of continuity of the provided products & services receives best points
Data Confidentiality	1	5	4	Most suitable terms of data confidentiality receive best points
Product Roadmap	2	4	3	Most detailed roadmap for future product receives best points

	VENDOR 1	VENDOR 2	VENDOR 3	
Product Development Life-Cycle	2	4	3	Most detailed & suitable life-cycle for product updates receives best points
New Release Process	5	4	3	Most comprehensive new release process receives best points
Average Score	**3**	**4**	**4**	**Average Score**
5. Licensing & Pricing Summary	**VENDOR 1**	**VENDOR 2**	**VENDOR 3**	**BASIS FOR SCORE**
License Fees	4	5	5	Most suitable fees (Compared with benefits) per organization's expectations receives best points
Maintenance Fees	1	5	4	Most suitable fees (Compared with benefits) per organization's expectations receives best points
Purchase Timeline	2	4	3	Most appropriate purchasing timeline per organization's goals receives best points
Licensing Period	5	4	3	Most appropriate licensing period per organization's goals receives best points
Other Fees	3	5	3	Most suitable fees (Compared with benefits) per organization's expectations receives best points
Average Score	**3**	**5**	**4**	

*Change weights based on company requirements. Total Score should = 1.00

CRITERIA SCORES	WEIGHT	VENDOR 1 WEIGHTED SCORE	VENDOR 2 WEIGHTED SCORE	VENDOR 3 WEIGHTED SCORE
1. Adherence to RFP Instructions	0.15	0.64	0.60	0.49
2. Company Information	0.15	0.57	0.66	0.51
3. Project and Requirements Understanding	0.20	0.72	0.88	0.76
4. Terms & Conditions	0.20	0.60	0.88	0.72
5. Licensing and Pricing Summary	0.30	0.90	1.38	1.08
Total Score	**1.00**	**3.43**	**4.40**	**3.56**

Workshops

Purpose

Workshop is a technique in which stakeholders collaborate for a set period of time to achieve a pre-determined goal. It is used to serve a wide variety of purposes such as planning, analysis, design, scoping, requirements elicitation, modelling, generate ideas for new features or products, reaching consensus on a topic, or to review requirements or designs.

Description

- Workshops typically include a representative stakeholder group, a defined goal, collaborative work, a defined work product, and a facilitator.
- It fosters trust, understanding, and strong collaboration among the stakeholders.
- Workshop is preferably facilitated by a skilled & neutral third-party facilitator or even a team member.
- A scribe may also be appointed to record the decisions and outstanding issues.
- A business analyst may perform the role of a facilitator, scribe, or participant in the workshops and there should be complete clarity on his/her role.

Elements

- Prepare for the Workshop – The activities carried out by business analyst in preparing for the workshop include defining the purpose, identifying participants as well as scribe & facilitator, creating & sending across the agenda, identifying methods to capture outputs, scheduling session & sending invites, arranging the required logistics and conduct pre-workshop interviews if required.
- Workshop Roles – Stakeholders who participate in workshop play one of below roles –
  - Sponsor – Not a regular participant in the workshop but accountable for its output.
  - Facilitator
    - Set up a professional ambiance so that the session is carried out formally.
    - Introduces the purpose, desired outcomes, and agenda of the session.
    - Establishes and put the ground rules in force.
    - Ensures that activities are carried out in a purposeful manner.
    - Facilitates conflict resolution and decision making.
    - Ensures all participants get a chance to participate and present their views.
  - Scribe
    - Documents the decisions taken in the workshop in an approved format.
    - Track any items or issues deferred in the session.
  - Timekeeper – Responsible to keep track of time spent on each agenda item.
  - Participants
    - Include key stakeholders and subject matter experts.
    - Provides their views and listens to the views of other participants.
    - Discuss the issues without bias.
- Conduct the Workshop – Workshop is conducted in a focused manner in accordance with ground rules like respecting each other's opinions, contributing without fail, limiting discussion on an off-topic, discussing issues & not people, and reaching consensus on decision making. The facilitator ensures that ground rules are followed, and activities carried out are aligned with purpose and desired outcome.

- Post Workshop Wrap-up – After the workshop session is over, the facilitator follows up on any open/deferred items, completes and distributes the document to all participants, and relevant stakeholders.

Usage Considerations

Strengths

- Facilitates in achieving quick agreement.
- Fosters collaboration, decision making, and developing shared understanding.
- Less costly as compared to carrying out multiple interviews.
- Quick feedback on issues and decisions.

Limitations

- Availability of all required stakeholders at the same time may be challenging.
- Highly dependent on the facilitator's expertise and participants' knowledge.
- Difficult to arrive at the right mix of participants for the workshop.

Real Life Example

A business analyst has been assigned to work on eliciting requirements for creating a mobile application. The objective is to present key analytics for all businesses of an Insurance company to the critical decision-makers.

In order to elicit requirements for the mobile application, business analysts decide to conduct a requirements workshop in which subject matter experts from all businesses of an insurance company like General insurance, home insurance, automobile insurance, health insurance, travel insurance, property and casualty insurance will join to bring in expertise from their respective areas. Also, the participation invite is extended to the Mobile UI/UX experts and Middleware (Interface) team from the insurance company to take key decisions on the UI/UX and APIs to be used for providing required data, respectively.

Business Analyst conducts the workshop with the representative stakeholder group in the presence of a facilitator. Key decisions on the functional, usability and API requirements are taken with shared understanding in a collaborative environment thereby ensuring that expertise of all stakeholders is utilized, and their needs are addressed.

Glossary

- **Backlog:** The backlog is used to record, track, and prioritize remaining work items.
- **Backlog Refinement:** A Periodic review of the entire backlog should occur because changes in stakeholder needs and priorities may necessitate changes to the priority of some of the backlog items. In many environments, the backlog is reviewed at planned intervals.
- **An Organizational unit (OU):** Any recognized association of people within an organization or enterprise.
- **Scope modelling:** Scope model is used to describe the scope of the analysis or scope of the solution. It allows the definition of "complete" scope, containing the boundaries of a business domain.
- **Request for information (RFI):** An RFI is typically the first and most broadly cast of a series of requests intended to narrow down a list of candidates.
- **Request for quotation (RFQ):** An RFQ is generally used to obtain pricing, delivery information, terms, and conditions from suppliers. In this case, requestors have a clear understanding of what they need, including requirements and specifications.
- **RFP:** An RFP, "Request for Proposal," is a document that asks vendors to propose solutions to a customer's problems or business requirements. An RFP is usually what follows an RFI; in fact, it's rare that a company will go from an RFI to an RFQ (for reasons that will become clear below). An RFP should contain much more specificity in terms of what a company's needs are by outlining the business goals for the project and identifying specific requirements that are necessary for the work being requested.
- **Subject Matter expert:** A subject-matter expert or domain expert is a person who is an authority in a particular area or topic. The term domain expert is frequently used in expert systems software development.
- **RACI Matrix:** Responsible, Accountable, Consulted, and Informed matrix (RACI matrix): A tool used to identify the responsibilities of roles or team members and the stakeholders.
- **Decision Analysis:** An approach to decision making that examines and models the possible consequences of different decisions and assists in making an optimal decision under conditions of uncertainty.
- **SIPOC:** A SIPOC diagram is a tool used by a team to identify all relevant elements of a process improvement project before the work begins. It helps define a complex project that may not be well scoped and is typically employed at the Measure phase of the Six Sigma DMAIC (Define, Measure, Analyze, Improve, Control) methodology.
- **Rough Order of Magnitude (ROM):** Almost always, the project manager begins by determining a rough order of magnitude (ROM) estimate, which is just what the name sounds like. This estimate gives a "ballpark," or order of magnitude, for the project.
- **Discount Rate:** In practical application, the discount rate can be a useful tool for investors to determine the potential value of certain businesses and investments who have an expected cash flow in the future.
- **Metric:** Quantifiable level of an indicator that an organization uses to measure progress.
- **Benchmarking:** Benchmarking is a process of measuring the performance of a company's products, services, or processes against those of another business considered to be the best in the industry, aka "best in class." The point of benchmarking is to identify internal opportunities for improvement.
- **Feasibility:** A feasibility study is an analysis that takes all the project's relevant factors into account including economic, technical, legal, and scheduling considerations to ascertain the likelihood of completing the project successfully.
- **Revenue Streams:** Revenue Streams are the various sources from which a business earns money from the sale of goods or the provision of services. The types of revenue that business records on its accounts depend on the types of activities carried out by the business.
- **Customer Segment:** Groups of customers based on common characteristics.
- **Customer Segmentation:** Process of dividing customers into groups based on common characteristics.

- **Value proposition:** A value proposition refers to the value, a company promises to deliver to its customers to make them buy their product.
- **Vendor:** A vendor, also known as a supplier, is a person or a business entity that sells something. Large retail store chains such as Target, for example, generally have a list of vendors from which they purchase goods at wholesale prices that they then sell at retail prices to their customers.

Case Study 1

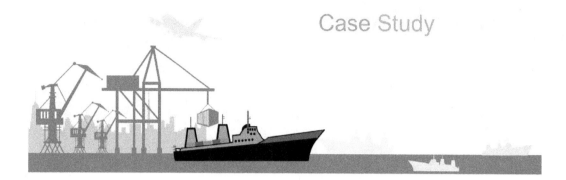

Case Study

Musteek corporation is a multinational company that deals with multiple products. They import and export these products and have a presence in more than 30 countries and 150 locations.

Managing the products and many transactions having international trade nuisances is becoming extremely difficult for the company.

The board of directors has given approval for an end to end process and operations automation. They have finalized Numen's infotech limited after due diligence.

Numens Infotech has formed a project team led by Mark Rossen as a project manager. Rohit Veer is the business analyst of the team. Both travel to the Musteek headquarters for meeting the customer representatives for the requirements gathering and analysis.

Rohit and Mark have identified the stakeholders as follows:

- Customer Project co-ordinator: Robert
- Head of finance: Samantha
- Technical Consultant: Jacob
- Risk Consultant: Ramesh Rowen
- Lead Tester: Narayan
- Service Manager: Martin
- Project Sponsor: Kent Brentwood
- UX lead: Sreenivas
- Functional SME: Shreyas
- Development Team head: Naresh
- Data entry team head: Johnson

Rohit has created the following stakeholder map. Not all stakeholders are shown on the map.

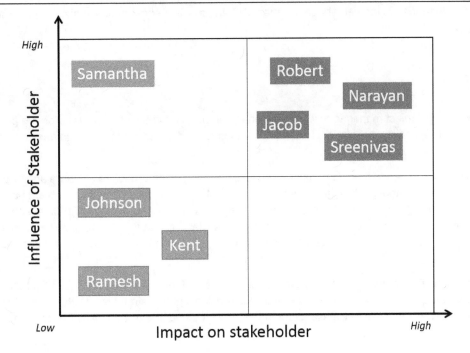

The estimated calendar months was 12 months. Unfortunately, the project ran into serious cost overruns and all the estimates had to be revised. Finally, the project was completed in 18 calendar months.

Case Study 1 Questions

Q1. Rohit has not put himself and Mark on the map. If you are asked to put them on this stakeholder map, where will you put them?

A) High impact, high influence
B) Low impact, low influence
C) High impact, low influence
D) Low impact, high influence

Q2. The project ran into serious cost overruns. Is there any issue with the stakeholder map, which might have contributed to the cost overrun?

A) Yes, the Project sponsor Kent is being shown in the low impact, low influence quadrant
B) The data entry team lead is being shown in the low impact, low influence quadrant
C) The Head of finance, Samantha is being shown in the low impact, high influence quadrant
D) Nothing is wrong on this stakeholder map

Q3. If the reasons for project cost overrun is related to poor risk mitigation strategies, what changes should be made in the stakeholder map to help focus on salvaging the project?

A) No changes required to be made on the map
B) The project sponsor should be moved to high influence and low impact quadrant showing his changed position
C) Ramesh should be moved from low impact to high impact category showing his changed position

TECHCANVASS

D) The lead tester Narayan should be moved to the low influence quadrant showing his changed position

Answers:

Q1 - Answer A: Project manager as well as business analysts have a major influence on the project as they lead the project from the vendor side. Also, the success and failure of the project impact them greatly as they are working on a single project.

Q2- Answer B: Data entry team lead uses a significant portion of the proposed software application and Johnson has been marked in low influence and low impact. This means that he and his team have every chance of not being included in the project requirements. This is because this group of stakeholders is only monitored and doesn't get involved. This can easily lead to gaps in the requirements or missed requirements and could be the reason for cost overrun (lots of defects cropping up during UAT by Johnson and his team)

Q3- Answer C: Ramesh was least affected by the outcome of the project as per the initial stakeholder mapping and that might have been a factor in the poor risk mitigation strategies. With changed position, Ramesh is now, rightly so, a key stakeholder in better risk management. So, this is the best answer.

Case Study 2

Ariva professional services is a top 20 resource management and recruitment firm in Australia. The company was set up almost 20 years back. The management believes in structured processes and methodologies.

In the last 5 years, the company has acquired multiple companies to grow inorganically. Acquisition of external companies leads to the need for merging processes of these companies. Despite the best of the efforts, the merger has not been smooth as the integration of processes is not yet completed. Employees of acquired companies and Ariva are using multiple processes and methodologies. This means that multiple versions of records are being maintained resulting in duplicate records for Ariva. The board of directors is fully aware of this.

A management firm XYZ has been hired to review the current situation and suggest an approach and a roadmap to unify the processes and methodologies across the organization.

Case Study 2 Questions

Q1. XYZ has suggested to create a central repository for all the processes, methodologies, and policies. All the IT projects, being carried out in Ariva, have been asked to apply these in their projects so that organization has a unified set of policies, methodologies, and procedures.

How will the ongoing projects use this new dictate?

A. Risk

B. Assumption

C. Constraint

D. Business Objectives

Q2. The project for creating a repository and getting it implemented in all the projects was initiated and a project manager was assigned to it. The project manager used the PERT approach and did the three estimations as 6 days (optimistic) to 20 days (pessimistic), and most likely as 10 days. What is the PERT estimate for this project?

A. 12 days.

B. 11 days.

C. 10 days.

D. 9 days.

Case Study Answers:

Q1-Answer C: This becomes a constraint for each of the projects as projects have align with these. It is not a risk as following these processes is a necessity and certainty and hence not a risk. It's also not an assumption for the same reason as above. Of course, it is not a business objective as each of the projects will have already defined business objectives.

Q2-Answer B: The formula to calculate PERT estimate = (Optimistic Estimate + 4 X most likely estimate + Pessimistic estimate) / 6

Case Study 3

Introduction

Phell Private Limited (going forward referred to as Phell) is an oil trading company that operates in 134 cities across 56 countries globally. The company has an employee headcount of around 195K people and around 1600 employees are responsible for forecasting the demand for oil, which is the primary product for Phell as it contributes to 78% of Phell's global revenues. Majority of Phell's employees are involved in registering and meeting oil product demand and these settlements are driven over telephonic conversations and Phell has an in-house IT team of around 100 people in maintaining and development of in-house portals for the company. The in-house IT team does not have a workload of more than 2 hours a day as all their activities are automated and they have many people in the team with great programming skills.

Production array and details

Product	Annual Consumption (Million Barrels Per Day)	Wastage Due to Inappropriate Forecasting	Wastage Cost/Day
Finished Motor Gasonline1	8.3223	2.764%	$ 574,973.8
Distillate Fuel Oil (Diesel Fuel & Heating Oil) 1	2.4566	1.255%	$ 77,053.3
Kerosene Type Jet Fuel	1.6242	1.773%	$ 72,004.8
Hydrocarbon Gas Liquids (HGL)	1.5643	4.027%	$ 157,501.5
Still Gas	0.6677	2.078%	$ 34,688.7
Asphalt and Road Oil	0.3242	3.664%	$ 29,694.6
Waxes	0.30142	1.922%	$ 14,483.5
Special Napthas	0.28854	2.576%	$ 18,578.9
Petrochemical Feedstocks	0.27831	3.356%	$ 23,348.6
Residual Fuel Oil	0.25792	1.163%	$ 7,499.9
Miscellaneous Products and Others 2	0.22031	1.980%	$ 10,906.1
Lubricants	0.18286	3.751%	$ 17,149.5
Kerosene	0.181	2.078%	$ 9,403.1
Petroleum Coke	0.17363	2.104%	$ 9,134.4
Finished Aviation Gasoline	0.09531	2.506%	$ 5,970.1
Total	16.9386		$ 1,062, 390.7

As-Is forecasting

The 1600 forecasters communicate with the customers daily to understand the demands across the product portfolios and they have joint responsibilities of facilitating sales. The people hierarchy in the forecasting team generally follows the practice of 6 heads to one head reporting and has 6 employee Career levels as CL1, CL2, CL3, CL4, CL5, CL6. The current headcount distribution at the global level is:

Carrel Level	Headcount	Annual Salary Total/day	
CL1	1	$	783
CL2	7	$	4,273
CL3	40	$	17,582
CL4	220	$	67,691
CL5	1332	$	368,855
Total	1600	$	459,184

At the lowest career level, around 1300 forecasters note the demands across the product portfolio and predict the demands for the next 12 months. These predictions are done manually in spreadsheets and all communications are happening over emails and there is a lot of time getting invested estimating the most accurate demand as people are spread globally across time zones. The information needs to be reviewed at several career levels before publishing the final demand forecast and despite efficient forecasters, the CEO of the company is worried as Phell witnesses a $1 Million daily wastage cost. The forecasting team is unhappy with the work-life balance as they invest a lot of time in the forecasting activities and run into working even on weekends and although forecasting been the primary responsibility, they do have other key responsibility areas to meet for ensuring that the demands are met end-to-end. The forecasters also serve as POCs between the in-house sales team and the primary customer heads. At times Phell also loses repeat business if the forecaster fails to dedicate communication time to the customer team.

Problem statement

The company is undergoing a wastage loss of around 1 million dollars every day due to manual forecasting and is inefficiently investing around 459K dollars as a daily salary for the forecasting team. The goal of the project is to Minimize the daily wastage cost and increase the productivity of the forecasting team.

Problem Solving

Mathew is the CEO of Phell and he decides in collaboration with Phil, who is the forecasting head at Phell to hire Business Analysis Aces Limited (BAAL) for addressing the situation at hand. Phil will be accountable for all the commercials and Jack is the lead business analyst from BAAL working on this project

Expectations from BAAL

1. End-to-end automation of oil demand forecasting
2. Data dictionary
3. Reference data management process definition
4. Stakeholder Matrix
5. User Stories
6. Reporting module

BAAL Solution Blueprint

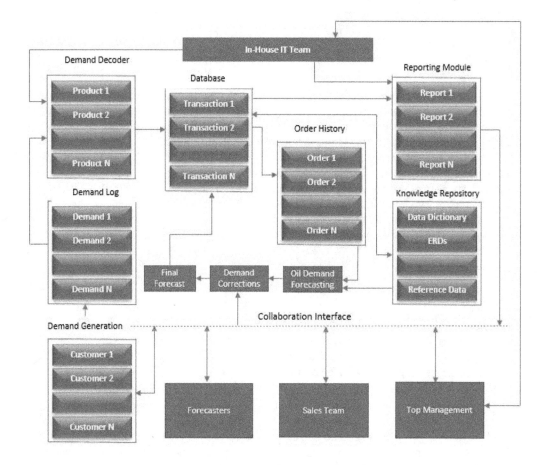

Case Study 3 Questions

Q1. As per the Gane-Sarson Notation and keeping the forecasting process as the central application, Demand Generation can be best described by which of the below-listed options?

    A. Input Data
    B. External Agent
    C. Data Source
    D. None of the above

Q2. Which of the below-listed technique is best suited for making reports for the Reporting module?

    A. Concept Modelling
    B. Data Flow Diagrams
    C. Data Modelling
    D. Data Mining

Q3. Which of the below-listed option is the best variation for the Database module?

    A. Strategic Data Model
    B. Conceptual Data Model
    C. Logical Data Model

D. Physical Data Model

Q4. Phil asked Jack to submit a report of expected solution benefits, costs of creating the solution, costs of operating the solution, and potential risk impact. Which technique will Jack use to make his report?

A. Estimation
B. Financial Analysis
C. SWOT Analysis
D. Risk Analysis and Management

Q5. With reference to the Sponsor definition in BABOK and information in the case study who is the Sponsor for BAAL? Select the best option.

A. Phil
B. Mathew
C. Both Phil and Mathew
D. Phell

Case Study 3 Answers

Q1-Answer: Option B. External Agent. The demands are generated by the customers. The demands they generate are indeed input data but the moment the focus becomes central to the forecasting process the Demand Generation module will be viewed upon as an External Agent.

Q2-Answer: Option D. Data Mining. Data mining is an analytic process that examines large amounts of data from different perspectives and summarizes the data in such a way that useful patterns and relationships are discovered. The Reporting Module is for Top Management.

A concept model is used to organize the business vocabulary needed to communicate the knowledge of a domain consistently and thoroughly. Data flow diagrams show where data comes from, which activities process the data, and if the output results are stored or utilized by another activity or external entity.

A data model describes the entities, classes, or data objects relevant to a domain, the attributes that are used to describe them, and the relationships among them to provide a common set of semantics for analysis and implementation.

Q3-Answer: Option D. Physical Data Model. Justification: This is a tricky question and someone who can answer this can be looked upon as a well-read BABOK individual.

One may argue that options B, C and, D are applicable, but the main point is in noting two things:
1. The best option
2. Keyword **the**, the moment this keyword is used before the actual name of a blueprint component, we land ourselves in the physical domain of the component which is in the solution.

Conceptual data model is independent of any solution or technology and can be used to represent how the business perceives its information. It can be used to help establish a consistent vocabulary describing business information and the relationships within that information.

Logical data model is an abstraction of the conceptual data model that incorporates rules of normalization to formally manage the integrity of the data and relationships. It is associated with the design of a solution.

Physical data model is used by implementation subject matter experts to describe how a database is physically organized. It addresses concerns like performance, concurrency, and security.

There is no such thing as Strategic Data Model, this is a misleading option which is a very tempting option which can cause an individual to lose out on the opportunity to score high.

Q4- Answer: Option A. Estimation. This is a very easy question to answer. If you get this wrong, then we are afraid that you have a long way to go before you take the actual exam.

Estimation is used to support decision making by predicting attributes such as:
• Cost and effort to pursue a course of action,
• Expected solution benefits,
• Project cost,
• Business performance,
• Potential value anticipated from a solution, and
• Costs of creating a solution,
• Costs of operating a solution,
• Potential risk impact.

Q5 - Answer: Option A. Phil. Sponsors are responsible for initiating the effort to define a business need and develop a solution that meets that need. They authorize the work and control the budget and scope for the initiative. Alternate roles are executive and project sponsor. Sponsors are accountable for the solution scope and can provide insight to be utilized when assessing change. Accountable as per BABOK: the person who is ultimately held accountable for the successful completion of the task and is the decision-maker. Only one stakeholder receives this assignment.

Case Study 4

In 2015 as per data shared by the apron control department at ABC airport, minimum of 1000 vehicles operate within its premises per day. All airlines and agencies that operate within the airport need these vehicles for aircraft maintenance, transporting luggage to the aircraft, catering service, etc. These vehicles are permitted within the airport with a temporary pass that is valid for a defined period. No vehicle is issued any permit that is valid for more than 12 months.

Besides issuing a vehicle permit, the apron control department also needs to issue driving permits which are valid for a maximum period of 12 months. Today all these permits are issued on paper and the records with respect to their expiry dates are maintained in spreadsheets.

BACKGROUND

Apron control department needs dedicated 320-man hours per week to manage this system which is manual and is open to many malpractices and errors. The minimum cost of a temporary pass which is valid for 1 day is Rs.200. The cost of this pass will also vary based on vehicle type: light or heavy. There are many parameters considered in determining the cost for each pass based on various conditions that are manually maintained and need to be updated on an annual basis depending on the policies set by the airport authority of the country. This is a regulatory body and notifies all the airports of the country to follow standard practices.

Air carriers need to pay for each pass issued by the apron control by cheque or they can also pay in cash. Sometimes passes need to be issued in bulk and payment is made at one go by these air carriers. Accounts are maintained manually and approximately 15% of cash transactions are not monitored since challans are issued in the form of manually written receipts and are subjected to manipulations. The data maintained in excel sheets need to be shared with the existing system called MAP which is an ERP and a repository for all financial transactions throughout the airport.

Various reports need to be shared with the higher management for maintaining transparency with respect to performance & revenue. The permit issued on paper cannot be renewed and all the required information needs to be entered manually for each field. Receipt books are printed for this purpose and the operators need to write each receipt every time they issue a new pass.

Often numbers that are projected at the start of the year for generating revenue from this model fall short of the expectations of the higher management. They believe that the current system lacks transparency, accuracy, and daily monitoring. They expect a system that can address these problems and needs to be implemented within a span of 1 year, followed by AMC (Annual Maintenance Contract) if required.

SOLUTIONING

Master Data Management

This module aims at enabling users to create and manage data that would determine the cost and type of the permit. The module will maintain a set of conditions in the system that can be updated by the user from time to time. The validity of each permit will be defined in this module.

User Management

User will be created and maintained in the system. Every user will have defined access rights to different modules in the system. There will be a set of user governance policies that will apply to each user in the system. The highest level of access will be configured for the system owner with administrative rights. Other users will create and update permits. Few reports generated from the system will be accessed by all users, whereas few will be accessed by a selective lot depending on the nature of data that can also contain sensitive information.

Permits Management

Users will create airside driving and vehicle permits online. The user will select the type and cost of the permit and print it from the system on the go. This interface will also enable the user to collect the payment by cheque or cash and make an entry in the system. It will also generate the necessary receipts that will be given to the applicant of the permit once she\he makes the payment through online banking, cheque, or cash.

Reports

This module enables automatic and manual generation of timely based reports. Users should be able to generate parameterized reports and should be able to perform customized sort and search.

Monitoring performance – BI

Dashboards created, will graphically represent the user and system performance. The module will display daily efficiency and revenue that the system generates based on the user and the company (applicant). It would also forecast future targets that need to be achieved.

Case Study 4 Questions

Q1. Answer the question below.

1. Often numbers that are projected at the start of the year for generating revenue from this model fall short of the expectations of the higher management.
2. Mangement believes that the current system lacks transparency, accuracy, and daily monitoring.
3. Approximately 15% of cash transactions are not monitored.
4. Lot of manual work is required for writing receipts.

Select the option that best describes the above 4 points.

A. Assess Risks
B. Define Future State
C. Analyze Current State

D. Define Change Strategy

Q2. Mathew told Robert that "The cost of making the application and maintaining it for the next 5 years is less than the currently assumed losses for one year and once the application is deployed it will minimize the losses to 10% of its original value." Which technique did Mathew use to arrive at this conclusion?

A. SWOT
B. Financial Analysis
C. Decision Analysis
D. Net Present Value

Q3. Master Data Management could be responsible for meeting which of the below option? Select the best answer.

A. Business Rules and Acceptance Criteria
B. Acceptance Criteria and Business Goals
C. Business Goals and Vision
D. Business Vision and Business Strategy
E. Business Strategy and Business Rules

Q4. Jane is a Business Analyst. She noted the following statements:

- Accounts are maintained manually and approximately 15% of cash transactions are not monitored.
- All the required information needs to be entered manually for each field.
- The operators need to write each receipt every time they issue a new pass.

The above statements reflect on which alphabet of the acronym SWOT?

A. S
B. W
C. O
D. T

Case Study 4 Answers

Q1-Answer: Option A. Assess Risks. Justification:

- The purpose of **Analyze Current State** is to understand the reasons why an enterprise needs to change some aspect of how it operates and what would be directly or indirectly affected by the change.
- The purpose of **Define Future State** is to determine the set of necessary conditions to meet Business needs.
- The purpose of **Assess Risks** is to understand the undesirable consequences of internal and external forces on the enterprise during a transition to, or once in the future state. An understanding of the potential impact of those forces can be used to make a recommendation about a course of action.
- The purpose of **Define Change Strategy** is to develop and assess alternative approaches to the change and then select the recommended approach.

Q2-Answer: Option B. Financial Analysis. Justification:

Net Present Value: Net present value (NPV) is the present value of the benefits minus the original cost of the investment. In this way, different investments, and different benefit patterns can be compared in terms of present-day value. The higher the NPV, the better the investment. NPV is an element of Financial Analysis and not a technique by itself, as most people are likely to mark it wrongly in the heat of the moment.

Q3- Answer: Option A. Business Rules and Acceptance Criteria. Business rules analysis is used to identify, express, validate, refine, and organize the rules that shape day-to-day business behaviour and guide operational business decision making. Acceptance criteria define the boundaries of a user story and help the team to understand what the solution needs to provide to deliver value for the stakeholders.

Master Data Management: This module aims at enabling users to create and manage data that would determine the cost and type of the permit. The module will maintain a set of conditions (should meet Acceptance Criteria) in the system that can be updated by the user from time to time. The validity of each permit will be defined in this module. (should meet Business Rules).

Q4-Answer: Option B. The S,W,O, and T stand for the following:

- Strengths (S): Anything that the assessed group does well. May include experienced personnel, effective processes, IT systems, customer relationships, or any other internal factor that leads to success.
- Weaknesses (W): Actions or functions that the assessed group does poorly or not at all.
- Opportunities (O): External factors of which the assessed group may be able to take advantage. May include new markets, new technology, changes in the competitive marketplace, or other forces.
- Threats (T): External factors that can negatively affect the assessed group.

Case Study 5

Adventus airlines is a new domestic airline in the United states and want to get its own travel management software. The airline will use the software for boarding pass and check-in management, ticket booking portal as well as loyalty management program.

Norita software solutions Inc has been contacted to develop the software. Norman is the business analyst for the project. Norman has created the use case model for the check-in features and is shown below.

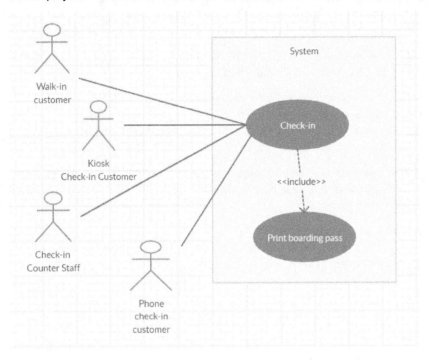

Fig 1: Use case model

Norman also wanted to represent the association between the use cases and so showed the following relationship. This diagram basically represents the parent-child relationship.

Fig 2: Actor relationships

Case Study 5 Questions

Q1. The check-in module use case model shows four actors and two use cases. Which of the following is true about the check-in module, based on the use case model?

A) The use case model shows all the customers flying their aircrafts

B) Printing of boarding pass is an optional use case for "check-in" use case

C) "Printing of boarding pass" is a special case for "Check-in" use case and happens only when needed

D) None of these

Q2. Figure 2 shows the relationship between two actors. As per the diagram, a Kiosk using traveller is a child of the walk-in traveller. Is it a correct representation of the relationship?

A) It correctly represents the relationship between the two actors

B) Kiosk and walk-in customers are just types of customers and not related in this way

C) Kiosk and walk-in customers are not different and so should not be shown independently

D) None of these

Q3. Norman asked his peer Nora to review the use case model as she had worked in the similar industry before. Put yourself in Nora's shoes and review the use case model. Which of the following review comments, you are likely to come up with?

A) There are too many actors shown in one diagram

B) Printing of boarding pass does not share include relationship with the check-in use case

C) Check-in counter staff is not a valid actor

D) Walk-in customer is not a valid actor

Case Study 5 Answers

Q1-Answer: A The case study does not state any other type of customer. So, A is the best answer. The case "printing of boarding pass" is included in the check-in use case and is hence mandatory. "Printing of boarding pass" is not a special case as we use extend for showing special cases.

Q2-Answer: B These two types of customers are different from how they interact with the proposed system. They do not share a parent-child relationship.

Q3-Answer: D Walk-in customers never interact with the software system. Check-in counter staff does all the activities on behalf of the walk-in customers. User of business service (walk-in customer) is different from the user of the system.

Exercises and Drills

Question 1: Match the following.

1. Catalogue of the stakeholders affected by a change, business need, or proposed solution, and a description of their attributes and characteristics related to their involvement in the initiative.	a. Personas
2. A group or individual with a relationship to the change, the need, or the solution.	b. Stakeholder Matrix
3. The role a business analyst takes when representing the needs of a stakeholder or stakeholder group.	c. Stakeholder List
4. A fictional character that exemplifies the way a typical user interacts with a product.	d. Stakeholder
5. Diagrams that depict the relationship of stakeholders to the solution or to one-another	e. Stakeholder Proxy
6. Diagrams that show how involved the stakeholders are with the solution	f. Stakeholder Map
7. Mapping the influence of stakeholders against their level of interest.	g. Onion Diagram

Question 2: Match the following.

1. Framework for scoping and planning, generally aligned to the business strategy.	a. Value, Performance Gaps, Risk
2. To achieve business goals or objectives, this is assessed for performance gaps and helps in prioritizing investments.	b. Capability Map
3. Graphical view of elements in Business Capability Analysis	c. Business Capability Analysis
4. Attributes that define a capability cell	d. High, Medium, Low
5. Attributes of a capability cell are classified	e. Capability

Question 3: Match the following tools.

1. Decision Matrix	a. Identifies final outcome of the tree.
2. Decision Tree	b. When there are more than 2 alternatives to choose from and is generally typed as simple or weighted.
3. Decision Node	c. Has different strategies
4. Chance Node	d. When there are multiple sources of uncertainty and is classified in terms of nodes
5. Terminator or End Node	e. Defines uncertain outcomes

Question 4: Match the following approaches to Prioritization.

1. Grouping	a. Prioritizing by Order from Most Important to Least Important
2. Prioritizing by classifying as High, Medium, or Low priority	b. Prioritizing by classifying as High, Medium or Low priority
3. Budgeting/Time Boxing	c. Stakeholder consensus on requirements to be prioritized

4. Negotiation	d. Prioritizing based on the allocation of a fixed resource (time or money)

Question 5: Match the key elements of a Business Model canvas with the examples.

Key Partnerships	IT Infrastructure
Key Resources	Internet
Channels	Technology Vendors
Customer Segments	Guaranteed delivery within 24 hours
Value Proposition	Customers in the age group of 40-50 who are worried about online transactions

Question 6: Match the following.

1.Business Rules	a. Directive for controlling, influencing, or regulating the actions of an enterprise and the people in it.
2. Business Policy	b. Analyzing large amounts of data to derive a pattern generally put as a mathematical model or equation.
3. Derivable from Business policy	c. Behavioural Rule
4. Rules the organization chooses to enforce as a matter of policy	d. business rule
5. Data Mining	e. Testable directive for guiding behaviour, shaping judgements or making decisions.

Question 7: Match the following.

1. A method of Qualitative research in which background information is gathered during requirement elicitation.	a. Data Mining
2. An approach to document analysis	b. Lessons learned
3. A session held at each milestone, that captures success, opportunities for improvement, failures, and recommendations for improving	c. Lessons Learned document
4. Document which is a result of Retrospective meeting	d. Document Analysis

Question 8: Match the following.

1. Connection between two components or solutions.	a. Interface Analysis
2. Elicitation technique that helps to identify interfaces to determine the requirements.	b. Methods for process improvement
3. Assessing process for efficiency and efficacy	c. Process Analysis Methodologies
4. Six Sigma, Lean are examples of	d. Process Analysis

5. Value stream mapping, statistical analysis and control, process simulation, benchmarking, and process frameworks.	e. Interface

Question 9: Match the following.

1. A file or a set of files which acts as a reference to data elements, their meanings, and allowable values.	a. Created by the business analyst, hence is system agnostic
2. A type of data dictionary which typically describes information in business terms and focuses on the meaning of terms and their relationship with other terms.	b. Created by Database architects and database administrators and refers to one database or one schema.
3. A type of data dictionary which typically describes the physical attributes of a data element.	c. Glossary
4. Logical data dictionary	d. Logical Data dictionary
5. Physical data dictionary	e. Physical Data dictionary
6. List of terms in business domain with their definitions and common synonyms.	f. Data dictionary/ Metadata Repository

Question 10: Match the following.

1. Examining a work activity first-hand as it is being performed	a. Elements of Observation.
2. An approach of observation, wherein the observer asks any questions as they arise while the activity is being done.	b. Passive
3. An approach of observation, wherein the observer asks any questions after the activity has done.	c. Active
4. Define objectives, Preparation, Conduct Observation, Confirm, and Present Observation results.	d. Observation or Job Shadowing

Question 11: Match the following.

1. A visual representation of OU, which describes the roles, responsibilities, and reporting structures that exist within the current state organization.	a. Organizational Chart
2. Type of Organizational model, wherein staff is grouped based on shared skills or areas of expertise.	b. Organizational Model
3. Type of Organizational model, wherein the OU is created to serve customer groups, geographical areas, projects, or processes.	c. Functionally-Oriented
4. Type of Organizational model, wherein the OU is a combination of functional and market-oriented.	d. Market- Oriented
5. OU, Roles/People, Line of Reporting are depicted as a part of Modelling	e. Matrix

Question 12: Solve the following.

1. Early model of the result.	a. Storyboarding [Type of functional]
2. An approach of the prototype, wherein the prototype made is not workable or extendable.	b. Prototype
3. An approach of the prototype, wherein the prototype made is workable or extendable.	c. Throw-away prototype

4. A method of prototyping in which the sequence of activities is portrayed visually and textually.	d. Evolutionary or Functional
5. A method of prototyping in which a draft of interface or process is made using paper and pencil.	e. Simulation [Type of functional]
6. A method of prototyping in which sequence of operations, focusing human aspects are depicted.	f. Paper Prototyping [Type of Throw-away]
7. A method of prototyping used to test various processes, scenarios, business rules, etc.	g. Workflow modelling [Type of functional]

Question 13: Match the following.

1. Organizing business vocabulary, that contains the knowledge of domain, is called	a. Elements of concept modelling
2. Concept modelling starts with _, typically containing noun concepts.	b. Concept Modelling
3. Noun concepts, Verb Concepts and Standard Connections together constitute?	c. Glossary
4. Basic concepts are called as Givens or	d. Standard Connections
5. Standard wordings that provide structural connections between noun concepts is called	e. Noun Concepts
6. Categorizations, Classifications, Partitive connections, Roles are types of	f. Verb Concepts

Question 14: Match the following.

1. Diagrams that depict the transformation of data.	a. Level 1
2. Highest level diagram that generally represents the entire system.	b. Level2, Level 3 etc.
3. This layer of abstraction in DFD (Data Flow Diagrams) depicts process with respect to the system.	c. Context Diagram (Level 0)
4. Breaking down the major processes of Level 1 diagram into further layers of abstraction.	d. Elements of DFD
5. Externals, Data Store, Process and Data Flow constitute	e. Data Flow Diagrams

Question 15: Match the following.

1.Diagram that is used to depict attributes of and relationships among the Entities, classes, data objects of the business need.	a. Cardinality
2. A rectangular box, that contains attributes and has relationships with other such boxes in data modelling	b. Attribute
3.A piece of information which has name, value and description.	c. Multiplicity
4. The minimum and maximum number of occurrences to which an entity may be related.	d. Entity/Class

5. The minimum and maximum number of occurrences to which a class may be related.	e. Data Model

Question 16: Match the following elements of Decision Modelling.

1. Compact, tabular representation of a set of business rules.	a. Decision Tree
2. Representation of a set of business rules in terms of leaf nodes and branches.	b. Decision Table
3. Visual representation of information, knowledge and decision making in complex business decisions.	c. Behavioural Rule
4. Business rule that is a claim of necessity and cannot be violated.	d. Decision Requirements Diagrams
5. Business rule that is a claim of obligation and can be violated.	e. Definitional Rule

Question 17: Match the following.

1. A minimal set of requirements that must be met for the solution to be worth implementing.	A. Evaluation Criteria
2. Set of requirements that will be used to choose between multiple solutions	B. Acceptance Criteria
3. The ability of a requirement to be tested against acceptance test case	C. Ranking
4. Process of determining the order of importance of all requirements.	D. Testability
5. Process of determining how well a solution meets a requirement using a scale.	E. Scoring

Question 18: Match the following.

1. Root cause of growing backlog	a. Product Backlog
2. Root cause of declining backlog	b. Sprint Backlog
2. List of tasks identified by the Scrum team to be completed during the Scrum sprint	b. Increase in demand/Decrease in productivity
3. List of all things that need to be done within the project	c. Decrease in demand/Increase in productivity

Question 19: Match the following dimensions of BSC.

1. Measures regarding employee training and learning, product and service innovation, and corporate culture.	a. Financial
2. Metrics that indicate how well the enterprise is operating and if their products meet customer needs.	b. Customer
3. Metrics on customer focus, satisfaction, and delivery of value.	c. Business Process

4. Financial measures needed to realize the strategy.	d. Learning and Growth

Question 20: Match the following on Financial Analysis Approaches.

1.	Prediction of expected total benefits minus expected total costs, resulting in net benefit	a.	Net Present Value
2.	A performance measure used to evaluate the efficiency of an investment or to compare the efficiency of some different investments	b.	Internal Rate of Return
3.	Sum of the present values (PVs) of incoming and outgoing cash flows over a period.	c.	Return on Investment
4.	Rate of return used in capital budgeting to measure and compare the profitability of investments, disregarding environmental factors like interest rates or inflation.	d.	Cost Benefit Analysis

Crosswords

Question 1: Complete the following crossword:

Across	Down
1. Studies conducted to compare Organizational practices with best-in-class practices. (12)	2. Researching information from customers to understand the need for a product or service. (Two words – 14)
3.Benchmarking and Market Analysis is used to improve Organizational processes. (10)	4.The main difference between focus group and brainstorming is that the former is _____ (10)
5. Brainstorming is generally conducted by a _____ (11)	
6. After the BA makes the Focus Group Plan, _____ is assigned to conduct the Focus Group. (9)	

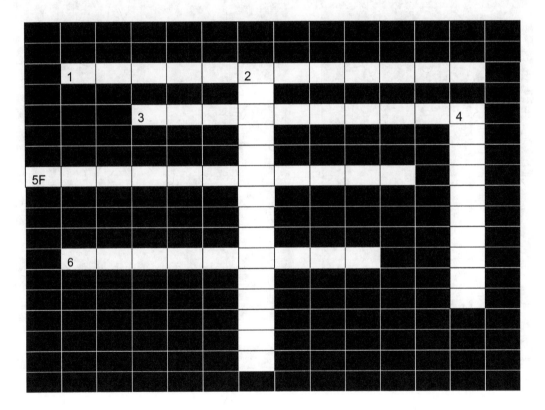

Question 2: Solve the following crossword.

Across	Down
1. It is generally categorized as predictive, diagnostic, or descriptive. (Two words-10)	1. The final step in data mining after data preparation, analysis, and modelling (10)
3. Deriving decision making from answers received when a user asks a question during data mining investigations are called _____ investigations. (10)	2. It is generally categorized as Behavioral or definitional. (Two words -13)
4. Deriving decision making from patterns discovery during data mining investigations are called _____ investigations (12)	

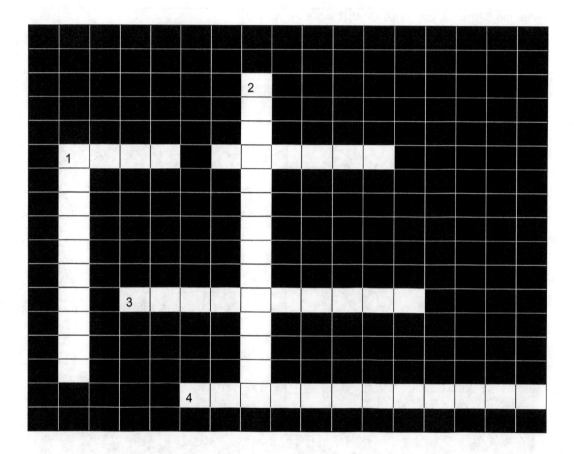

Question 3: Solve the following crossword.

Across	Down
1. The notation of DFD, wherein the process is represented by a circle. (Two words -11)	2. The notation of DFD, wherein the process is represented by a rectangle with rounded corners. (Two words – 10)
3. A variation of data model, used generally by SME's to describe database, such that performance, concurrency and security are taken care of. (8)	4. A variation of data model, that is independent of any solution or technology. (10)
	5. An abstraction of a solution independent model, which incorporates normalization rules while designing solution. (7)

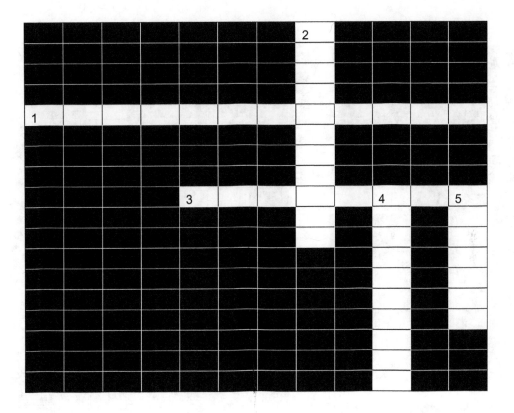

Question 4: Solve the following crossword on methods of Estimation.

Across	Down
1. Examining the components at a high level in a hierarchical breakdown. (two words – 7)	2. Using calibrated parametric model of the element attributes being estimated. (10)
	3. Using lowest-level elements of a hierarchical breakdown to examine the work in detail. (Two words -8)
4. High level estimate, based on limited information, acronym. (3)	4. Repeated estimates throughout an initiative or project. (Two words -11)
5. Uses a combination of expert judgement and history. (5)	6. Each component of the estimate is given three values- Optimistic, Pessimistic and Most Likely. (4)

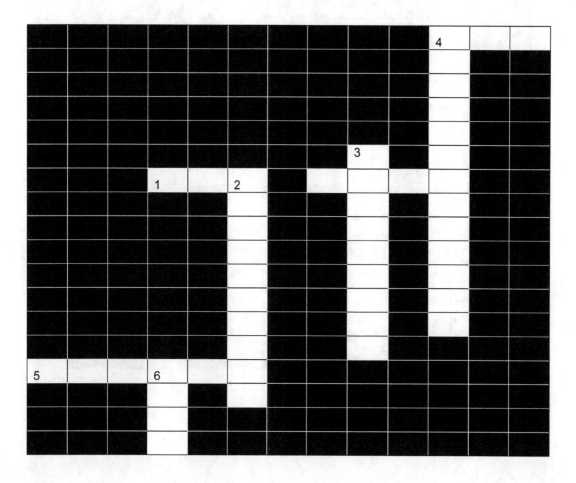

Answers

Answer 1: 1-c, 2-d, 3-e, 4-a, 5-f, 6-g, 7-b

Answer 2: 1-c, 2-e, 3-b, 4-a, 5-d

Answer 3: 1-b, 2-d, 3-c, 4-e, 5-a

Answer 4: 1-b, 2-a, 3-d, 4-c

Answer 5: 1-c, 2-a, 3-b, 4-e, 5-d

Answer 6: 1-e, 2-a, 3-d, 4-c, 5-b

Answer 7: 1-D, 2-A, 3-B, 4-C

Answer 8: 1-e, 2-a, 3-d, 4-c, 5-b

Answer 9: 1-f, 2-d, 3-e, 4-a, 5-b, 6-c

Answer 10: 1-d, 2-c, 3-b, 4 -a

Answer 11: 1-b, 2-c, 3-d, 4-e, 5-a

Answer 12: 1-b, 2-c, 3-d, 4-a, 5-f, 6-g, 7-e

Answer 13: 1-b, 2-c, 3-a, 4-e, 5-f, 6-d

Answer 14: 1-e, 2-c, 3-a, 4-b, 5-d

Answer 15: 1-e, 2-d, 3-b, 4-a, 5-c

Answer 16: 1-b, 2-a, 3-d, 4-e, 5-c

Answer 17: 1-b, 2-a, 3-d, 4-c, 5-e

Answer 18: 1-c, 2-d, 3-b, 4-a

Answer 19: 1-d, 2-c, 3-b, 4-a

Answer 20: 1-d, 2-c, 3-a, 4-b

Crosswords

Answer 1: 1-Benchmarking, 2-Market Analysis, 3- Operations, 4- Structured, 5-Facilitator, 6-Moderator

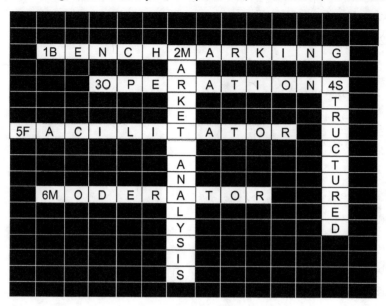

Answer 2: 1 Across -Data Mining, 1 Down- Deployment, 2- Business Rules, 3- Supervised,4- Unsupervised

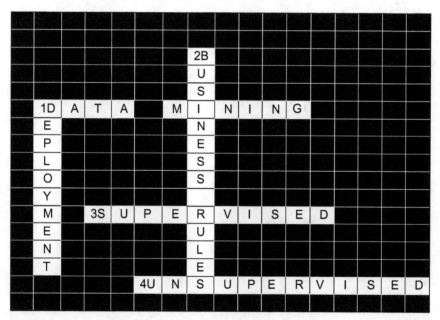

TECH**CANVASS**

Answer 3: 1-Yourdon-Code, 2-Gane-Sarson, 3 -Physical,4-Conceptual,5-Logical

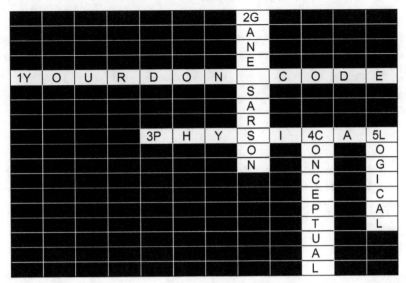

Answer 4: 1- Top Down, 2-Parametric, 3-Bottom Up, 4 Across – ROM, 4 Down- Rolling Wave, 5- Delphi, 6- PERT

TECHCANVASS

Mock Questions

Q1. As part of his job of analyzing data anomaly, Tony has tried to understand a pattern of data mismatches, its timing, and root causes of these anomalies. What technique Tony has used in his analysis task?

A. Concept modelling
B. Data modelling
C. Data mining
D. Data lineage

Q2. Purnima Wagh is a business analyst. She has evaluated the organizational capabilities thoroughly. She is now ready to create a business case to recommend a solution approach to help the customer achieve the desired objectives. What does a business case include?

A) Needs and goals
B) Potential Value
C) Solution Options
D) Solution Design

    A. All four
    B. A, B, and C
    C. A, B, and D
    D. B, C, and D

Q3. Acceptance and evaluation criteria refer to two different aspects. The acceptance criteria are different in nature than the evaluation criteria. Which of the following statements describe the two appropriately?

    A. The acceptance criteria are used to define the parameters for requirements whereas evaluation criteria are used for everything other than requirements.
    B. Acceptance criteria define the criteria for accepting a solution whereas Evaluation criteria are a set of measurements that are used to evaluate multiple solution options.
    C. Acceptance criteria are defined for customers so that there is an agreement on the acceptance of the software. Whereas the evaluation criteria are defined for any stakeholder for evaluating software or a solution.
    D. The term is used collectively to define a singular concept. This concept relates to defining the value attributes which are used to define the expected qualities of a solution.

Q4. A warehouse needs to be automated for managing the movement of stocks and its management. Which of the following techniques may not be useful for requirements elicitation for this proposed system?

    A. Brainstorming & observation
    B. Business rules analysis & brainstorming
    C. Observation & Benchmarking and Market Analysis
    D. Document analysis and, data mining

Q5. Ramesh Jain, the lead business analyst of Ryan Corporation, is creating the business architecture for a large multi-national bank. He is conducting interviews to understand the existing state capabilities. What is the next step for him to come out with recommendations/solutions to transition to the future state?

    A. Creating a Business Case
    B. Conducting Business Rules Analysis
    C. Creating Concept Modelling

D. Conducting Business Capability Assessment

Q6. What is TRUE about the Include relationship between the use cases?

A. Include relationship shows the parent-child relationship
B. Include relationship shows two use cases which can only be used together and not independently
C. Include shows the mandatory relationship between use cases
D. Include shows the optional relationship between use cases

Q7. A system has the following requirements: Once the member enters all the credit card details and clicks on Submit button, the details are submitted to the payment gateway to complete the transaction. Identify the actor or actors in this case.

A. Member
B. Member and payment gateway
C. Member, site, and payment gateway
D. Payment Gateway

Q8. Which of the following is not TRUE about the user story?

A. It is used to represent functional requirements
B. It is not used to represent non-functional requirements
C. It is a textual representation of requirements
D. It also includes the reason why functionality is needed

Q9. Rekha is the business analyst for an insurance project. During the requirements elicitation phase, she was not only able to get the details of requirements but was also able to build a good rapport with a couple of stakeholders. Which requirement elicitation technique Rekha might have used?

A. Focus Group
B. Workshop
C. JAD session
D. Interview

Q10. A reputed restaurant chain has hired a software development firm to develop the food ordering app. The business analyst of the project wanted to understand the overall system and its boundaries to start with. Which of the following diagrams, the BA can create?

A. Process Flow Diagram
B. Use-Case Diagram
C. Context Diagram
D. Concept Model

Q11. A business analyst is conducting an impact analysis for major changes in a system. He also wants to understand all the existing interfaces of the system. The BA wants to go through all the available system documentation for information on the interfaces. Which specific model/diagram should the BA look for in this context?

A. Context Diagram
B. Conceptual Model
C. Use-Case Diagram
D. Mind Map

Q12. Shikha is conducting the elicitation activities with a multi-national company, based out of Geneva. She is talking to the department heads and line managers. To have a better understanding later, she needs to identify key domain-related terms, concepts, and relationships between these. Which of the following does she need to create to capture the above details?

A. Glossary

B. Process Analysis
C. Data Modelling
D. Concept Modelling

Q13. The creation of a glossary should take place in the early stages of a project in order to facilitate knowledge transfer and understanding. The terms are added to the glossary based on the following factors:

A) The term is unique to a domain
B) There are multiple definitions for the term
C) There is a reasonable chance of misunderstanding
Choose the right option from the following which represents the correct factors for adding terms to the glossary.
  A. A and B
  B. Only A
  C. Only C
  D. All of the above

Q14. An HNI customer is defined by two parameters. Their annual revenue must be more than USD 1 million and every year they must place an order of USD 150,000 and above. Otherwise, they are categorized as standard customers. What does the above statement represent?

  A. Definition rule
  B. Behavioural rule
  C. Business constraints
  D. Assumption

Q15. One of the requirements in an HR system is as follows: A user can access the application using credentials but can only access it from one device at a time. Which of the following correctly describes this?

  A. It is a constraint
  B. It is a risk for the system
  C. It is a business rule for the system
  D. It's an assumption

Q16. A business analyst follows an operations manager, working on the shop floor to understand the nature of his job. Which of the following correctly describes this activity?

  A. Conducting Survey
  B. Conducting Observation
  C. Conducting a focus group study
  D. Conducting Reviews

Q17. How easy is the user interface (UI) for the business and for end-users? What does this statement represent?

  A. This is an example of evaluation criteria
  B. This is an example of acceptance criteria
  C. This is an example of a test case
  D. This is an example of a requirement

Q18. All unit test cases must be run successfully, and results are shared to verify. This is an example of?

  A. Requirements
  B. Test Scenario
  C. Verification
  D. Acceptance Criterion

Q19. Agile teams use a backlog document. What is the purpose of using the backlog document?

A) Keeping a track of items to be done
B) To keep a record of the priority of requirements to be done
C) To maintain traceability of requirements

    A. All the three options
    B. A and B
    C. A and C
    D. B and C

Q20. An organization Incarta Inc has multiple factories across the European region producing, storing, and supplying components for manufacturing heavy machines. They have hired ANZ IT solutions to develop a supply chain management system. Ron Jenkins is the lead BA for the project. Which of the following elicitation techniques he should opt for?

    A. Interviews
    B. Survey
    C. Workshop
    D. Observation

Q21. Ron Jafferson has been deployed to prepare specifications for an MIS system by Zyan Inc. The stakeholder has asked him to assess and justify the solution. So, he is preparing a business case. Which three key elements will be included in the business case?

    A. Needs, Requirements, Solution
    B. Needs, Desired outcomes, and Recommended solution
    C. Requirements, solutions, and costs
    D. None of these

Q22. Focus groups are a specialized way of requirements elicitation. It is useful for getting information from a group of people about a specific product, service, or opportunity. However, it is not effective in some cases. Choose such a situation where it is not effective.

    A. People behave differently than what they say about their behaviour
    B. Maybe disruptive to the performance of the participant and the overall organization
    C. Does not prevent the risk of failure as the partnership evolves
    D. Subjectivity may bias the evaluation outcome

Q23. Jude is working as a Business analyst. He needs to create a method that will promote a common understanding of the business domain and better communication among all stakeholders. Which technique will help Jude?

    A. Functional Decomposition
    B. Interface Analysis
    C. Glossary
    D. Process Analysis

Q24. Which term is used to describe a technique which brings together a wide range of different stakeholders and an independent facilitator?

    A. Workshops
    B. Survey
    C. Review
    D. Brainstorming

Q25. On a class diagram, what does the multiplicity represent?

A. The number of attributes held within each class.
B. The minimum and maximum number of operations in each class.
C. The minimum and maximum number of objects in each class.
D. The business rules for an association between two classes.

ANSWERS

Q1. Answer C: Correct Option C. Data mining helps in identifying patterns and trends. (Section 10.14.1 BABOK)

Option A -Incorrect. Concept modelling is related to business vocabulary to be utilized during business communication.
Option B - Incorrect. Data modelling is used to understand the existing database or to build a new database model.
Option D - Incorrect. This is partly correct as this data lineage deals with the consistency of data across the process flow.

Q2. Answer B: Solution design is not a part of the business case as it is not ready when business cases are developed. However, Needs, goals, potential value and the solution options are included in a Business case. So, option B is correct. Section 10.7.2 of BABOK lists down the elements for which a Business case is created.

Q3. Answer B: (Section 10.1, BABOK) Option B is the correct answer. Typically, we use acceptance criteria to define the parameters for the acceptance of any artefact of a project, be it requirements or design even code. Evaluation criteria are used to evaluate alternatives and help decision making. Both of them can be used for any type or stage of the project. So, option C is not correct as it restricts the definition of acceptance criteria to customers only. Option A is also not correct as it restricts the definition of acceptance criteria to requirements.

Q4. Answer D: Option A, B and C are the techniques that may be used for the warehouse management system. Observation plays an important role in observing the process and exploring the possibility of improvement. Brainstorming is a common technique and can be used in any project. Business rules analysis as well as, Benchmarking and Market Analysis, are also the valid techniques.

There is no information on data for the proposed project. So, data mining is not a suitable elicitation technique. There is no specific section in BABOK for this answer, but you can check the respective techniques.

Q5. Answer D: (Section 10.6.3.5) From the given options Conducting Business capability assessment is the best option. It provides input about where the organization wants to go and can also produce a set of recommendations or proposals for solutions to reach that state. A business capability assessment helps to formulate a set of recommendations or proposals to reach the desired future state and hence option d is the correct answer.

Q6. Answer C: (Section 10.47.3.1 – Include) Include relationship is used to show shared logic amongst multiple use cases. It is also referred to indicate mandatory relationship.

Let us say, use case A and B have INCLUDE relationship. This means that Use case A cannot be completed without completing use case B. This means that there is a mandatory relationship. Therefore, option C is correct.

Q7. Answer B: Actor is a person or a system external to a solution to interact with the solution itself. In this case, Member is the primary actor in the transaction, and payment gateway is the secondary actor whereas payment gateway is the solution. Both are actors (external entities), who participate in the completion of the payment transaction, and hence the correct answer is option b. (Section 10.47.3.2 BABOK)

Q8. Answer B: User stories can be used to represent functional as well as non-functional requirements. For example, we can write a user story for a non-functional requirement as follows: As a user, I want the site to be available 99.999 percent of the time so that I can use it anytime to make a purchase. Thus, the correct answer is option b. (Section 10.48.3.2 of BABOK)

Q9. Answer D: Correct Option D, Section 10.25.1. The interviews can also, be used for establishing relationships and building trust between business analysts and stakeholders in order to increase stakeholder involvement or build support for a proposed solution. Thus, the correct answer is option d.

Q10. Answer C: The context diagram also known as level 0 data-flow diagram, is drawn in order to define and clarify the boundaries of the software system. It also helps in defining the boundaries of the system. (Section 10.13.2)

Q11. Answer A: Correct answer is A. Context diagrams also show the interfaces. (Refer to the Section 10.13.1) Use case model does not depict interfaces. Concept model represents the key concepts of a system and relationships between the concepts whereas Mind map is an obvious incorrect option.

Q12. Answer D: Choice A: Glossary of terms is about creating the common set of terms relevant to a project but does not show the relationships. choice B: Process analysis is used to understand the current process and identify improvement opportunities. Choice C: Data modelling is used to understand entity relationship. Choice D: Correct answer. The noun concept represents the terms and concepts whereas verb concepts represent connections between the noun concepts (Relationships) and both these noun and verb concepts are part of concept modelling. (Refer to section 10.11.3.1 and 10.11.2.2)

Q13. Answer D: All the factors are necessary. (Refer to section 10.23.3 of BABOK)

Q14. Answer A: (Section 10.9.3.1) Definitional rules often prescribe how information may be derived, inferred, or calculated based on information available to the business. In this case, the given statement defines the rule for an HNI customer. So, the correct answer is A.

Q15. Answer C: This is an example of a rule to be developed in the system and since it is to be developed as a system behaviour, it is considered as a behavioural business rule. Thus, option c is the right answer. (Section 10.9.3.2 of BABOK)

Q16. Answer B: This is an observation technique where requirements and nature of work is investigated by shadowing the stakeholder, as he/she performs day to day activity. It is also known as job shadowing. (Technique 10.31, BABOK)

Q17. Answer A: This statement represents an evaluation criterion for evaluating multiple solution/design options. Evaluation criteria are the measures used to assess a set of requirements in order to choose between multiple solutions. (Section 10.1.1, BABOK)

Q18. Answer D: This is an example of acceptance criterion and not others. As per BABOK 10.1.1, Acceptance criteria are used to define the requirements, outcomes, or conditions that must be met in order for a solution to be considered acceptable to key stakeholders.

Q19. Answer B: Backlog document is not used for traceability rather; it is used to have an updated and prioritized list of items to be done by the team. The other two purposes are valid. Section 10.2.2. So, Option B is correct.

Q20. Answer B: Survey seems to be the best bet from the given options. The customer has factories spread across multiple countries. Since it is a supply chain automation project and each factory have a role to play, the requirements elicitation needs to involve all these stakeholders. Surveys are the most effective technique in the given scenario. (Section 10.45.1)

Q21. Answer B: A business case will have Needs, Desired outcomes, and Recommended solution and option b mentions all the above, and hence it is the right answer. (See Business cases in Techniques section. Section 10.7)

Q22. Answer A: (Section 10.21.4.2 of BABOK - The limitations of Focus groups) - In a group setting, participants may be concerned about issues of trust or maybe unwilling to discuss sensitive or personal topics. This may lead to inaccuracy of collected data. The above-mentioned limitation explains option a mentioned in the question and thus option A is correct.

Q23. Answer C: A glossary defines key terms relevant to a business domain. (BABOK - Techniques - Glossary - Section 10.23.1)

Q24. Answer A: This elicitation technique is a Workshop where stakeholders are brought together along with a facilitator, to achieve a pre-defined goal. (Section 10.50.2 BABOK)

Q25. Answer D: Multiplicity actually shows the relationship between the classes as specified by the business. For Example, a customer may place one or many orders. So, correct answer is D. (Figure 10.15.2, BABOK)

Perspectives

Perspectives provide the context to the business analysis activities for a project. It means that the tasks and techniques become more specific as per the perspectives. The perspectives included in the BABOK® Guide are:

- Agile,
- Business Intelligence,
- Information Technology,
- Business Architecture, and
- Business Process Management.

BABOK guide describes each perspective with a common structure. The structure comprises of the following elements:

- Change Scope
- Business Analysis scope
- Methodologies, approaches and Techniques
- Underlying competencies
- Impact on Knowledge areas

Agile Perspective

Overview	Describes the business analysis activities in the Agile context.
Change Scope	➤ A business analyst engages with the business sponsor to define the features in line with the business objectives. This is further broken down into a list of tasks with priority order in consultation with stakeholders ➤ The scope is constantly evolving in Agile projects. The backlog list is reviewed and re-prioritized continually. ➤ Change is expected at any point of time and rapid response to change is desired. Short iterative delivery based on prioritized backlog list allows to incorporate changes in the upcoming iterations with minimal impact. ➤ In case of major change, the entire project may be re-assessed and even may be adjourned, if needed
	➤ **Breadth of change:** Initiatives using agile approaches can be undertaken within a single department or can span across multiple teams, departments, and divisions of an organization. ➤ Agile mindset is a cultural transformation of an organization as opposed to adopting a new practice or methodology ➤ **Depth of change:** Agile project or initiative can be part of a larger program in an organization like organizational transformation and change, Business process re-engineering or business process change ➤ **Value and Solutions delivered:** Agile initiatives deliver the value and the solution just like any other initiative; however, the approach is different than the other projects. Agile approach is iterative and highly collaborative. This approach is about short iterative delivery and rapid customer feedback. The solution evolves over a period.

	➢ **Delivery Approach:** Agile approaches focus on people interactions, transparent communications, and ongoing delivery of valuable change to stakeholders. However, there could be specific characteristics to each Agile approach specific to the initiative. The teams may also adopt a hybrid approach.
	➢ **Major Assumptions: The major assumptions are:**
	  o Changes at any point in time in the project is acceptable
	  o A business problem can be decomposed into needs to find the suitable solution
	  o Agile initiatives have customers and SMEs, fully believing in the agile approach
	  o The changes in the team is not welcome
	  o The teams could be co-located for more efficient results. However distributed teams with appropriate communication channel can be also work as efficiently
	  o The team members play multiple roles within the team if needed.
	  o The team works with the mindset of continually improving the delivery through regular inspection
	  o Agile teams are empowered and self-organizing

Business Analysis scope	➢ **Change Sponsor:** The sponsor of an agile initiative must have a buy-in for the agile philosophy like adaptive planning, uniform duration iterations and his/her own involvement
	➢ **Change targets and agents:** A change agent (a stakeholder) is similar as any other initiative. It does not change because of being agile. The stakeholders are:
	  o Agile Team leader
	  o **Customer representative or product owner**
	  o **Team members**
	
	➢ **Business Analyst position:** A business analyst may be working in the agile team (with or without the designation):
	  o A business analyst working on the team,
	  o The customer representative or product owner, or
	  o Distributing these activities throughout the team
	
	➢ **Business Analysis outcomes:** Open communication and collaboration is one of the principal outcomes of successful business analysis in an agile project.

Approaches and Techniques	o **Approaches:** Agile itself does not represent any methodology but it is an umbrella term. **Some of the** agile approaches include Crystal clear, Disciplined agile delivery, Dynamic Systems Development Method (DSDM), Evolutionary Project Management (Evo) and more… o **Techniques:** The commonly used techniques within agile approaches are: Behaviour driven development (BDD), Kano Analysis, Lightweight Documentation, MoSCoW prioritization and more…
Underlying competencies	➢ In adopting the agile mindset and philosophy, the business analyst develops competencies in: o Communication and collaboration

	<ul><li>Patience and tolerance</li><li>Flexibility and adaptability</li><li>Ability to handle change</li><li>Ability to recognize business value</li><li>Continuous improvement</li></ul>
Impact on knowledge areas	<ul><li>**Business planning and monitoring:** In agile approaches, adaptive planning approach is used rather than predictive planning approach. An initial plan is developed, which is modified to account for change prior to the start of the net iteration.</li><li>**Elicitation and collaboration:** This is a progressive event in agile approaches. The most common pattern is an initial elicitation activity that establishes the high-level vision and scope of the solution, and an initial milestone-based plan for the delivery of the product.</li><li>**Requirement lifecycle management:** Scope of work gets more detailed and specific over a period. As that happens, the prioritization of the requirements is taken into consideration for development.</li><li>**Strategy Analysis:** Agile team members use strategy analysis to help understand and define product vision, and develop and adjust the development roadmap, in addition to conducting ongoing assessments of related risks.</li><li>**Requirements analysis and design definition:** In agile projects, Analysis and design are performed on a just-in-time basis. Analysis is performed before and during the iteration for estimation and construction, respectively.</li><li>**Solution evaluation:** Throughout an agile project, the stakeholders and agile team continually assess and evaluate the development solution as it is incrementally built and refined.</li></ul>

Business Intelligence Perspective

Overview	Business intelligence focuses on the transformation of data into value-added information. The Business Intelligence Perspective highlights the unique characteristics of business analysis when practiced in the context of transforming, integrating, and enhancing data.

Change Scope	➤ **Breadth of change:** Business intelligence initiative involves creating a uniform and consistent view of data by establishing **"Single point of truth"** for data coming from diverse sources. To achieve that. a business intelligence initiative may also involve the **development of infrastructure services in the organization**, such as data governance and metadata management.
	
	 ➤ **Depth of change:** Business intelligence initiatives focus on decision making at various levels in the organization (**Executive, management, and process levels**) and the information needed to make the decision. The initiatives also focus on investigating the business implications at all the other levels.
	
	 ➤ **Value and Solutions delivered:** The **value of a business intelligence initiative** is in its ability to provide timely, accurate, high value, and actionable information to those people and systems who can use it effectively in making business decisions. Increased revenue and reduced costs are the primary indicators of improvements in company performance.
	
	 ➤ **Delivery Approach:** The infrastructure services that provide data management, analytics, and presentation capabilities, facilitate a phased or incremental development strategy in respect of:
	    o The inclusion, coordination, and control of different data sources, and
	    o The analysis and development of business information and insights.
	
	 ➤ **Major Assumptions: The major assumptions are:**
	
	    o Existing business processes and transactional systems can provide source data that is definable and predictable,
	    o The cross-functional data infrastructure that is needed to support a business intelligence solution has not been precluded by the organization on technical, financial, political/cultural, or other grounds, and
	    o the organization recognizes that process re-engineering and change management might be needed to effectively realize the value from a business intelligence solution.

Business Analysis scope	➤ **Change Sponsor** is typically the highest-level role from the organizational unit affected by the change.
	
	 ➤ **Change targets and agents:** The targets of a business intelligence initiative are the business decisions made by people or processes at multiple levels in the organization that can be improved by better reporting, monitoring, or predictive modelling of performance-related data.
	
	 ➤ **Business Analyst position:** A business analyst will participate as:
	    o Liaison between the stakeholders and solution providers
	    o Enterprise data modelling
	    o Decision Modelling

	<ul><li>○ Specialized presentation design (Dashboards)</li><li>○ Ad hoc query design</li></ul> ➤ **Business Analysis outcomes:** The major outcomes of the business analysis activities are:<ul><li>○ Business process coverage</li><li>○ Decision Models</li><li>○ Source logical data model and data dictionary</li><li>○ Source data quality assessment</li><li>○ Target logical data model and data dictionary</li><li>○ Transformation rules</li><li>○ Business analytics requirements</li><li>○ Solution Architecture</li></ul>
Approaches and Methodologies	➤ **Methodologies:** The business analysts work within or alongside the methodologies applicable to other disciplines or perspectives. ➤ **Approaches:** there are a few less formal and potentially overlapping approaches that map to business and technical contexts. **Types of Analytics:** There are three types of data analytics that represent incremental solutions<ul><li>○ Descriptive Analytics</li><li>○ Predictive Analytics</li><li>○ Prescriptive Analytics</li></ul>**Supply and Demand Driven** The objectives and priorities of a business intelligence initiative can be based on the technical goals of improving existing information delivery systems (supply-driven) or on the business goals of providing the appropriate information to improve decision-making processes (demand-driven). *Supply-driven: assumes the view of "for a given cost, what value can we deliver?"* *Demand-driven: assumes the view of "for a given value, what cost do we incur?".* **Structured and Unstructured Data** Business intelligence initiatives consider two types of data – structured and unstructured.
Underlying competencies	➤ In addition to the communication and analytical competencies, the business intelligence systems outcomes may further be enhanced by:<ul><li>○ Business data and functional usage</li><li>○ The analysis of complex data structures and their translation into standardized format</li><li>○ Business processes affected including KPIs and metrics</li><li>○ Decision modelling</li><li>○ Data analysis techniques</li><li>○ Logical and physical data models</li><li>○ ETL best practices</li><li>○ Business intelligence reporting tools</li></ul>

Impact on knowledge areas	➢ **Business planning and monitoring**
	  ○ A business intelligence initiative may require establishing an underlying data infrastructure to support the solution, or it might be an enhancement based on the infrastructure of an existing solution.
	  ○ Scope Modelling is frequently used to differentiate between these alternatives and plan the relevant business analysis activities accordingly.
	
	➢ **Elicitation and collaboration:** The cross-functional nature of business intelligence typically requires business analysts to employ specialized documentation tools and techniques to elicit types of requirements from stakeholders, both business and technical.
	For example,
	  ○ Interviews with individual stakeholders identify the information and analytic insight required to support their decision making.
	  ○ Data models and data dictionaries provide definitions of the structure and business rules of existing systems data.
	➢ **Requirement lifecycle management:** This initiative typically requires implementation of infrastructure services. This creates structural dependencies within the solution, affecting the prioritization. It is often possible to achieve efficiencies by implementing related requirements at the same time.
	
	➢ **Strategy Analysis:** Business analysts can use high-level conceptual data models to map the current state of corporate information, to identify information silos, and to assess their related problems and opportunities. Business analysts can define change strategy options based on business needs and priorities, impact on the business operations, and the usability of existing infrastructure components.
	
	➢ **Requirements analysis and design definition:** Models of an existing system's data and reverse-engineered modelling is used in this initiative. Reverse-engineered modelling is used Where existing systems documentation is non-existent or out of date. A future state data model demonstrates how the source information is generically structured in the proposed solution.
	➢ **Solution evaluation**
	  ○ A common enterprise limitation with the introduction of a business intelligence solution is the under-utilization of the information resource and analytic functionality that the solution provides.
	  ○ Business analysts explore and evaluate opportunities for additional value that are enabled by a business intelligence solution.

Information Technology Perspective

Overview	The information technology perspective focuses on changes in the information technology systems. The initiative could be small bug fixes or enhancements or as large as re-engineering the entire IT infrastructure.
Change Scope	The reasons for changes in the IT systems could be as follows: - Create a new organizational capability - Achieve an organizational objective by enhancing an existing capability - Facilitate an operational improvement - Maintain an existing information technology system - Repair a broken information technology system **Breadth of change:** Information technology initiative may focus on a single system or on multiple systems. These systems may be: - A commercial off-the-shelf (COTS) system developed by an organization and implemented here - A customized software by an external vendor Business analysts working in IT carefully consider the context for any information technology change. **Depth of change:** Due to the level of detail required in these types of initiatives, business analysts elicit and analyse how the organization works as a whole and how the IT system will support those operations. **Value and Solutions delivered:** The *importance of an information technology initiative* is in its ability to deliver value to an organization. IT systems changes can deliver value by one or more of the following: - Reduction of operating costs - Decreasing wasted effort - Increasing strategic alignment - Increasing reliability and stability - Automating manual processes - Repairing issues and more **Delivery Approach:** *Information technology initiatives* vary from being small to large and complex ones. Depending on the duration of the initiative, a Business analyst may get involved for a short period or many Business analysts may get involved. **Major Assumptions:** The major assumptions are: - Business capabilities and processes that use an IT system are delivering value to the organization, - Business analysts working from other perspectives can integrate their work - with the work of the IT business analysts, and - IT systems changes are usually driven by a business need, although some initiatives may originate from within technology developments
Business Analysis scope	**Change Sponsor for information technology initiatives** is typically by sponsors or IT department or both. These changes should align to organizational strategy and business goals.

Change targets and agents: The targets of **information technology initiatives** could be a department, process, application, or a function. Business analysts keep an eye on the business and technical impact of the change.

Business Analyst position: The functions of the business analyst may be played by one or more Business Analysts with the following skills/background:

- Experience of working with the Business Users
- Worked as a liaison between the technical team and the business group which uses the application
- A subject matter expert (SME) experienced with the current software implementation
- A software user experienced with the daily activity of how the software is used and can focus on usability
- A systems analyst who has experience within the business domain but does not have experience with the specific application and more.

Business Analysis outcomes: The major outcomes of the business analysis activities in the information technology initiative are:
- Defined, complete, testable, prioritized, and verified requirements
- Analysis of alternatives,
- Business rules,
- Gap analysis,
- Prototypes
- Process analysis and models
- State Models
- Decision Models
- Scope and Context models
- Data Models

Approaches and Methodologies	**Methodologies:** Methodologies may vary widely but they usually are either Adaptive or Predictive or in the continuum between these two. Some of the established methodologies used in Information Technology initiatives are as follows: - **Organization Specific:** A home grown methodology based on the other initiatives in the organization. - **Requirement Engineering:** Establishes a structured approach for requirements development and management and is used in predictive, adaptive, and agile environments. - **Structured System Analysis and Design (SSADM):** A development methodology which is predictive in nature. It focuses on requirements from solutions as the central theme. - **Unified Process (UP):** An adaptive development approach. The inception and elaboration phases are of interest to business analysts. UP is not considered agile but is an adaptive methodology.
Underlying competencies	A business analyst may possess skills as mentioned below to be able to perform his/her tasks:

	o **Specific IT dev skills:** Programming, Database, Creating an architecture, software testing and so on.
	o **Non-**IT skills: Systems Thinking, Negotiation, Facilitation and influencing skills for working with the stakeholders
Impact on knowledge areas	**Business planning and monitoring** • A business analysis approach is key to the identifying the resources and time for business analysis activities. • A business analysis plan is prepared (which is part of overall project plan) to conduct business analysis activities. **Elicitation and collaboration:** Business analysts practicing in an IT environment may utilize any of the techniques identified in the Elicitation and Collaboration knowledge area. In addition, the following techniques can also be very useful: ▪ Investigation using organizational process assets, market research etc ▪ Simulations using statistical modelling and mock-ups ▪ Experimentation like proof of concepts, prototypes etc. **Requirements lifecycle Management:** IT initiatives frequently experience major discoveries while creating the change. It is through exploration that the business analysts discover the implications of the new functionality provided by the solution. Business Analysts work closely with the stakeholders to develop a consistent approach to manage regular changes to the requirements (or to evolution of requirements). As technical systems are changed over time, it is helpful when each version of each requirement is stored in some way and accounted for. Traceability makes it possible to find the source and owner of each requested function and feature, as well as why, when, and how it changed over time. **Strategy Analysis:** Business analysts analyses and work to understand all the various aspects that may be impacted by the change. A BA starts by understanding the current state of the organization. The future state defines the changed state of the organization. Defining future state helps in defining the scope of work and the change strategy. There are uncertainties associated with the future state and these are identified as risks. **Requirements analysis and design definition:** Business analysts elaborate business and technical requirements, break down and define stakeholder needs, and identify the value to be realized by stakeholders once a technical solution or change is implemented. As part of requirements analysis, an IT business analyst may partner with another business analyst with a different focus, such as an enterprise business analyst or business architect, to ensure that the IT requirements align to business or organizational strategy.

Solution evaluation: Solution evaluation focuses on solution components and the value they provide. One aspect of solution evaluation within an IT context is software testing or solution testing.

Business analysts also focus on the business objectives and value to ensure that the solution component or solution achieve these. This is validated by using performance measures and comparing the actual values with the expected values.

Business Architecture Perspective

Overview	Business architecture models the enterprise to show how strategic concerns of key stakeholders are met and to support ongoing business transformation efforts. Business analysis activities focus on the business architecture context. Business architecture follows certain fundamental architecture principles: • Scope • Separation of concerns • Scenario driven • Knowledge based

Change Scope	➢ **Breadth of change:** In the business architecture context, the business analysis activities may be carried out:
	  o Across the enterprise as a whole
	  o Across a unit (Line of business)
	  o Across a single functional unit (department)
	
	➢ **Depth of change:** The business architecture initiatives do not work at *operational or process level*, rather focused on the executive level of the enterprise. It provides the context to other initiatives.
	
	➢ **Value and Solutions delivered:**
	  o The insights provided by business architecture help keep systems and operations functioning in a coherent and useful manner and add clarity to business decisions.
	  o The architecture itself can be used as a tool to help identify needed changes.
	  o The function of business architecture is to facilitate coordinated and synchronized action across the organization by aligning action with the organization's vision, goals, and strategy.
	  o Business architecture provides a blueprint that management can use to plan and execute strategies from both information technology (IT) and non-IT perspectives.
	➢ **Delivery Approach:** Business architecture creates a planning framework that provides clarity and insight into the organization and assists decision makers in identifying required changes.
	  o The business architecture may define current state, future state or transition state(s) for each change.
	  o Business architects play an important role in communicating and innovating for the strategy of the organization.
	
	➢ **Major Assumptions: The major assumptions are:**
	  o A view of the entire organization that is under analysis,
	  o Full support from the senior leadership
	  o Participation of business owners and subject matter experts (SMEs),
	  o An organizational strategy to be in place, and
	  o A business imperative to be addressed.

Business Analysis scope	➢ **Change Sponsor:** the sponsor of a business architecture initiative is a senior executive or business owner within the organization. However, the sponsor may also be a line of-business owner.

	➢ **Change targets and agents**
	     o Change targets are: Business capabilities, business value streams, initiative plans, investment decisions, and portfolio decisions.
	     o The change agents could be - management at all levels of the organization, product or service owners, operational units, solution architects, project managers, and business analysts working in other contexts
	
	 ➢ **Business Analyst position:** A business analyst will participate to:
	     o Understand the entire enterprise context and provide balanced in
	     o Provide a holistic, understandable view of all the specialties within the organization.
	 ➢ **Business Analysis outcomes:** The general outcomes of the business analysis activities are:
	     o The alignment of the organization to its strategy
	     o The planning of change in the execution of strategy, and
	     o Ensuring that as change is implemented, it continues to align to the strategy.

Reference models and Techniques	➢ **Reference Models:** Reference models are predefined architectural templates that provide one or more viewpoints for an industry or function that is commonly found across multiple sectors (for example, IT or finance). o Examples are - ***Business Motivation Model (BMM)***, ***Control Objectives for IT (COBIT)***, ***Information Technology Infrastructure Library (ITIL®)*** ➢ **Techniques:** Commonly used techniques in the business architecture context are – ***Business Motivation Model*** (BMM), ***Business Process Architecture***, ***Customer Journey Map***

Underlying competencies	➢ Some of the competencies needed by business analysts working in business architecture context are:
	     o A high tolerance for ambiguity and uncertainty,
	     o The ability to put things into a broader context,
	     o The ability to transform requirements and context into a concept or design of a solution.
	     o The ability to suppress unnecessary detail to provide higher level views,
	     o The ability to think in long time frames over multiple years,
	     o The ability to deliver tactical outcomes (short term), which simultaneously provide immediate value and contribute to achieving the business strategy (long term), & More...
	 ➢ These are in addition to the underlying competencies described in BABOK v3

Impact on knowledge areas	➢ **Business planning and monitoring**
	     o The business analyst needs to understand the following from organizational perspective:
	        ▪ Strategy and direction,
	        ▪ Operating model and value proposition,
	        ▪ Current business and operational capabilities,
	        ▪ Stakeholders and their points of engagement,
	        ▪ Plans for growth, governance, and planning processes,

- Culture and environment, and
- Capacity for change.

➢ **Elicitation and collaboration:** The business analysts have to deal with lots of ambiguity and uncertainty in these initiatives. So, they consider changes in organizational direction based on external and internal forces and changes in marketplace environment.

  o In these initiatives, Business analysts elicit inputs such as strategy, value, existing architectures, and performance metrics.

  o Ensuring stakeholders understand and support the organization's strategy is an essential function within the discipline of business architecture. Business architects may impose scope and constraints on a project or initiative to ensure the activity aligns to the organization's strategy, which may be viewed unfavourably.

➢ **Requirement lifecycle management:** It is essential that business analysts working in the discipline of business architecture have executive support and agreement of the work to be undertaken. An architecture review board comprised of senior executives with decision-making powers can review and assess changes to the business architecture.

  o Business analysts also identify possible emerging changes in both internal and external situations (including market conditions) and decide on how to incorporate these changes into the business architecture of the organization.

➢ **Strategy Analysis:** Business architecture can play a significant role in strategy analysis. It provides architectural views into the current state of the organization and helps to define both the future state and the transition states required to achieve the future state. Business architects develop roadmaps based on the organization's change strategy.

➢ **Requirements analysis and design definition**

  o Business analysts working in the discipline of business architecture employ expertise, judgment, and experience when deciding what is (and what is not) important to model. Models are intended to provide context and information that result in better requirements analysis and design.

  o Design is done in conjunction with understanding needs and requirements. Business architecture provides the context to analyze the strategic alignment of proposed changes and the effects those changes have upon each other.

➢ **Solution evaluation:** Business analysts working in the discipline of business architecture analyze the results of measurements and factor these results into subsequent planning.

Business Process Management Perspective

Overview	The Business Process Management Perspective highlights the unique characteristics of business analysis when practiced in the context of *developing or improving business processes*.
Change Scope	Business analysts focus on bringing changes to process (or processes) to achieve the business objectives, expected through the change. BPM lifecycle comprises of the following activities: <ul><li>Designing</li><li>Modelling</li><li>Execution and Monitoring</li><li>Optimizing</li></ul><ul><li>➢ **Breadth of change:** Individual initiatives may improve specific processes and sub-processes. These processes could result after decomposing more complex and large processes.</li><li>➢ **Depth of change:** BPM Frameworks are used to analyse and to have in-depth understanding of the organizational processes.</li></ul> <ul><li>➢ **Value and Solutions delivered:**<ul><li>○ The goal of BPM is to improve operational performance (effectiveness, efficiency, adaptability, and quality) and to reduce costs and risks.</li><li>○ Business analysts frequently consider transparency into processes and operations as a common core value of BPM initiatives.</li><li>○ Some of the drivers for BPM initiatives are:<ul><li>▪ Cost reduction initiatives</li><li>▪ Increase in quality</li><li>▪ Increase in productivity</li><li>▪ Compliance initiatives etc.</li></ul></li></ul></li><li>➢ **Delivery Approach:** The delivery approach for BPM initiatives across organizations ranges from a set of tactical methods focused on improving individual processes to a management discipline that touches all the processes in an organization. Organizations conduct periodic assessments of key processes and engage in ongoing continuous improvement to achieve and sustain process excellence. There are several BPM implementations mechanisms are:<ul><li>Business process re-engineering</li><li>Evolutionary forms of change</li><li>Substantial discovery</li><li>Process benchmarking</li><li>Specialized BPMS applications</li></ul></li> <li>➢ **Major Assumptions: The major assumptions are:**<ul><li>○ Processes are generally supported by information technology systems, but the development of those systems is not covered by most BPM methods.</li><li>○ BPM initiatives have senior management support.</li></ul></li></ul>

	o BPM systems require a tight integration with organizational strategy, but most methods do not tackle the development of strategy which is outside the scope of this perspective. o BPM initiatives are cross-functional and end-to-end in the organization.

Business Analysis scope	➢ **Change Sponsor:** The sponsor of business process initiatives are executives (top level executives) with focus on strategic objectives. These strategic objectives then help in connecting to the business processes.
	➢ **Change targets:** The possible change targets for business process management initiatives are:
	    o Customer
	    o Regulator
	    o Process Owner
	    o Process Participants
	    o Project Manager
	    o Implementation Team
	
	➢ **Business Analyst position:** A business analyst in a BPM initiative may assume the roles of:
	    o **Process Architect:** A process architect is responsible for modelling, analysing, optimizing, deploying, and monitoring business processes.
	    o **Process Analyst/Designer:** They perform analysis and assessment of as-is processes, evaluate alternate process design options, and make recommendations for change based on various frameworks.
	    o **Process Modeller:** A process modeller captures and understands the "AS-IS" and "TO-BE" processes. (SEE THE DIAGRAM 11.5.1 from BABOK v3)
	➢ **Business Analysis outcomes:** The general outcomes of the business analysis activities in this initiative are:
	    o **Business process models:** Business process models start at the highest level as an end-to-end model of the whole process and can become as specific as modelling specific work flow. Business process models serve as both an output and a starting point for the analysis of the process.
	    o **Business Rules:** Business rules guide business processes and are intended to assert business structure or control the behaviour of business.
	    o **Process performance measure:** Process performance measures are parameters that are used to identify process improvement opportunities.
	    o **Business Decisions:** Business decisions are a specific kind of task or activity in a business process that determine which set of options will be acted upon by the process.
	    o **Process performance Assessment:** The success of any BPM initiative rests on the intention and capability to continuously measure and monitor the performance of targeted business processes.

Frameworks, Methodologies & Techniques	➢ **Frameworks:** Commonly used frameworks for BPM initiatives are: *ACCORD, Enhanced Telecommunications Operations Map (eTOM), Governments Strategic Reference Model (GSRM) etc.*

	➢ **Methodologies:** Commonly used methodologies for BPM initiatives are: *Adaptive Case Management (ACM), Business Process Re-engineering (BPR), Continuous Improvement (CI), Lean etc.* ➢ **Techniques:** Commonly used techniques are – *Cost Analysis, Critical to Quality, (CTQ), Cycle-time Analysis, Define Measure, Analyze Design, Verify (DMADV) etc.*

Underlying competencies	➢ Some of the competencies needed by business analysts working in BPM context are:
	   ○ Strong negotiation skills,
	   ○ Ability to resolve conflicts,
	   ○ Ability to work as a neutral & independent facilitator; .
	   ○ The ability to communicate well
	➢ These are in addition to the underlying competencies described in BABOK v3

Impact on knowledge areas	➢ **Business planning and monitoring**
	   ○ Progressive elaboration is common in the planning of BPM initiatives since the amount of information available for full planning may be limited in the initial stages.
	   ○ A common cause for the failure of BPM initiatives is the failure to plan for ongoing monitoring of the effect of changes to the process.
	
	➢ **Elicitation and collaboration:**
	   ○ During elicitation, the business analyst focuses on cause and effect of both changing existing processes and keeping the processes as they are through the elicitation and collaboration effort.
	   ○ As an existing process is changed, the effect of any process improvements identified on the organization, people, and technology are considered.
	   ○ Process changes can have significant impacts across the organization, so managing stakeholders and their expectations is particularly critical.
	➢ **Requirement lifecycle management:** The impact of BPM activities on requirements life cycle management is significant as it can drive out business requirements resulting in new design, coding, implementation, and post-implementation changes.
	➢ **Strategy Analysis:** In a BPM context, strategy analysis involves understanding the role the process plays in an enterprise value chain.
	It involves describing the current state, future state & the change strategy.
	➢ **Requirements analysis and design definition**
	   ○ Requirements analysis and design definition will focus on defining the to-be process model.
	   ○ The requirements architecture is likely to include the process model, associated business rules and decisions, information requirements, and the organizational structure.
	➢ **Solution evaluation:** As processes are evaluated for different scenarios, they can be refined, and the results are monitored.
	Solution evaluation tasks provide insight into the understanding of the impact of process improvements and the value delivered by business process change.

Glossary

- **Blueprint** - Business architectural descriptions and views are called blueprints. Business architecture provides a blueprint to management for planning and executing strategies
- **Business Process Management drivers** - Business needs are referred to as BPM drivers. Examples include increase in quality, cost reduction, increase in productivity, compliance initiatives, faster processes, etc.
- **Process transformation** - The main aim of BPM initiatives is process transformation, which is nothing but identifying, prioritizing and optimizing the business processes to deliver value to stakeholders
- **BPM Lifecycle** - Includes the following activities: Designing, Modelling, Execution & Monitoring, and Optimizing
- **Business Intelligence** - BI (Business Intelligence) is a set of processes, architectures, and technologies that convert raw data into meaningful information that drives profitable business actions.
- **Business Architecture** - Business Architecture reveals how an organization is structured and can clearly demonstrate how elements such as capabilities, processes, organization and information fit together.

Exercises and Drills

Question 1: Match the following techniques with the correct descriptions/concepts.

1. Value Stream Mapping	A. A model that is used to assess ideas in the context of customer and value.
2. Relative Estimation	B. A delivery approach that focuses on enhancing the stakeholder and team member communication by using concrete examples to represent product needs.
3. Real Options	C. A project delivery framework which focuses on fixing cost, quality, and time at the beginning while contingency is managed by varying the features to be delivered.
4. Purpose Alignment Model	D. Fact based and time series representation of stream of activities required to deliver a product or service to the customer.
5. BDD	E. Representing the size of a user story without using hours or days as unit of work.
4. Dynamic Systems Development Method (DSDM)	F. An approach to help people know when to make decisions rather than how.

Question 2: Match the following techniques used within agile approaches with their description.

1. Personas	A. A lessons-learned technique which focuses on continuous improvement.
2. MoSCoW	B. A technique for understanding which product features will help drive customer satisfaction.
3. Retrospectives	C. Helps provide a way to reach a consensus on relative importance of a user story in the product.
4. Kano analysis	D. Provides a visual and physical view of sequence of activities to be supported by a solution.
5. Story mapping	E. Fictional characters or archetypes that exemplify the way users interact with a product.

Question 3: Match the following.

1. Supply driven	A. Approach based on business goals of providing the appropriate information to improve decision making processes. Assumes the view of 'for a given value, what cost do we incur?
2. Demand driven	B. Data such as text, audio, images, video where the structure and relationships are not predefined.
3. Structured data	C. Approach based on technical goals of improving existing information delivery systems. Assumes the view of 'for a given cost, what value can we deliver?
4. Unstructured data	D. Numerical and categorical data where the structure and relationships are predefined.

Question 4: Complete the crossword.

Across	Down
1. Technique to create requirements which are at the appropriate level of detail (13)	3. A visual way to represent a sequence of activities to be supported by a solution is known as Story _____ (7)
5. A way to represent how a specific user type interacts with a system. These are fictional characters (8)	2. A visual way to represent sequence of activities that represent user interactions with a system or business, known as story _____ (8)
	4. A textual structure to represent requirements (9)
	5. A consensus-based estimation technique known as planning _____ (5)

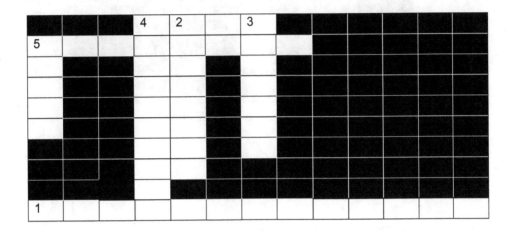

Answers

Answers:

Answer 1: 1-D, 2-E,3-F,4-A,5-B,6-C

Answer 2: 1- E, 2- C, 3 – A, 4 – B, 5 – D

Answer 3: 1 – C, 2 – A, 3 – D, 4 – B

Answers 4:

			4U	2B		3M						
5P	E	R	S	O	N	A	S					
O			E	A		P						
K			R	R		P						
E			S	D		I						
R			T	I		N						
			O	N		G						
			R	G								
			Y									
1D	E	C	O	M	P	O	S	I	T	I	O	N

Mock Questions

Q1. You are a business analyst for a project, which is in the maintenance phase. You are working on a series of enhancements to the existing system. The enhancement needed change in the architecture of the system, which you are documenting. Which of the following need not be included in your document?

A. Change in the operational model
B. Change in the organizational structure
C. Change in the business model
D. Change in the database design

Q2. A business analyst has been tasked by senior management of a company to analyze the company's business infrastructure and develop blueprints for the transition. The future transition state is aligned with business goals. Which of the following techniques will be useful for the BA?

A. Architectural Mapping
B. Process Mapping
C. Business Model Canvas
D. Business Cases

Q3. A business analyst is working on a business intelligence project. A business intelligence project involves dealing with lots of data. What are the types of data, the business analyst will be dealing with in this project?

A. Primitive and non-primitive data
B. Structured and Unstructured data
C. Predictive and adaptive data
D. Logical and physical data

Q4. Maria is the primary agent for an agile project. She is responsible for making sure that the change being executed is going to satisfy customer needs. What is the role that Maria is playing?
A. Iteration Manager
B. Customer Representative
C. Usability Expert
D. Scrum Master

Q5. There are several approaches to perform business analysis activities in Agile projects. Which of the following is not a valid one?

A. Activities performed by a product owner
B. Activities performed by a business analyst as a team member
C. Activities performed by each member collectively
D. Activities performed by the business stakeholders supporting the agile team

Q6. Ramesh is the product owner of a project. His responsibility includes conveying the organization's vision and needs to the agile team in an easy to comprehend manner. Which of the following competencies is essential for the product owner?

A. Ability to recognize business value
B. Continuous improvement
C. Patience and tolerance
D. Communication and collaboration

Q7. A Business analyst is part of an initiative which aims to help an organization decide regarding: **How much down-time a production server must allocate for planned maintenance?** Which level of the organization is going to get benefitted from this initiative?

A. Executive Level
B. Management Level
C. Process Level
D. Executive Board level

Q8. A Business analyst is part of an initiative that aims to help an organization make key decisions regarding employee performance and increments. Which level of the organization is going to get benefitted from this initiative?

A. Executive Level
B. Management Level
C. Process Level
D. Operations level

Q9. A team has developed an application that is going to help the management in creating a rules-based scenario for simulating various business situations. It will help the management in identifying the elements needed to achieve the desired outcome. Which of the following represents this type of application?

A. Data Models
B. Decision Models
C. Business Rules Models
D. Scenario Models

Q10. A Business analyst is brainstorming with the stakeholders. The agenda is to enhance the IT systems so that better services can be provided to their customers without increasing the prices of these services. What is this referred to as?

A. Demand-driven BI initiative
B. Data-driven BI initiative
C. Supply-driven BI initiative
D. Decision-Matrix-driven BI initiative

Answers

Q1. Answer D: Changes in database design are not relevant in this case as the data model is not part of business architecture. It is a conceptual question and need not have a direct section mapping to BABOK. (Refer 11.4 of BABOK - Third Paragraph - Last Sentence)

Q2. Answer C: Blueprints are elements of the Business Architecture (BABOK 11.4 - 3rd paragraph). Business architecture provides architectural views of the current state and helps in defining the future state and transition states. Section (BABOK 11.4.5.4). As the BA is asked to create the Blueprints (which are elements of business architecture), the BA needs to use the techniques as mentioned in this section 11.4.5.4. Business model canvas is listed as one of the techniques here and is the right answer. Thus, the correct answer is option C.

Q3. Answer B: Business intelligence approaches involve two types of data: Structured and Unstructured data. Thus, the correct answer is option b. (Section 11.2.3.2 - Structured and Unstructured Data.)

Q4. Answer B: A customer representative or a product owner is an active team member responsible for ensuring that the change being developed addresses the requirements for which it has been mandated and helps meet the customer's needs. The correct answer is option B. (Section 11.1.2.2. Customer representative or product owner:)

Q5. Answer D: Section 11.1.2.3. This section describes the approaches of performing business analysis activities in Agile teams. As per BABOK, A product owner or a business analyst in the team, perform the business analysis activities besides, the activities can be shared by the team. However, the activities performed by the business stakeholders are not counted towards business analysis activities. So, it is incorrect and hence the correct answer is option D.

Q6. Answer D: The product owner needs to communicate the organization's expectations to the team members effectively. It helps the team to align themselves with the vision and needs - an essential element for a project's success. Communication and collaboration are one such competency that defines the above-mentioned activities. So, option D is the correct answer.

Q7. Answer B: The focus of this initiative is tactical. Generally tactical level is beneficial for the middle level in an organization. (All the levels are described in section 11.2.1.2)

For more information: Strategic information is used at the very top level of management within an organization. These are typically a long term (5 years to 20 years). For example, the decision to sign a long-term maintenance contract to save costs over a 10-20-year period. A tactical decision is short term (6 months to 5 years) and involves decisions at the middle management level.

Q8. Answer B: The focus of this initiative is tactical and not strategic. The decisions about employee performance and their increments are always short term as the organization wants to see the benefits immediately. Also, these decisions are used by middle-level management to boost team confidence and morale. (The levels are described in section 11.2.1.2. So, the correct answer is B.

For more information: Strategic information is used at the very top level of management within an organization. These are typically a long term (5 years to 20 years). For example, the decision to sign a long-term maintenance contract to save costs over a 10-20-year period. A tactical decision is short term (6 months to 5 years) and involves decisions at the middle management level.

Q9. Answer B: The decision models bullet point describes - what decision models are? These types of applications help in using different business rules to simulate an outcome. This simulation also helps in identifying the components needs to achieve an outcome. (Section 11.2.2.4)

Q10. Answer C: As per BABOK, supply driven approach focuses on **for a given cost, what value can we deliver?** The question also refers to the discussion on improving the quality of service without changing the price or at the same cost. Thus, this refers to a supply-side consideration (the company which is providing the service). Hence the correct answer is option c. (Section 11.2.3.2 of BABOK - Supply and demand-driven section.)